Western Apache Heritage

WESTERN APACHE HERITAGE

PEOPLE OF THE MOUNTAIN CORRIDOR

Richard J. Perry

University of Texas Press, Austin

First Edition, 1991

Requests for permission to reproduce material from this
work should be sent to Permissions, University of Texas Press,
Box 7819, Austin, Texas 78713-7819.

∞ The paper used in this publication meets the minimum
requirements of American National Standard for Information
Sciences—Permanence of Paper for Printed Library Materials,
ANSI Z39.48-1984.

Library of Congress Cataloging-in-Publication Data

Perry, Richard John, 1942–
    Western Apache heritage : people of the mountain corridor /
by Richard J. Perry. — 1st ed.
        p.   cm.
    Includes bibliographical references and index.
    ISBN 0-292-76524-X (cloth). — ISBN 0-292-76525-8 (paper)
    1. Western Apache Indians—History.   2. Western Apache
Indians—Social life and customs.   3. San Carlos Indian
Reservation (Ariz.)—History.   I. Title.
E99.A6P47   1991
979.1'55—dc20   90-48543
                                                            CIP

Contents

Maps

Photographs

Preface

I first came to San Carlos in 1963 as an undergraduate, having somehow in Cambridge, Massachusetts, acquired a summer job in Arizona as an "instructional aide" for the Bureau of Indian Affairs. Excited and a bit apprehensive about the prospect of going to live on an Apache reservation, I arrived with myriad colorful preconceptions about the people in whose midst I would soon be spending the summer. In the course of a rather average childhood in the 1940s and 1950s, I had absorbed much of the standard folklore about "The Old West" to which most of my generation had been exposed—fantasies that were especially compelling to those of us who never had been west of Buffalo.

Needless to say, my preconceptions—about the West, about the people of San Carlos, and about my own role in that setting—were drastically adjusted in the face of reality. The countryside was formidable, spectacular, and more beautiful than I had imagined. The people were occupied with their own daily problems of living, which were considerable. Although I treasured the occasional friendly gesture, these were so rare that from the point of view of the people of San Carlos, it seemed, my presence there was not a cause for enthusiasm and in fact could just as well have been dispensed with. I learned also that my association with the Bureau of Indian Affairs was not particularly helpful for developing acquaintances among people of the Apache community.

Yet the people of San Carlos were anything but dour. In the face of terrible poverty, they laughed easily and often, though at times with a humor that showed the barbs of deep anger. I began to perceive something about the complexity of human relationships there and, with time, came to glimpse some of the richness underlying the outward appearance. I was lucky early in the summer to meet Marshall Durbin, who was doing linguistics research in San Carlos and kindly introduced me to the joint family with whom he was staying. Acquaintance with these people is something for which I shall always be grateful. Years later when I returned to San Carlos to complete my doctoral research in anthropology, this time with my wife, Pat, and two small children, the same people welcomed us again. In a climate in which intercultural communication could be difficult indeed, they received us into their midst and treated our children as their own.

In trying to learn and understand something of Apache culture and society, I was intrigued by the difficulty of reconciling San Carlos of the 1960s and 1970s with the Apache past. Partly, of course, this was because the people I saw every day in San Carlos were real, whereas much of the popular image of the past is fallacious. Still, although much of the older culture continued to affect the present— almost everyone, for example, still spoke in Apache rather than in English—the lives of the people were tremendously different from what they had been a century or two before. The problem of change versus continuity came to seem increasingly provocative.[1] The pages that follow represent the pursuit of that interest. They are an attempt to demonstrate the continuity of modern San Carlos with the past centuries, to see the present in perspective against the backdrop of long-term processes of culture change.

Despite long-standing Anglo-American assumptions that cultural diversity tends to be residual, at best, in the modern United States, the San Carlos community represents far more than the dying embers of a once-viable cultural system. To be sure, historical events have stifled the autonomy these people once exercised. Many of the decisions that most affect their lives are made elsewhere, whether in Washington or in the regional offices of the Bureau of Indian Affairs. But the continuity of tradition that has extended over the centuries does not seem likely to end abruptly in the foreseeable future. As long as the people continue to exist, their sense of reality and of the nature of their existence will derive in part, as among all humans, from their own past.

Apache traditions do not evince a preoccupation with the chronological events of their own ancient history. For the past couple of centuries, their history has been interwoven with the affairs of other peoples, both native and Euro-American. But culture patterns far more ancient have always permeated Apache life, carried from generation to generation over centuries and thousands of miles from the Subarctic to the Southwest. The people's traditional accounts of migration do not extend beyond northern Arizona, but their culture shows remarkable continuity with their ancient northern homeland. Even without conscious memory of it, the past remains an aspect of their present.

We know that the people referred to as Apache came from the western Subarctic, probably not more than a millennium ago. What were they like then? What led them southward? When did it happen? What was the milieu in which they survived? What experiences did they undergo in the intervening centuries, perhaps leaving indelible, enigmatic traces in the present?

Much of what we would like to know we can never learn. But the evidence of the Apache past has been enriched over the last few decades, to the extent that now we can piece together an outline with some confidence. Some of the Apaches' heritage survives in the language and in other facets of life: beliefs about the nature of life itself and the human soul, for example, and a special concern with the power of femaleness. Changes are pervasive, too, and no less interesting. In this book a synthesis of evidence from archaeology, linguistics, ethnohistory, and the ethnographic record will help reconstruct an Apachean continuum from the Subarctic Proto-Athapaskan baseline through the long series of segmentations, divergences, migrations, and ecological changes that led to the San Carlos Reservation.

Before going on, though, there is an obligation to present some justification for this enterprise. The Western Apache have no cultural tradition of any Subarctic homeland or migration into the Southwest. Impressions of a time when the people lived near the Hopi and Navajo in northern Arizona seem to be the farthest extent of Western Apache chronological history, and ethnohistoric sources indicate that this took place as recently as the 1860s (Schroeder 1974, IV, 478, 479, 482).[2] Few human populations without written records have retained the details of their own history much deeper into the past, although many conjure ancient eras to account for the construction of the present. The Apache prohibition on mentioning the names of the dead no doubt inhibited recollection of past experiences over generations. But of far greater importance than a chronology of events are the timeless axioms and concerns, the ways of defining and dealing with reality, whose origins at a particular point in space or time are not relevant, and perhaps even are meaningless, to people for whom they continue to be a part of life.

In the 1930s the Western Apache insisted that they had always had clans. They considered clans to be such an essential aspect of the human condition that they found it difficult to believe that other groups of people lack them (Goodwin 1969:105, 109).[3] Evidence that many of the Western Apache clans originated in northern Arizona only a few generations ago, as the legends of clan migration from localities in that region attest, has implications that may be interesting to an outsider with a linear concept of time[4] and possibly even intriguing, in a whimsical way, to some Apache people as well. But this chronological measure of duration does not occupy the same conceptual realm as the timelessness of the principles of interpersonal relationships embodied in the clan system. The perceived ancientness of the clans is as much a reflection of their importance to the society as an indication of their chronological age.

The elemental principle of the clan system—that people related by descent through women have something special in common—is indeed an aspect of Apache life with ancient roots, whatever the structural forms that have developed on that basis. Even though many of the clans had their beginnings only a few generations ago, they convey a strength drawn from the past that is comparable to Apachean concerns with female puberty which may already have been ancient, even in terms of linear time, in early Athapaskan prehistory.

Why, then, should an outsider try to construct a model of the Apache past, operating from the perspective of linear time and hoping to detect the chronological sequence of events and processes that can suggest relationships of cause and effect? The Apache past belongs to the people themselves. Our attempt to uncover and interpret it involves a certain audacity.

But the experiences of any group of people are a part of a broader human heritage. The culture history of the people who came to be known as Western Apache is a history of human survival, resilience, and change, and our attempt to understand it tells us a little more about the human condition. How the people dealt with the problems of survival over millennia, not only maintaining life but perpetuating a distinctive quality of life, a sense of the way things should be and the way the universe works, refined and modified from an ancient heritage, is a matter of importance to all people.

The Apache are an important people. Perhaps this is an odd assertion for an anthropologist to make. One of the few things most anthropologists would agree upon is the view that people should not be differentiated in terms of their relative "importance." Given anthropology's preoccupation with the fine and variegated tapestry of the human experience, the most minute cultural esoterica warrant attention worthy of a jeweler's glass and can provoke years of heated debate. The concept of relative importance may rest more comfortably with some historians and political scientists, who can look to the impact of one or another population on the subsequent affairs of the world.

But in many ways the Apache experience has special significance for the rest of us. Their impact on the popular ideology of the United States has been wildly disproportionate to their numbers. At any particular time in the past, the scattered bands of Apache who dominated an area the size of France and fiercely maintained their sovereignty in the face of Spanish, Mexican, and Anglo-American armies for four centuries would hardly fill a quarter of the seats in a modern football stadium. The Apache of Arizona, whose name in historical myth came to be equated with ferocity, probably were never more numerous than the population of a small modern American town.

Much has been written on recent Apache history, particularly the "Apache Wars" and the period of turmoil in the Southwest that spanned three hundred years or so and the early reservation period. In that era the Apache came to be seen as the scourge of the region, a source of terror and targets of the genocidal policies of several governments (e.g., Thrapp 1968; Worcester 1979). This is not meant to be a reiteration of these studies, nor is it intended to be a detailed, full-scale ethnography of the Western Apache. For such information Grenville Goodwin's (1969) *Social Organization of the Western Apache* probably never will be surpassed, and time has only enhanced its indispensability to anyone interested in these people.[5] In addition, Keith Basso (1970) has written a concise, accessible study of the Western Apache community at Cibecue.

Some day, we hope, a member of the Western Apache population will write a detailed account of his or her own culture that will be far more penetrating and insightful than any outsider could produce. The intention here, though, is to view the seamless continuity of Western Apache culture in deeper diachronic perspective—to catch a glimpse of the processes of change, the slow, inexorable trends, and the poignant accidents of choice that led the people from the mountain corridors of the North to the San Carlos community in Arizona. It is one of my greatest hopes that should this reconstruction stand the test of the new evidence that continues to accumulate, it will be of interest to the Western Apache and meet with their approval.

This is a study of culture change and its implications for survival. It gives special consideration to the food quest, on which everything else depends. This basic facet of human existence, in which strategies are addressed to the possibilities of subsistence, is the essential interface between the biological aspects of being human and the unique qualities of humanity. It is the realm in which rational choices, gambles, skills, knowledge, presuppositions, attitudes, and traditions operate in the natural world to maintain life. From the Subarctic to the Southwest, the food quest is a common thread, its changes and continuities often reverberating in the shifts, adjustments, and continuities of culture.

Much of the discussion that follows is based on ethnographic reconstruction. Chapter 4 presents the method in some detail, and documentation of the ethnographic data on which the reconstruction is based, drawn from thirty-one Athapaskan groups and the linguistically related Eyak, appear in the appendices with citations for anyone wishing to examine them.

In closing, I must reiterate my gratitude to the people in San Carlos who welcomed us with kindness, generosity, and patience and express my gratitude to former teachers and colleagues who have provided valued guidance and advice in my study of the Western Apache. Among those I wish to thank especially are Professors D. Glynn Cochrane, William Mangin, Michael Freedman, and Robert Bettarel. Although they have not seen the present work, their assistance has contributed to it greatly. I must also thank reviewers of the manuscript. Charles Bishop provided valuable insights and constructive criticism. Philip Greenfeld and James Clifton read the manuscript and shared some helpful reactions. I also thank my colleague Robert Carlisle, Professor of History at St. Lawrence, for his encouraging comments early on. And special thanks to Barbara Cummings of the University of Texas Press for her fine work in copy-editing the manuscript.

I would like to express my gratitude to Pat Perry, who was with me in San Carlos in 1970. I owe a great deal to the late Marshall Durbin, whose enthusiasm for anthropology and linguistics and whose affable friendship in San Carlos many years ago gave direction and impetus to my own studies. I am grateful to Professor Alice Pomponio for her encouragement and advice on sections of the manuscript. Assistant Professor of History Martha May provided insight from another discipline. Finally, I would like to express appreciation to Laura Hacker, who was our undergraduate departmental assistant and premiere anthropology major at the time this manuscript was written, for her work on several of the photographs that appear in this book. Thanks, too, for the help of Anne Noonan, student assistant for the Department of Fine Arts at St. Lawrence University. Although none of these people should be held responsible for the conclusions I have offered in this book, their support, rigorous criticism, and painstaking advice did much to enhance whatever quality this work may have.

Field research on which some of this study is based was made possible by National Institutes of Health fellowships 1 FOI MH43646-OIAI and 3 FOI MH43646-OIAISI from the National Institute of Mental Health.

Western Apache Heritage

CHAPTER 1

From the Present into the Past

On an autumn morning not long ago, sunlight touched the houses and brush ramadas below an Arizona mesa, and silence hung in the crystalline blue morning air. Here and there on the sand a dog dozed, showing life in a dreaming twitch or a throaty sigh. A mile away a pickup truck started, disturbing the quiet pool of cold stillness and whining through its repertoire of gears until the drone faded in the distance. A rooster shrieked, answered by another. A dog barked, provoking a chorus of barks from other house clusters. Morning was irrevocable.

An old woman appeared. The long gray hair that spilled down her back framed a soft face creased and darkened by an Apache lifetime. The folds of her blue gingham dress almost touched the ground, swaying gently against her stride as she walked over the dusty ground around a clump of tumbleweeds. She drew a fringed red shawl over her head and shoulders against the chill and carried an aluminum pot to a faucet near the house. Cold water rushing from underground drummed on the bottom of the pot, shattering the quiet and softening to a gurgle as the pot filled.

A fleeting tang of woodsmoke flavored the air, and the sun colored and warmed the houses. A baby cried. A dog stretched and wandered off, and a woman's voice scolded someone unseen.

From another house, whooping laughter subsided into conversation. A shirtless man stepped into the sun and tossed water from a pan, the sheet glassy in the sunlight, missing a sleepy dog. Setting the pan down, he coughed and spat and walked drowsily toward a rough board outhouse.

Children appeared in new clothes. Their black hair shone in the sun, and their breath steamed in tiny clouds as they chattered through the powdery dust to the blacktop road. Eventually a yellow school bus would labor and grind its way around the mesa, emerging at last into view. Another day had begun for the Apache.

For most people in San Carlos, this day would not be much different from the days preceding or following it. Some would find checks for cattle sales waiting at the post office. Old people's arthritis might act up with the cooler weather. A horse was liable to escape and trot nervously among the clusters of dwellings, scattering chickens as spindly-legged dogs happily took up the chase. A baby might be born. Boys, having stayed home to shoot basketball at a rusty rim and backboard set up on a pole, might be lectured by an older relative for skipping school. For someone this might be the last day. But for most, life would change only slightly, imperceptibly.

For the Apache this was only the latest in an unbroken chain of hundreds of thousands of days stretching back over mountains to the north through countless small changes and momentous events and human experiences beyond recollection. This study is an attempt to understand the processes of change and continuity, to understand how the past led to the present.

San Carlos in the Apachean Context

There are plenty of hypotheses about the origins of the term Apache. It appears in Spanish documents in the early 1600s. It might be derived from the Zuni *apachu* (enemy), or from the Nahuatl term for raccoon. The term could have originated in the late 1500s with the Ute word *awatche*, picked up by the Spanish expedition of Juan de Oñate, or it might have come from the Yavapai word *apache* (persons) (D. Gunnerson 1974; Schroeder 1974, I, 239). Whatever its derivation, though, Apache is a name the people were called by others. The people of San Carlos refer to themselves as *nde* (people) in their dialect of Apachean. *Nde* has the same historic roots as *dine*, as the Navajo to the north call themselves, and the same origins as *dene* in the Subarctic dialects of Canadian Athapaskan and *ten'a* and *d'ana* in Athapaskan languages of Alaska. The Western Apache share a past with these distant peoples, remote from San Carlos.

In its contemporary sense, Apache is a broad category that includes not only the people of San Carlos but all of the speakers of Athapaskan languages in the Southwest and the southern Plains. In recent times these people consisted of a handful of distinct populations who came to be referred to as "tribes." The Jicarilla Apache inhabited the Sangre de Cristo Mountains and margins of the southern Plains in northern New Mexico. The Lipan Apache once lived in the mountains and plains to the southeast into Texas. The Chiricahua were southernmost of the surviving Apache, and their sphere of

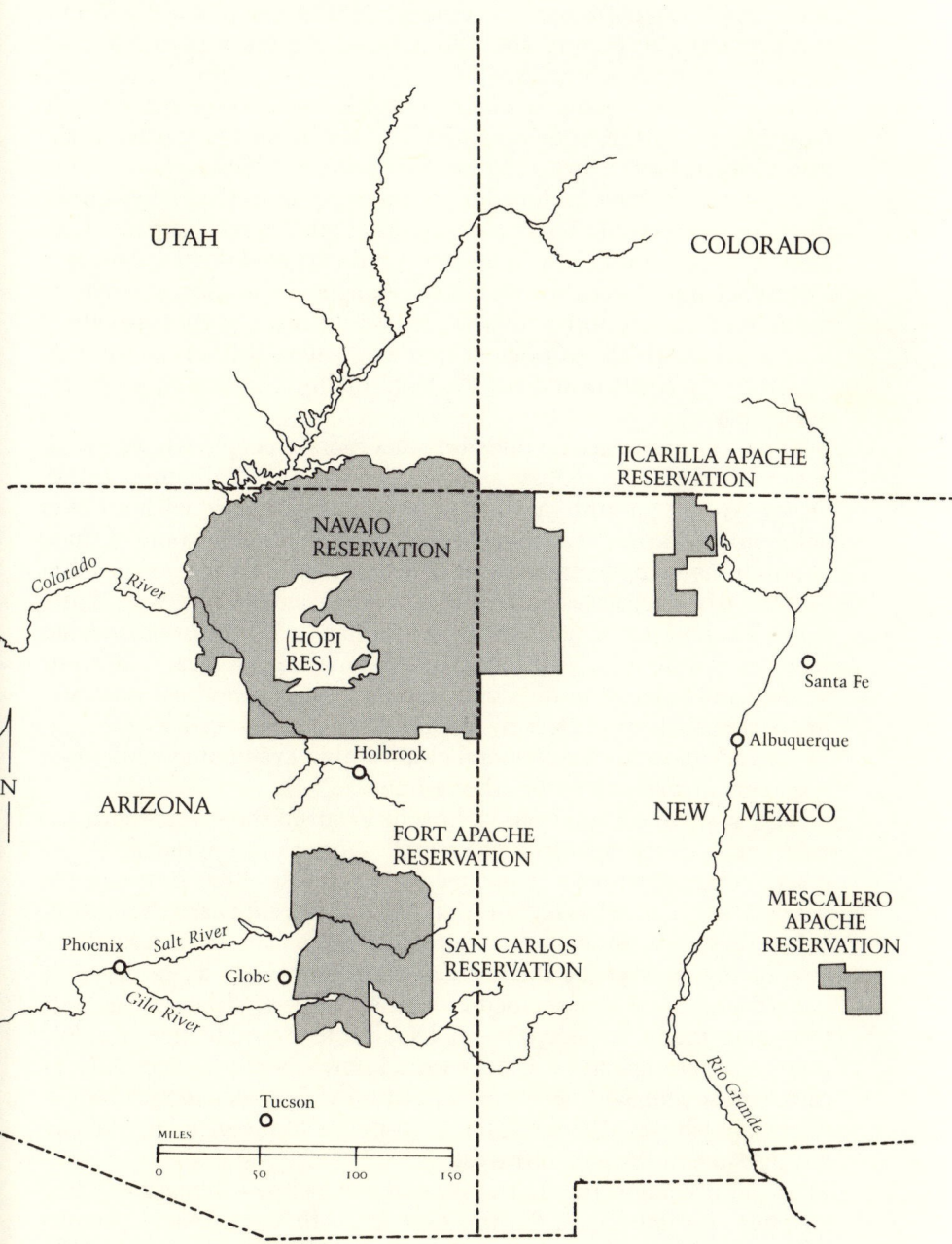

Map 1. Apache reservations in the Southwest

activities overlapped parts of Arizona, New Mexico, and the Mexican provinces of Sonora and Chihuahua. The Mescalero Apache's domain centered in southern New Mexico east of the Rio Grande. Navajo territory included much of northern Arizona and parts of New Mexico, Utah, and Colorado. And the Western Apache, in the mid-nineteenth century, held most of eastern Arizona.

Most writers have included the Kiowa Apache of the Plains among these groups as well. Referred to in early French documents as "Gattaka" or "Tska-taka," they may never have entered the Southwest at all but separated from the rest of the Apache population when all of them lived farther north.[1] By the nineteenth century, they had allied themselves with the Kiowa and were engaged in the buffalo-hunting and horse-raiding life-style of the High Plains (Gunnerson and Gunnerson 1971).

Some of these Apache divisions incorporate people whose grandparents and great-grandparents belonged to entirely different bands. Other Apache groups may have existed in the past without ever being noted in the historic records. It is probable that some of these populations were destroyed through the hostilities of the period or by Old World diseases introduced through encounters with Europeans.[2] Early Spanish accounts refer to many *rancherías* of Apaches whose relationships with modern divisions are not clear, and some of the bands named in old documents probably owe their existence in written history to fleeting, sporadic encounters with Europeans. Many may have been ephemeral clusters that evaporated when their members dispersed to join other groups.

The Spanish designations of Apache bands in the seventeenth and eighteenth centuries often were little more than references to the places where Spaniards happened to run across them. Some of the band names referred to regions that the Spanish supposed the Apache inhabited, even though their domains often were inaccessible to anyone but the Apache themselves. Sometimes Apache groups were named after men who seemed to be their leaders, although such appearances might be deceptive, and such roles could be fleeting. And many of these apparent leaders were known to chroniclers only by nicknames that had been bestowed by the Spanish themselves or were Spanish translations of terms from one of the many native languages spoken in the Southwest.

Social divisions among the Apache have shown remarkable persistence in some cases. For the most part, though, Apache populations have diverged, merged, and separated along different fault lines and converged to form new aggregates. The various Western Apache bands of the nineteenth century have left their traces in the linguistic differences that mark the speech of modern San Carlos.[3] But in general, Apache history is a tale of individual alliances and ad hoc affiliations that confound our attempts to trace any neat continuity of social divisions back through the centuries. In the historic record, Apache groups apparently disappeared, showed up suddenly without known antecedents, underwent changes in reputation, and loomed importantly before disappearing again. Their identity sometimes blurred in the eyes of observers. To this day debate continues over whether certain groups, mentioned in documents but long since gone from the Southwest landscape, were Apache. Yet all the while, they somehow maintained an essence of continuity from an ancient tradition. The processes involved in these changes remain a challenge to analysis.

But what is it that we are trying to fathom, after all? The issue amounts to what people over a series of generations chose to do. They formed aggregates to which other people they happened to encounter gave names. They dispersed and in different places joined others with whom they felt a common purpose. Underlying what seems to have been an organizational chaos, a special kind of order persisted over the centuries. It depended upon the continuity of interpersonal ties, in shared self-definition, and in a perception of commonality through bonds of reciprocal obligations. It persisted in the mutual predictability of behavior among those who understood the same social rules. It resided in an approach to reality colored by shared understandings.

None of this relied very much on the maintenance of political boundaries or highly structured corporate bodies. Perhaps one could say that the boundaries were cultural rather than political. They were maintained through a network of individual obligations, preferences, and affiliations rather than any sense of membership in some corporate group or another.

Apachean cultural continuity has been a manifestation of the capacity to change. Individuals have made choices based on knowledge drawn from the past and concepts instilled by previous generations about the way things ought to be and how people should act. Their options allowed shifts in behavior to fit new circumstances, not so much constrained by the past as impelled by it.

The capacity to change through the recognition of a spectrum of possibilities reflects strategies compatible with a food quest that was attuned to a mountainous environment, enabling the ancestors of the Apache to exploit a variety of ecological niches and food sources. In that sort of milieu, flexible response has clear advantages. In succeeding centuries this opportunism allowed generations of people who faced myriad climates, situations, ecological zones, and unfamiliar peoples to survive. From the time Athapaskans departed the region of their ancient cultural heritage in northeastern Asia to the present, when they face such concerns as the next school board elections in Globe, Arizona, the people who came to be known as Apache represent an epic tale of human persistence.

We have no solid evidence that the Apache were in the Southwest until the sixteenth century (Dyen and Aberle 1974: 213–214; Forbes 1959).[4] Their presence after that was felt throughout the region. Had they been there much before 1500, it seems likely that they would have been noted by other groups and mentioned to the earliest Spanish expeditions of the 1540s. In their early years in the Southwest, they still shared a fairly homogeneous culture despite the diverse subdivisions that came to characterize the several Apache populations in more recent times. Even before they arrived in the region, though, there was at least a minor differentiation between the eastern and western sections of the population.

The western groups (Navajo, Western Apache, Chiricahua, and Mescalero) differ from the eastern (Jicarilla, Lipan, and Kiowa Apache) in the structure of their kinship systems (Opler 1936). There is also a general east-west linguistic difference among the Apache divisions. The sound /t/ in the western dialects became a /k/ among those of the Jicarilla, Lipan, and Kiowa Apache (Hoijer 1938; Hockett 1977), which indicates that long before these various groups became distinct, there was an old dichotomy between the eastern and western sectors. On the other hand, these differences are shallow compared to the profound cultural similarities among all of the Apache groups. In many ways they are little more than slight variations on a fundamental unity. All of the Apache divisions speak dialects of a single language. Kiowa Apache stands out as the most divergent, but considering its geographic separation, this is not particularly surprising. It still, nonetheless, is considered a dialect of the same language (Hoijer 1956).[5]

Most of the apparent differences developed among the Apache groups after they arrived in the Southwest. The historic Jicarilla and Lipan Apache descended from the easternmost section of the Proto-Apachean population, with the ancestors of the Lipan, in particular, exploiting food resources of the eastern side of the Rocky Mountains and the adjoining plains. The recent past of the Jicarilla is fairly well documented. They underwent remarkable changes and shifts in their subsistence focus during their centuries in the Southwest, and their activities ranged from sedentary farming to buffalo hunting (D.

Gunnerson 1974; J. Gunnerson 1969; Opler 1936, 1938, 1944, 1946; Schroeder 1974, I; Tiller 1983).

The western portion of the broad Apache population gravitated into other territorial niches, with ancestors of the Chiricahua and perhaps some of the Mescalero apparently in the vanguard of an expansion to the south and west.[6] The Western Apache descended into eastern Arizona below the Mogollon Rim from the mountainous areas to the north or northeast, probably during the early 1600s.[7]

In their territory in Arizona, the Western Apache continued their process of segmentation. The various small aggregates of people became associated with particular mountainous locales, and eventually they developed their own regionalisms and distinct identities. The process gave rise to a handful of scattered populations held together by kin ties and a sense of local affiliation, with subtle differences in dialect and perhaps still subtler differences in cultural style that grew as time passed (e.g., Goodwin 1969: 8, 9). Relationships among these aggregates varied at times from gregarious hospitality to feuds and mutual hostility.

Sorting out these local Western Apache divisions has been complicated. Disagreement among scholars reflects the fluid process of adaptation to circumstances that has characterized Athapaskan-speaking peoples in general. To develop a better understanding of the processes that led to the present situation of the San Carlos population, though, it is helpful to locate their recent precursors. In this case the subdivisions also reflect something of the divisions the Apache population saw among themselves.

Grenville Goodwin (1969: 1–62), who spent a decade with the people in the 1930s and gathered a rich bank of information from the old people of his day, refers to the local Western Apache clusters as "groups" whose members considered themselves to be subdivided into smaller distinct, localized "bands." He places the White Mountain group in the northeastern sector of Western Apache territory, divided into eastern and western bands. To the west of the White Mountain bands, he places the Cibecue group, subdivided into the Carrizo, Cibecue, and Canyon Creek bands. South of the Cibecue and west of the White Mountain groups was his San Carlos group, with their territory bisected by the Gila River. The San Carlos group included the Pinal, Arivaipa, San Carlos, and Apache Peaks bands.

Goodwin also includes the Northern Tonto, who occupied an area to the northwest of Western Apache territory, and the Southern Tonto, adjoining them to the southeast, as additional Apache populations. Subsequent research has indicated that these people were predominantly Yavapai, non-Apachean speakers who associated closely with some of the Western Apache during the pre-reservation period. In the late nineteenth century, some government and military officials mistakenly came to consider them to be Apache. Some of them lived on the San Carlos Reservation for a time and intermarried with Apache (Schroeder 1974, IV, 395–441).

As a result of later archival research, Albert Schroeder has modified Goodwin's groupings. He suggests that during prereservation times the Western Apache consisted of the three major groupings of Arivaipa, Pinal, and Coyotero, with the Coyotero perhaps subdivided into White Mountain and Gila drainage subgroups (Schroeder 1974, IV, 640).[8] Within the Western Apache sphere, though, these divisions are neither very ancient nor deep. They are based more on locality than on any other factor, and their minute cultural differences stem mostly from their recent dispersal into local territories. The uncertainty surrounding them tells a great deal about the fluid nature of this population who moved over thousands of square miles in their various activities and whose relationships with one another at times included intermarriage, raiding alliances, and sporadic feuds.

Although the Western Apache have lost most of their territory, the modern reservations are located in or near their old domains. Many of the people associated with Goodwin's Cibecue and White Mountain groups, often referred to in the early literature as Coyotero, inhabit the large Fort Apache Reservation to the north of San Carlos. The people of the San Carlos Reservation are mainly descendants of Pinal and Arivaipa, with a few Coyotero, the former two comprising bands of Goodwin's San Carlos group.[9] But these distributions are not particularly rigid. The population of San Carlos includes people from many of the other Apache divisions, as well as some non-Apache people.

An Approach to the Past

If the present is a consequence of the past, then it is liable to be incomprehensible without some sense of what has gone before. Although we can never retrieve or understand completely most of the forgotten events and experiences that led to the emergence of the Western Apache over the centuries, we can reconstruct many aspects of the past. How did the Apache come to be as they are?

One way to approach Apache culture history is to examine the relationships among the various Athapaskan-speaking groups of recent times. If they all stem from a common origin, why did they diverge, and when? What conditions might have given rise to the expansions of the population, their movements, and their segmentations into different groups?

It is useful to view Athapaskan culture history in terms of a "radiation model" analogous to the biological phenomenon of adaptive radiation. This refers to a situation in which a successful species or population expands into a variety of niches at the margins of its range, with the result that in the process of adaptation to the situations they encounter, local contingents alter to produce variants of the former parent population. As applied to the Athapaskan case, this is no more than a metaphor and should not be pushed too far, but it does provide a model for the process involved in Athapaskan segmentations and culture change.

Beginning with a population who shared a single cultural system some time in the past, Athapaskan peoples migrated vast distances. Inadvertently, perhaps, many of them found themselves in foreign ecological settings and faced conditions that changed, imperceptibly in some cases and drastically in others. They were exposed to novel ideas. They altered some of the patterns of their food quest, and through time they adjusted their beliefs and patterns of behavior in a variety of ways until considerable cultural diversity had developed. But throughout this process, they retained echoes of a common heritage. These traces that remain, in conjunction with other evidence, are important clues to the past.

Culture change is one of the most complex and elusive phenomena imaginable. It does not lend itself to the controlled experimentation of laboratory analysis with replicable results, as the ideals of the "hard" sciences demand. But in the Athapaskan dispersal, we have a different sort of controlled situation. The Athapaskan radiation model has an exciting potential to illuminate some of the dynamic properties of culture.

In the broader scope of human prehistory, this process of population movement, segmentation, and dispersal has been the rule rather than the exception. But in many ways the Athapaskan case presents an unusual opportunity to reconstruct the past, not only to examine some of the changes that took place but to explore some of the reasons. What can account for the alternative directions of change that these groups followed? Can this tell us anything about cultural developments that are likely to occur under particular conditions? Is prediction possible?

The past relationships among Athapaskan-speaking peoples have presented an interesting problem for generations of scholars. Research began in an intensive way early in this century when it was realized that the Athapaskan languages share a clear "genetic" relationship.[10] This was intriguing in its own right, but it was also an essential precondition for the unraveling of Apachean culture history. There is general agreement now that all of these languages stem from a common parent language. This ancient language, the population who spoke it, and their associated cultural and social phenomena are referred to as "Proto-Athapaskan" (Young 1983 : 393).

Athapaskan-speaking peoples today inhabit a remarkable variety of ecological zones and regions, many of which are separated by thousands of miles. Their territories range from the mountains and barren grounds of the interior of Alaska and Canada through the mild northern California and southern Oregon coast to the broken, hot rugged deserts and mountains of the Southwest. In many ways Athapaskan cultures are so different from one another that, without the insights of linguistics, it is unlikely that anyone would have suspected, much less been able to establish, a common heritage among them (e.g., Driver 1961 : 578). Linguistic evidence continues to provide crucial insights into Athapaskan relationships, and since the fact of a common base is established, we can employ other kinds of evidence to flesh out the shared cultural heritage that this implies.

Biological data support the idea that Athapaskan-speaking peoples share a common past. A specific blood antigen designated "albumin Naskapi," for example, is common among the Athapaskan-speaking populations of the western Subarctic, and it occurs with a high frequency in the Southwest only among Athapaskan-speaking peoples (Lampl and Blumberg 1979). On the basis of twenty-four blood group gene frequencies, the geneticist Emoke Szathmary (1977 : 117) concludes that there is "little or no significant genetic differentiation among Athapaskans."

If the linguistic and biological evidence for common Athapaskan origins are compelling, though, the archaeological evidence leaves much of the mystery intact. Attempts to trace Athapaskan continuities deep into the past have to rely on evidence that is both scarce and ambiguous. Continued work by researchers in the Subarctic promises to clarify the processes of Athapaskan cultural development in that crucial region, but some of the general characteristics of Athapaskan cultures pose inherent problems for archaeological research.

In recent historic times and far into the past, most Athapaskan-speaking groups have been extremely mobile, returning periodically to favored spots but rarely occupying any site continuously for extended, unbroken lengths of time. This mobility has been an effective means of coping with the conditions of the food quest and is a typical characteristic of hunting peoples. But such a living pattern

Map 2. Distribution of Athapaskan and Eyak peoples

means that at any particular site, the accumulation of debris that might be useful to the archaeologist is likely to be sparse.

Athapaskan peoples also have tended to be receptive to innovation, especially with regard to technology, which normally constitutes most of the data accessible to the archaeologist. As a result, some of the aspects of material culture most visible to archaeologists, such as the styles of projectile points, have changed rapidly and erratically. In the nineteenth century, a single group of Navajo used several different types of arrow points at the same time (Farmer 1940). At an archeological site in Alaska that Athapaskan-speaking Tanaina occupied within the memory of living people, the artifacts were identical with those of nearby Eskimo groups (Townsend 1970, 1973). And the Western Apache often used implements that they found at prehistoric sites (Gregory 1981: 264).

Throughout the Subarctic in recent centuries, Athapaskan peoples have used bone points with barbs along one side, bird bone drinking tubes associated with female puberty seclusion, and a few other characteristic artifacts. But beyond the range of recent periods and particular regions, there does not seem to be any particular diagnostic form such as a distinctive type of stone point that can be associated definitively with Athapaskan speakers. Consequently, the Athapaskan present in the archaeological record is elusive. The puzzle remains a serious obstacle to clarifying the prehistory of this population in the Subarctic. One researcher characterizes Athapaskan prehistory as "a thing of many strands" (A. Clark 1981: 119), and in the words of another, it remains "an enigma" (Donohue 1977: 89).

Through trade, raiding, and the influence of ideas, Athapaskan groups have adopted many features from neighboring peoples, albeit selectively. The archaeological data show that trade in obsidian from a single source occurred throughout much of the interior of Alaska for thousands of years, which suggests that many other kinds of mutual influences pervaded among these populations as well (A. Clark 1977: 131). This openness to innovation is an interesting characteristic in its own right. Why have Athapaskan people been so ready to change? Is this a general receptivity to innovation, or has their acceptance been more selective in any consistent way?

The Navajo, for example, have been referred to as "some of the outstanding learners among American Indians" (Underhill 1953: 226). After World War II, a study that compared Navajo and Zuni communities' reactions to returning veterans substantiated this impression. While the Zuni were rather cautious about the harmful influences that returning veterans might bring into the community from outside, the Navajo appeared far more interested in the possibility of benefiting from new ideas (Adair and Vogt 1949).

As to northern Athapaskan groups, James VanStone (1974:125) notes "the importance of cultural flexibility as an Athapaskan adaptive strategy. . . . Indians moving into different environments in most cases readily borrowed techniques and technologies from the people already present and accommodated those techniques within Athapaskan culture. Traditional Athapaskan culture must be thought of as essentially an accommodating culture, and accommodation, in turn, greatly facilitated survival in a demanding environment." For people migrating into a variety of ecological zones where other people already had developed successful ways of exploiting the local resources, this characteristic had some clear advantages.

Paradoxically, though, if we conceive of culture as learned, shared knowledge and belief manifest in observable behavior and material artifacts, we can discern a conservative aspect of Athapaskan cultures as well. To some degree it appears in language. Athapaskan dialects and languages have been notably resistant to outside influence (Sherzer 1973).[11] In Alaska, for example, the long period of contact between the Athapaskan-speaking Ingalik and coastal Eskimo people led to extensive borrowing of material culture, but Eskimo influence on the Ingalik language has been surprisingly slight (Krauss 1973b).

Some aspects of intellectual and belief systems among Athapaskan speakers also have shown remarkable persistence. We might have expected beliefs to be especially unstable through time, especially among populations without written language. For ideas to be perpetuated, they must be transmitted orally from generation to generation. On the other hand, beliefs might be less directly affected by the changes in ecological relationships caused by migration, shifts in the food quest, adjustments in social organization, or innovations in technology, and therefore might be more likely to be passed on over generations through a variety of circumstances. A concept of a living, sentient universe, for example, or a belief that ghosts whistle in the dark, may be as feasible in one ecological zone as another. The same may not be true of particular forms of social organization.

Morris Opler (1983a:380), a noted scholar of the Apache, has suggested that there is a "basic Apachean culture pattern." He notes that where outside influences acted upon various Apache groups throughout history, "the basic ideas and content were reworked to harmonize with Apachean conceptions and purposes." Joseph Jorgensen (1983:691) points out that "the Athapaskan speakers who probably began moving into the Southwest during the early sixteenth century maintained considerable similarities even though they came to occupy a vast area." As to the Northern Athapaskan populations, VanStone (1974:125) writes that despite numerous influences from surrounding groups, "there are deep cultural similarities among all northern Athapaskan speakers."

What can we make of all this? Why should many of the least tangible aspects of life be so tenacious and durable, while material culture, the "hardware" of a people, is so changeable? We could surmise that in a sense, culture tends to be conservative. Beliefs about the "truths" of life and the universe, concepts of the way things work and why, tend to persist from generation to generation unless something dramatic occurs to undermine or refute them. For the most part, these beliefs are not empirically testable hypotheses but intellectual "givens." They are guides for interpreting reality.

Time-honored interpretations of reality in some cases might come to seem inadequate for dealing with novel situations. Conventional obligations and responsibilities can become burdensome in new circumstances. But these aspects of culture tend to continue through time because a sense of the way things are, or ought to be (providing the basis for a definition of the self in the context of the universe), often involves considerable emotional commitment and psychological investment. Ways of living, if they do not prove to be catastrophically inadequate, survive from generation to generation because they work, or seem to. They are associated with the past and are deeply identified with the people themselves.

We can see continuities of this sort in the cultural similarities that persist among the widely separated Athapaskan-speaking populations. Many of these old patterns have been modified, to be sure, but they continue to share enough resemblances to accommodate ethnographic comparison. This in turn can shed light on the earlier common culture base from which they developed. It is possible to illuminate some important gaps in the Athapaskan past and tentatively, at least, to fill them by examining some of the features that historic Athapaskan groups still have in common, after allowing for the likelihood of coincidence or borrowing from other cultures. In the pages that follow, we shall piece together information from a range of sources to gain a sense of the shared Athapaskan cultural heritage and examine some of the processes that have led to the present.

Athapaskan diversification can be approached in a number of ways. The food quest provides one continuous, common thread from the beginning to the present. Throughout Athapaskan culture history, the simple need to obtain food has imposed constraints on options and has influenced choices, fostering the development of certain cultural features. In the Subarctic it affected the movements and actions of local populations and no doubt tempered the tone of relationships among them. It played a part in the migration decisions of Athapaskan peoples and, in some cases, led them into circumstances that fed back in turn upon the culture, consequently stimulating other kinds of changes.

The use of mountain ranges, the independent movements of small groups, buffalo hunting, farming, and the raiding complex in the Southwest—all were part of Apachean cultural processes that we can view from the perspective of strategies for getting food and their repercussions on the rest of the cultural system. Conversely, the evident continuance of some ancient cultural features throughout these changes is of equal interest.

This focus on the food quest does not imply that the nature of subsistence has any particular deterministic power over other aspects of culture, but it does provide a "handle," a device for dealing with a complex array of data. It is both a fundamental aspect of life and a phenomenon articulated in complex ways with other aspects of human existence. For social life to continue—and for humans there is no life but social life—culture patterns must be at least minimally compatible with food-getting techniques and strategies feasible in the immediate surroundings. Complex and systemic relationships exist between subsistence and other aspects of life. Each of them is liable to set constraints and to influence the direction of change that can occur in the other, and change in any of these aspects is likely to have further repercussions, whether subtle or dramatic.

Some of the strategies of historic Athapaskan groups in the western Subarctic would have been successful in the same region thousands of years earlier. It is a region with many ecological zones, encompassing a range of food sources that tend to be mobile and often are thinly scattered, but which also can be sporadically rich. It is a setting of mountainous terrain inhabited by caribou and other game, salmon rivers, and in a few places, with access to the Pacific Coast. For people who lived in that setting, a strategy of operating in autonomous, freely moving population clusters with a capacity to exploit seasonal and ad hoc sources of food has had proven success.

Because of the wild fluctuations in the numbers of Subarctic game animals and the meager overall carrying capacity of the land, the constraints on human inhabitants are severe. Large groups of people could not have existed in any one locality for very long. Rigid

territorial boundaries would have inhibited the necessary movements of people in search of food. Moreover, since a particular game
species might be abundant one year and rare the next in any one
area, specialized focus on a narrow range of food sources would have
been a poor strategy indeed. The conditions of the Subarctic impose
flexibility on the food quest, and a capacity to take advantage of unpredictable and far-flung opportunities requires easy movement.
Such a capacity has characterized most Athapaskan groups in recent
times.

In most of the Subarctic, the food quest favored mountain ranges,
where the greatest variety of ecological niches can be tapped within
a minimal distance. This allows utilization of a range of secondary
food sources as well as access to such important game as caribou,
which can be found in different places at various times of the year.
(Appendix B documents the mountainous locales of Athapaskan-
speaking populations.)

From southern Alaska, the Proto-Athapaskan population could
have expanded their territory along mountain ranges for over a thousand miles to the north, northeast, and the southeast without leaving the same ecological setting.[12] With a mountain adaptation and
"mixed bag" food quest in the North, the Cordillera leading into the
Rocky Mountain chain became a corridor stretching south toward
the region that eventually would be known as Apachería.

Nothing more than the pursuit of their traditional patterns would
have been necessary to lead the people south into regions where, as
the climate slowly changed, they shifted the emphases of their food
quest to make use of the available resources. Retaining their ancient
and well-tested strategies as they moved into the Rockies, the people
would have found Subarctic fauna such as caribou becoming scarce
during the course of a long warming trend that began by the first few
centuries A.D. Increasingly, their subsistence activities would have
to have been directed toward other game including mountain sheep,
mountain goats, elk, deer, or perhaps buffalo at lower elevations.
Many of the old hunting techniques from the North, such as collective game drives, are adaptable to a variety of species.

By the sixteenth century A.D., the mobility of the people and the
free movement of small groups that they had maintained throughout these changes led them still farther along the mountain chain
toward the Southwest core area. It is possible that they had never encountered sedentary agricultural peoples before they spied the adobe
villages of Pueblo farmers. But soon they incorporated this resource
into their subsistence pattern through trading with the agricultural
peoples of the region and, later, by raiding. The self-sufficient, inde-

pendent mobility of the scattered Apache groups with their preference for mountainous areas was well suited for this way of life.

When the Western Apache later chose to grow crops of their own, they merely added cultivation to their subsistence rounds. Most of them managed to avoid a specialized commitment to agriculture that could have curtailed their free movements. Even so, the growth of their dependence on raiding and their partial reliance on planted crops not only had repercussions among the Apache themselves but in the wider network of relationships throughout the Southwest. Eventually these dynamic processes led to the suppression of raiding and farming. Their eventual loss of control over their territory and the external administration of their society ended their autonomous food quest and eventually, following the eclipse of their political sovereignty, imposed a structure of oppression.

The next chapter will consider the diversity of historic Athapaskan cultures in order to provide a basis for ethnographic comparison. Chapter 3 deals with Proto-Athapaskan conditions during the earliest phase in North America, and in chapter 4 some aspects of Proto-Athapaskan culture are reconstructed. Subsequent chapters consider the spread of the Athapaskan population toward the south and the separation of the Proto-Apache from the northern groups. Later, we shall examine the entry of the Apache population into the Southwest and the culture change that occurred as a consequence, leading to the reservation period and the modern community of San Carlos.

CHAPTER 2

The Athapaskan-speaking Peoples

The people with whom the Western Apache share a common linguistic heritage are scattered over the western half of North America. Despite the variety of locales that Athapaskan-speaking populations inhabit, though, they fall into three major geographic groups. The northernmost, thinly dispersed from northern and western Alaska toward the western edge of Hudson Bay, are referred to as Northern Athapaskan or, in Canada, Dene, in recognition of a term by which some of them refer to themselves.

On the Pacific Coast other Athapaskan speakers inhabit a densely populated area on both sides of the California-Oregon boundary. Generally the people of this enclave are referred to as Pacific Coast Athapaskan. A still smaller population in the state of Washington once spoke Athapaskan languages called Kwalhioqua and Tlatskanai. These languages have been lost without ever having been adequately recorded, although they shared significant features with Northern Athapaskan languages (Krauss 1979:870). The third contingent are the Apache, often referred to collectively as Southern Athapaskan.

The range of diversity among these groups is striking, but some generalizations about Athapaskan cultures are possible. It is worth examining what these groups have in common, regardless of their geographic differences, in order to establish a basis for reconstructing the common heritage they share deep in the past. Most of these populations in all three regions live in or near mountainous areas (see Appendix B). In the North some of them have expanded eastward into the flatlands to exploit the barren ground caribou herds, and in historic times they engaged in the fur trade. But considerable evidence exists that this spread to the east is fairly recent.

Most Northern Athapaskan peoples still live in the mountainous interior of Alaska and the Yukon Territory and in the Cordillera running parallel to the Pacific Coast into the Rockies. On the California

Mountainous terrain in southeastern Arizona

and Oregon coast, Athapaskan speakers exploited mountainous ter-ritories in conjunction with the coastal zones. Most Athapaskan groups in the Southwest inhabited mountainous terrain as well. Even those who spent considerable time on the Plains, such as the Lipan and Jicarilla, returned periodically to the mountains.

A typical Athapaskan social organization has involved small and very mobile autonomous groups without any rigid overall political structure to unite them. In all of these regions, the primary basis for interaction has been individual ties within and between clusters of people rather than membership in well-defined corporate groups. With the important exception of the Pacific Coast groups, if Atha-paskan populations recognize any principle of unilineal descent at all, it is matrilineal. In that case marriages typically occur between members of different matrilineal descent groups, often arranged by intermediaries, who generally are older relatives of the couple. Some form of bride service, in which a man is expected to hunt for his new wife's parents for a period of time, is usually part of the marriage agreement. In some groups, particularly in the Southwest, where the couple reside with the wife's parents, this is an implicit aspect of the preferred matrilocal residence pattern. (The distribution of these characteristics among Athapaskan peoples is documented in Appendix C.)

Most Athapaskan systems of cosmology involve a belief that both living and inanimate objects are invested with a "power" that inherently is neither good nor bad, but capricious, unpredictable, and potentially dangerous because of its strength. Such power may interact directly with humans, generally through dreams, and affect them in various ways (see Appendix E for the distribution of these features).

Femaleness also is a pervasive ideological concern among Athapaskan peoples and tends to be viewed as a potentially dangerous force. It expresses itself in various restrictions on women during menstruation and childbirth, with menstrual seclusion and special ritual recognition of girls' puberty (see Appendix C for documentation).

Beliefs about life and death among Athapaskan peoples often involve concepts of multiple components of the soul. One of these is threatening and is subject to a specific complex of avoidance measures. The other is associated with wind or air. (Appendix D documents these features.) Conversely, a concern with health and long life also is a widespread theme. Among both Northern and Southern Athapaskan groups, this theme was often associated with female puberty rituals and rigorous physical training for young people (de Laguna and McClellan 1981:659; McKennan 1981:572; Goodwin 1969:461).

Northern Athapaskan

The territory of Northern Athapaskan peoples is ringed by the barren ground beyond the tree line along the Arctic Coast to the north and the west coast of Alaska, an extensive region inhabited by Inupiaq- and Yupik-speaking Eskimos. One could say that in northwestern Canada and most of Alaska, the coastline and tundra were the domain of Eskimos and the interior that of Athapaskan peoples. The width of coastal Eskimo territory varied throughout that expanse, and it has fluctuated in the past, reaching its thinnest point in western Alaska near Norton Sound, where the coast faces Siberia across the Bering Strait. Within historic times, no Athapaskan-speaking group in the North had access to the sea except for the Tanaina, whose territory embraced Cook Inlet and included the site of the present city of Anchorage.

Toward the south, the northern Athapaskan population was scattered along mountainous terrain into British Columbia, again blocked from the coastline along the full length of their distribution by Pa-

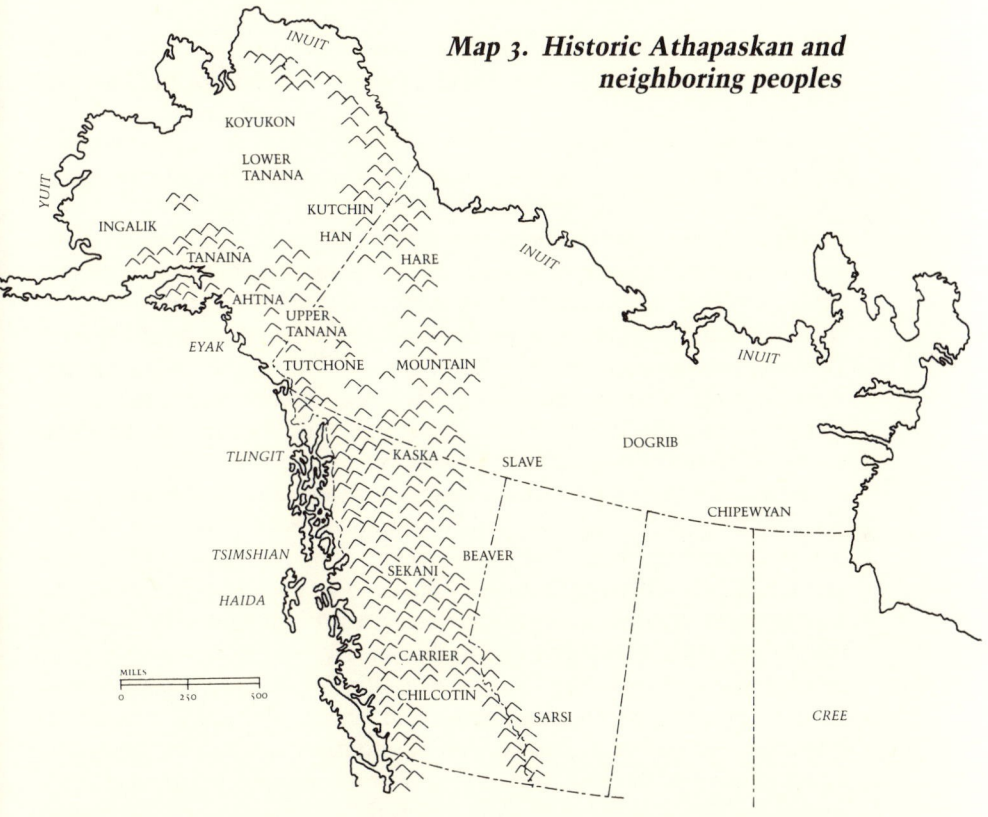

Map 3. Historic Athapaskan and neighboring peoples

cific Eskimo, Eyak, Tlingit, Haida, Gitksan, and Tsimshian peoples. Athapaskan-speaking peoples also spread eastward from the Cordillera into the flatlands as far as the vicinity of Hudson Bay, although as mentioned earlier, this appears to have been a secondary expansion. These small, scattered aggregates ranged over broad distances in their quest for food and distributed themselves very thinly over this vast territory to the east, with some tracts all but uninhabited for much of the year. The overall distribution of this population of Northern Athapaskans raises questions about the process of dispersal. Where did it start? Where was the point of departure likely to have been?

To start this search for Athapaskan beginnings, it is useful to scan the expanse of the western Subarctic and consider the distribution of peoples throughout the region. Language is a useful means of unraveling relationships among these local populations.

We can subdivide the Northern Athapaskan territory in a number of ways. The Alaska-Yukon boundary is one basis for a regional dichotomy. As far as native peoples are concerned this line is an accident of history, but it does roughly separate Athapaskan speakers of

Alaska, whose languages are extremely different from one another, from the Canadian Athapaskan speakers to the south and east, whose dialects are far more similar. The greater diversity among the languages in Alaska suggests that they have been separate much longer than the languages and dialects to the east (Dyen and Aberle 1974:804; also Adams, Van Gerven, and Levy 1978:507).

Tanaina, which is spoken in southern Alaska, is the most divergent. It is about equally distant from all other Athapaskan languages, including the Pacific Coast and Southern Athapaskan groups.[1] Ahtna, Ingalik, and Koyukon, spoken in Alaska, also are deeply split among themselves.[2] Since these Alaskan languages show the most profound linguistic differences, indicating that the splits among them are very old, it seems likely that the early homeland of Proto-Athapaskans was somewhere in Alaska.

When we consider linguistic distinctions and the implications they have for cultural boundaries, though, it is important to keep in mind that the most realistic way to view the Northern Athapaskan groups is to see them as a nearly continuous, thinly spread linguistic community. Within this population, abrupt contrasts are less common than differences that gradually shade into one another. In a few cases, sharp changes divide one neighboring Athapaskan language from another, but Michael Krauss and Victor Golla (1981:69) point out that "whatever the language boundaries, the network of communication in the Northern Athapaskan dialect complex is open-ended." There are breaks in mutual intelligibility between Tanaina, Kolchan, and some other Alaskan languages and their neighbors, but the few demarcations of that sort do not produce anything resembling a neat pattern of "tribal" divisions in an ethnic or sociopolitical sense (Krauss and Golla 1981:73, 74).

We can also draw a distinction between groups that inhabit the Arctic drainage region—so designated because of the direction of river flow to the east of the mountains—and those of the Pacific side. Many Athapaskan peoples of the Arctic drainage, particularly Chipewyan, Dogrib, Slave, and, formerly, Yellowknife, inhabit relatively flat country and hunt caribou, moose, and in earlier times, wood buffalo. A few Athapaskan groups on the Arctic drainage side of the Cordillera, such as the Kaska and Sekani, inhabit more mountainous terrain (see Appendix B).

In many parts of the Pacific drainage, the natural food supply is enriched by the presence of salmon that migrate up the rivers flowing west into the ocean. The climate of the Pacific side tends to be milder as well, catching the effects of the Japanese Current in warm

Two young Ahtna women around 1900 (National Anthropological Archives, Smithsonian Institution)

westerly winds that the Cordillera shields from the eastern flat-lands. As a consequence, extreme winter cold is less a factor on the western side than it is east of the mountains, where the temperature can drop to 60° F. or more below zero.

Throughout this territory the quality and type of food available to Athapaskan peoples varies widely. Effective exploitation of food sources across the Subarctic required mobility and prevented popu-lations from achieving densities comparable to those in many other parts of North America. And in the Arctic drainage region, the need for mobility was still more extreme, requiring an even thinner dispersal.

To the east of the Cordillera, Athapaskan peoples developed sys-tems of kin ties with a bilateral basis, giving equivalent recognition to relatives on the mothers' and the fathers' sides. This allowed people to maximize the scope of their relationships: their options to call upon ad hoc affiliations as the need arose were as wide as pos-sible. This system afforded flexibility in the people's capacity either to coalesce into large temporary aggregates or to disperse easily into smaller clusters. In one sense this pattern is an extreme end of the spectrum of the more general Athapaskan tendency to operate in small autonomous groups (Helm 1965).[3]

With the exception of these Arctic drainage Athapaskans, though, a matrilineal principle of descent with matrilocal residence, at least initially after marriage, predominated as a Northern Athapaskan pattern. In historic times the Ahtna had from eight to ten matrilineal clans grouped into two divisions, or moities. Marriage of a man with a woman of his father's clan was the preferred form. This system produced a situation in which, ideally, pairs of clans would be "continually linked in marriage" (de Laguna and McClellan 1981:653). The Tanaina also had matrilineal clans and moieties (Townsend 1981:633). In the interior of Alaska, Tanana clans were grouped in a "tripartite" system (McKennan 1981:572). Bride service was common throughout the area (see Appendix C).

Along the Pacific drainage side of the Cordillera, many Athapaskan groups show strong influence from coastal peoples. The Tlingit, Haida, and Kwakiutl exemplify a distinctive and long-established Pacific Coast culture complex—a way of life resting on a population density made possible by a rich, dependable food supply that allowed such developments as a formalized emphasis on social rank and group stratification, stable residence in large, substantial buildings of cedar planks and beams, and art forms in carved wood that were both intricate and monumental. This is the area associated with totem poles and the socially pivotal feasting known as the potlatch.

Public ceremonies and feasts in this area expressed group definition and specified, acknowledged, and validated rights and status proclaimed through emblems and symbols often referred to as crests. Throughout the Pacific Coast, wealth regulated and maintained formalized relationships among large, compact, sedentary populations who relied on resources that were rich, but localized and unevenly distributed.

The influence of this venerable and well-established cultural style appears among some Athapaskan groups in their ceremonial feasting, crest groups, and possibly even their moiety systems. Some researchers have argued that the origin of Athapaskan unilineal concepts of descent stem from this coastal influence. The Athapaskan-speaking Carrier of British Columbia, for example, show many effects of contact with the coastal Tsimshian and Gitksan. The Carrier matrilineal clans, grouped in clusters or phratries associated with specified ranks, crests, and ceremonial feasting, are clearly reminiscent of the Pacific Coast pattern. The Carrier names of crests, titles, and phratries are Tsimshian words. The Carrier, unlike the neighboring Tsimshian and Gitksan, have no traditions of their own about the origins of these socially important features.

Vernon Kobrinsky (1977) suggests that in former times Carrier social organization involved loosely defined aggregates of kin who had no more than a vague sense of territorial boundaries. This would be a familiar Athapaskan pattern. The more elaborate, sharply bounded clans and phratries with their ceremonial appurtenances, he argues, may have been a more recent development. But why would the Carrier have acquired such a pattern? The ceremonial complex of non-Athapaskan peoples on the Pacific Coast developed among densely settled salmon-fishing populations. In this kind of setting, a complex and sharply defined structure of relationships with denoted "chiefs" and "a ranked array of lesser nobles" served as a way to "regulate problems of space, population, wealth, power, and philosophy through the parliamentary institution known as the potlatch."[4]

The Carrier, having moved toward the coast from the inland Cordillera, and having gained access to some of the rich resources that already were being exploited by these long-established salmon-fishing peoples, chose to emulate much of what they saw. Certain aspects of the social organization of the Pacific Coast—crests, ranks, and specified individual rights with publicly understood criteria— were intimately associated with that particular resource base. Kobrinsky (1977) sees much of the "Tsimshianization" of the Carrier social organization as a result of the stimulus of a "newly adopted salmon economy."

But the Carrier did not adopt everything that they observed among the neighboring groups, and Kobrinsky (1977) observes that "ordinarily one would expect that lengthy exposure to Gitksan tutelage would have resulted in more thorough reproduction of their ways." Yet despite intense influences from exposure to other cultural systems, Athapaskan peoples have tended to select items and ideas judiciously. Generally, they have modified and made them over to fit the Athapaskan context.[5]

As to whether Carrier matrilineal clans are a result of influence from other peoples, it should be noted that wherever unilineal descent groups do appear among either Northern or Southern Athapaskan populations, they have almost always been matrilineal (see Appendix C). Non-Athapaskan embellishments on the Carrier social organization seem clear, but they were added to an Athapaskan culture base that among other things involved a concept of defining relationships through women (see Appendix C). As such, the matrilineal clans themselves mainly represent elaborations on an underlying theme, stimulated by interactions with foreign groups.

The quality and concentration of the food supply has been one important aspect of the conditions that led to the development of these general Athapaskan cultural features. Throughout the Northern Athapaskan range, clear-cut matrilineal descent occurs most often in the relatively rich areas. Indeed, groups with systems of matrilineal descent inhabit the entire length of the Pacific drainage (Dyen and Aberle 1974:289). Bilateral organization, on the other hand, is more common in relatively sparse areas. The Kutchin provide an interesting illustration of this. Their territory spans a region from the mountainous terrain in Alaska to somewhat flatter country in the Yukon. In historic times, at least, matrilineal descent among this population tended to become weaker toward the more barren lands in the east.[6]

Nowhere, though, was the food supply stable, concentrated, or predictable enough to allow people to pursue a specialized food quest of the sort that developed among non-Athapaskan salmon-fishing coastal peoples or Eskimo groups, with their focus on marine mammals. Of the Northern Athapaskan groups, only the Tanaina had access to the Pacific in historic times, via Cook Inlet. The Katchemak Bay area in their territory may have been the richest of any of the regions inhabited by Northern Athapaskan peoples (Osgood 1937:17, 46). Yet even the Tanaina maintained a broad, multifaceted food quest and extensively utilized inland resources, such as caribou, in addition to sea mammals. In earlier times the reliance on inland food sources probably was even greater (Hosley 1977).

With the introduction of guns and the incursion of nonnative peoples into the Tanaina area near the turn of the century, caribou and other game became scarce in some regions. At the same time, the introduction of a device called the "fish wheel" made it possible to harvest salmon from the murkier main streams of the major rivers. Fishing in earlier times had depended more on spearing and traps in smaller, clear tributaries, and the appearance of dogsleds during the fur trade era created a demand for fish for dogfood. But in prehistoric times caribou and other inland game would have received greater attention, and a more varied subsistence pattern was probably more typical of Athapaskan populations.

Plants that can be utilized as food by humans are sparse in the Subarctic compared to regions to the south.[7] Animal populations tend to be sparse as well, especially on a situational basis. Some of the most important species range over great distances and, for a number of reasons, tend to fluctuate wildly in numbers over the years. This instability in numbers as well as location is associated partly, at least, with the nature of Subarctic vegetation and the overall paucity of biomass. This results in a need for large animals such as caribou that feed on plants to cover extensive terrain. The herds must move over vast distances to live, and the fluctuation in their numbers is due in part, at least, to a short food chain that provides few buffering factors. Natural vagaries at the lower end can have pronounced repercussions.

People in the western Subarctic regions who depend entirely on the natural food supply must cope with these fluctuations and make the greatest possible use of whatever food is available to them. In that kind of situation, easy mobility is essential to make the maximum use of food resources, and in most areas the population must be thinly dispersed. To deal with these unpredictable aspects of the food supply, a strategy of nonspecialization, keeping one's options open to all opportunities, is a rational policy. Conversely, overdependence on any particular food source would likely be disastrous over a few generations.

That positive strategy of maintaining wide options, avoiding overcommitment to particular resources though overspecialization, is well suited to a preference for mountainous terrain in which a variety of ecological niches are accessible at different altitudes within a minimal distance. Catherine McClellan and Glenda Denniston (1981:372) describe such a setting in vivid terms: "The Subarctic Cordillera is a magnificent high plateau country. In it are large and small rivers and lakes, flood-plains and muskeg swamps, patches of meadow, and vast stretches of boreal forest, but there are also alpine tundra, bare slopes of scree, craggy mountain peaks, small glaciers, and huge icefields."

To exploit this region's resources, Athapaskan peoples used traps, snares, gill nets, and weirs made of sinew, spruce and willow roots, twisted grass, rope made from the hair of mountain goats, and *babiche*, a cordage made from caribou hide. The range of game sought by the Athapaskan-speaking Kaska exemplify the food sources to be exploited in this area. Caribou, moose, black and brown bears, mountain sheep and goats, beavers, muskrats, lynx, ground hogs, gophers, martens, rabbits, porcupines, squirrels, a variety of birds including geese, ducks, owls, eagles, cranes, swans, loons, spruce hens, willow grouse, ptarmigan, and several types of fish were eaten, as well as a variety of berries in season (Honigmann 1964:31).

Despite this apparent cornucopia of food, though, Kaska traditions refer often to starvation. Severe food shortages were not uncommon (Honigmann 1964:32). The Cordilleran food quest was a matter of exploiting varied econiches with "distinctive subsistence and deployment patterns, which combine big and small game hunting and fishing with some gathering into an annual round of high mobility." But as McClellan and Denniston (1981:373) note, "Starvation has been reported for all Subarctic Cordillera groups, including the Chilcotin farthest to the south."

The collective game drive may be one of the oldest of the many techniques the people in this area used to obtain food. It involved taking advantage of the herding behavior of these animals to drive them into a V-shaped enclosure. The objective was to move a herd into an area encompassed by widely separated, flaring wings of the structure in which, as the animals moved forward, the channel ahead of them narrowed increasingly to a spot where waiting hunters hidden behind mounds of brush could easily kill large numbers of them. Most Athapaskan groups used variations of this for hunting caribou. Gathering in large camps for the hunt late in the summer, people could provide themselves with a good supply of meat and skins to help carry them through the cold months.

Samuel Hearne's (1911:309) vivid description of a Chipewyan game drive on the barren grounds in the late eighteenth century has the immediacy of an eyewitness account. The Chipewyan employed the drive technique in the summer. It was necessary to locate the herd far in the distance and quickly deploy drivers around and behind them before they could become alarmed. Once the animals had been spotted, the hunters would hide downwind at chosen spots and "lie concealed in small circular fences, made with loose stones, moss, &c." Other people would erect sticks fifteen or twenty yards apart, "which they carry with them the whole summer for the purpose" (Hearne 1911:309). These sticks were topped with lumps of moss and pendants, probably made of bark, that would swing and twirl in the breeze and frighten the caribou and keep them from breaking through the lines.

The women and boys divided into two groups and circled widely upwind to meet far behind the caribou, "which are drove right forward." As the animals finally stampeded through the narrow end of the drive, hunters hidden in the camouflaged blinds would leap up to kill as many as they could. Many things could go wrong with even the best-laid plans, but Hearne (1911:310) maintains that the technique usually was extremely productive.

The game drive, probably a very ancient device, occurred widely among Athapaskan groups. The Koyukon of northern Alaska used it well into the nineteenth century. One Kutchin game drive structure had a narrow enclosure about a mile long, with flaring wings extending far into the distance, and contained about ten thousand poles (J. Wright 1976:30). Hearne, in his centuries-old account, claims that the Chipewyan used the technique only on the barren grounds, but the principle was far more flexible and could be used in different types of terrain for other game. In southern Alaska the Ahtna generally used their caribou drive structures, or "fences," in mountainous areas above the tree line (de Laguna and McClellan 1981: 648).

Snowshoes were another important aspect of Athapaskan technology. Probably no other cultural innovation in preindustrial times had greater significance in opening vast regions of the northern hemisphere to human exploitation. The basic idea of snowshoes may have arisen in Siberia, but the refined, netted version was the result of a series of Athapaskan innovations and improvements on the basic pattern (Davidson 1937). The upturned leading edge, left foot and right foot forms, and complex patterns of netting apparently developed in the Northern Athapaskan region and later spread eastward through the Subarctic into the eastern woodlands.

Efficient snowshoes would have allowed a secondary expansion of Athapaskan peoples from the Cordillera eastward into the flatlands. With this improved means of travel, Athapaskan peoples could hunt the tremendous herds of barren ground caribou that winter in the forests to the south and migrate north to spend their summers on the tundra (Dyen and Aberle 1974: 276).

These constraints and possibilities, which rest ultimately on the resource base, affected the range of organizational choices open to Athapaskan peoples. Small clusters of people who were able to move freely, with a capacity to disperse and coalesce easily, would have been able to respond to the vagaries of the environment in the most efficient manner. A general ethic of individual autonomy seems to have been inherent in this mode of living.[8]

The free movement of small groups was not hindered by any rigid restriction to bounded territories or association with permanent villages. In central Alaska, for example, the Tanana retained base camps, but the people rarely lived there for any extended time. The disparate seasonal demands of the food quest required that they cover an expansive territory on a regular basis, on foot. People might travel to caribou drives or fishing spots fifty miles or more from their base camps, and in some cases groups of fifteen to seventy-five persons covered territories of up to five thousand square miles (Holmes 1971: 101; Hosley 1981: 540). Typically, villages or base camps were favored spots where the people living in a particular region could gather periodically, often during the winter. But rather than stable residential units, they tended to be geographic reference points and social centers of gravity for wide-ranging activities.

These aspects of Athapaskan social life in historic times represent sensitive responses to subsistence needs, but for some other widespread Northern Athapaskan cultural features, the food quest is less clearly or directly accountable. Some of these aspects of Athapaskan cultures, perhaps, stem from an ancient, shared cultural stratum. Throughout the western Subarctic, for example, Athapaskan peoples considered their surroundings to be permeated with life or "power." All objects and animals were considered to be imbued with this power, which was not necessarily considered good or evil but could be either.

Koyukon belief portrayed the universe as filled with capricious, unpredictable beings and forces that could either help people or harm them (A. Clark 1970). In Tanaina thought, inanimate objects or matter, such as snow, fire, or water, had will and motivation that could affect the fortunes of human beings. In a literal sense the universe of Northern Athapaskan peoples was alive.[9] Among the Peel River Kutchin, according to Cornelius Osgood (1936:154), "This 'liveliness' of the surroundings demands a respectful attitude but is not always fearful."

The belief systems of Northern Athapaskan peoples included vaguely anthropomorphic, multifarious spiritual beings that exhibited a wide range of attitudes toward humans. Generally they were as unpredictable as the environment itself on which the people depended for survival. Conception of a being referred to as *nakani* (a threatening, wild, manlike creature that lived in the woods) occurred throughout the region.[10] The Tanaina called this being *nandina* ("bad man," or "bad Indian") (Osgood 1937:171). People tended to visualize the *nakani* as humanlike, and perhaps in some ways it personified the threat that strangers in the forest posed to small isolated groups. Many believed that the *nakani*, like some strangers who were fully human, sometimes ran off with women and children.

Northern Athapaskan groups also shared a general ideological concern with femaleness. Throughout the region women were secluded during menstruation, with particular emphasis on a young woman's first menses. Comparable practices occur sporadically throughout the New World, and such customs may have very ancient origins. Among Athapaskan speakers the woman usually would be secluded in a small hut some distance from the group, attended by her mother or some other older woman.

There was a widespread concept that such a condition imbued her with a quality dangerous to men and, to some extent, even to the woman herself. The dangers to men posed by physical contact with a woman in this condition could involve loss of strength and poor luck in hunting, and if she touched a man's hunting weapons they could lose their effectiveness. Some groups believed that the failure to observe the proper restrictions at such times could result in the men, or even the young woman herself, suffering from painful, aching joints (Honigmann 1964 : 124).[11]

The special transpersonalized quality of this condition in women is implicit in the personal restrictions that applied to the woman. There seems to have been little tendency to attribute personal malevolence to her. The danger lay in the power that imbued her. Because of this, women usually were not supposed to touch themselves during this period but instead used special scratching sticks, often kept on a cord around the wrist. Various Athapaskan peoples believed that for a woman to scratch herself with her nails at this time would cause her hair to fall out or cause sores to break out on her skin. For this reason, too, her hair could be combed only by her mother or another older woman attending her.

Menstruation imposed various dietary restrictions as well. Generally, the woman in seclusion could not eat fresh meat. Some groups extended this restriction to bear meat of any kind, the heads of moose or caribou, and other specific types or portions of game. Almost everywhere in the western Subarctic, young women in seclusion were not supposed to drink cold water. Many of the Northern Athapaskan groups believed that if a young woman in seclusion were to touch any water directly with her lips, hair would grow around her mouth. She used a bone drinking tube to avoid this.[12]

A young woman's gaze had special importance at such times. Among the Tanaina, Kutchin, and others, a young woman in seclusion wore a special hood that covered her eyes to prevent her from gazing out over the woods, which would offend the game.[13] In some groups a woman wore her hair pulled over her face for the same reason. Tanaina believed that if a young woman looked at a boy during this time he might be killed on a hunt (Townsend 1963 : 216). A general celebration sometimes marked a young woman's return from seclusion.[14]

Childbirth also entailed restrictions. Probably the most widespread general measure was a prohibition on the presence of men at the scene of delivery. Among the Kaska, a male shaman who attended a difficult birth would stand only at the woman's head (Honigmann 1964 : 117). Kutchin men often left on hunting trips when their wives were in labor, and after the birth, the couple slept separated by a partition for a few weeks. The Tanaina used a separate hut for childbirth, and among the Ahtna, birth involved thirty days' seclusion (Osgood 1936 : 139; McKennan 1981 : 571; de Laguna 1981 : 657). (See Appendix C for the distribution of the cultural features mentioned above.) Clearly some perceived essence of femaleness was a subject of concern and warranted special recognition throughout the area.

Certain principles are implicit in these practices and beliefs. Most patently, there is an emphatic concern with the cognitive opposition between maleness and femaleness. But more than that, these practices are consistent with a general recognition of power or spiritual essence associated with all things and beings. Femaleness was considered another type of power that could ebb and flow over and above the individuals who might be imbued with it. During times of menstruation and childbirth, femaleness was most evident and hence was felt to be present to a heightened degree. Inherently neither good nor evil, it was nonetheless concentrated at such times and therefore dangerous because of its power.

Men were especially vulnerable to this power. Maleness was cognitively associated with hunting, and success in hunting demanded not only skills and physical strength but a tenuous personal power. It could be manifest in phenomena ranging from luck in gambling to rapport with game animals. Generally fleeting and uncertain in any case, diminution of this power could result in debility, poor luck, and ultimately, starvation. Femaleness, the opposite of maleness, could neutralize it.

Hunting was truly a matter of life and death for Northern Athapaskan peoples. Despite the skills and efforts an individual might employ, success depended on factors beyond direct human control. Weather conditions, the sparseness of game and the movements of animals over vast areas, and natural fluctuations in the numbers of animals could play havoc with even the best hunters' efforts to get food. Often, bad luck could be life threatening.

Because the hunting success necessary for survival was so vulnerable to the imponderables of chance, it was a potential source of great anxiety. It is not surprising that this aspect of life, the most fundamental requisite for existence in the Subarctic, would have been associated with a multitude of restrictions to cope with a realm of chance factors that otherwise were beyond human control.[15]

A number of cultural and ecological factors, then—the ancient and widespread concern with femaleness, the vital importance of hunting, and the implications of this activity as an aspect of the sexual division of labor—combined to generate an array of symbolic devices that at crucial points emphatically dissociated the complementary, but opposed, realms of maleness and femaleness. These concerns are far from unique to Northern Athapaskan cultures, of course. A dissociation of women from hunting weapons occurs among hunting peoples in many parts of the world. But in many respects the Athapaskan pattern of shared features is distinctive.

There seems to have been no general Athapaskan ritual recognition of boys' puberty, although there was a scattering of diverse practices. Some of the easternmost Athapaskan populations, whose involvement in the fur trade led to contact with the Algonkian-speaking Cree, observed a vision quest for boys, involving solitary fasting and meditation. This is a familiar pattern among Algonkian speakers of the eastern Subarctic, and it seems likely that these Athapaskan peoples borrowed this custom from the east. In a few other Athapaskan-speaking groups, boys went through what appears to have been a version of the female ritual, with seclusion, scratching sticks, and food restrictions. This sometimes involved physical training to promote strength.[16] But no discernible pattern associated with male puberty occurs throughout the Northern Athapaskan region with anything approaching the consistency of the female pattern.

Other aspects of belief occur widely among Athapaskan groups. Commonly, the human soul consisted of two components. One was associated with air, vapor, or the breath identified with life and which disappears at death. The other component, usually translated into English as the "shadow," was a reflection of the person's physical being. Among the Kaska the shadow tended to linger near the scene of death or the grave and sometimes appeared at night as a ghost, referred to as *mezi*. The term for the other component, *tajuc*, translates as "soul" or "wind." Either one or the other component, most often the shadow, was threatening, in some cases because it sought out the shadows of surviving relatives out of loneliness, or because it was inherently evil (Honigmann 1964 : 136).[17]

Northern Athapaskan peoples employed a variety of devices to keep the threatening aspect of the soul separated from the living. People no longer spoke the name of the deceased, particularly close relatives,[18] and often they avoided words that resembled the name.

There was much variation in ways of disposing of the body, sometimes even within the same group. In early historic times, cremation was widespread.[19] One gets the impression that what happened to the remains of the deceased was less important, ultimately, than the measures taken to ensure that the dead would not cause trouble for the living. Accommodations to the spiritual essence predominated over disposal of the substance of the remains.

Usually the survivors removed the body from the dwelling through a hole made in the wall or through a window, or in a few cases, through the smoke hole in the roof. Such practices are widespread throughout the Northern hemisphere and often involved the idea that the living and the dead should not follow the same path (Hosley 1981:539). The relatives abandoned or destroyed the dwelling in which death occurred. This may not have been a severe material hardship for mobile hunters, although they also left the personal property of the deceased at the grave, often purposely damaging it. This may indeed have been a serious loss.

These patterns reveal a consistent underlying concern with the severance of ties between the living and the dead. On the other hand, beliefs in reincarnation also were widespread throughout the Northern Athapaskan region (see Osgood 1937:167 for the Tanaina version). Despite some variation, it was usually the "breath" or "air" aspect of the soul that was reborn. When this occurred, the child might resemble its former self in some way, or display idiosyncrasies of a deceased person that older people who had known the individual might recall. Many Northern Athapaskan peoples believed that children sometimes had memories of an earlier life, and some groups considered children who were born with teeth to be reincarnated. (See Appendix D for the distribution of features associated with concepts of life and death.)

Northern Athapaskan groups shared many other cultural features. Throughout the Subarctic, people used sweat houses for therapeutic or recreational purposes, but generally they did not have the strong religious connotations associated with them in many non-Athapaskan societies. Facial tattooing was common among women, with widely varying designs that most frequently were centered around the mouth. In many groups the human gaze had considerable power and significance, and the Ingalik, for example, taught their children that to look directly at someone was offensive (Osgood 1959:66).[20] This also was a special concern in the context of female puberty seclusion, when the gaze of young women was especially powerful and dangerous.

These Northern Athapaskan cultural similarities are tempered with myriad regional responses to outside influences. We noted earlier that Athapaskan peoples in general have been receptive to many kinds of cultural innovations, and in the Subarctic the expanse of Athapaskan territory on all sides bordered different ecological zones and peoples. The influences for change have been diverse. On the southern margin, for example, the Athapaskan-speaking Sarsi in the early historic period shifted to a full-time Plains focus. Adopting horse nomadism and directing their food quest to buffalo hunting, they allied themselves with the Algonkian-speaking Blackfoot.

The Pacific Coast influence of the Tsimshian, Haida, and Tlingit is evident along the western margins of the Northern Athapaskan territory. Intermarriage intensified cross-cultural influences among these groups. We noted earlier that salmon fishing allowed many Athapaskan peoples of the Pacific drainage to maintain larger and more stable communities than would have been feasible in the interior and permitted them to incorporate traits reminiscent of the cultures of the Pacific Coast. The ceremonial feast known as the potlatch and other identifiable coastal features manifest this influence, from the Tanaina of southern Alaska southward to the Carrier and Chilcotin in British Columbia.

Athapaskan peoples of the northern periphery, such as the Tanaina, Ingalik, and Koyukon, borrowed a great deal of Eskimo technology, although Eskimo influence on these cultures is less apparent in other respects. Considering their long adjacency, the apparent mutual influences are surprisingly slight, but this could be a result of differences in the ecological focuses of these populations. Krauss points out that there are no detectable Eskimo loan words in Apache, nor are there Athapaskan loan words in the Greenland Eskimo dialects that spread eastward within the last millennium or so. This could be an example of Athapaskan conservatism when it comes to borrowing words from other languages, but it might also reflect a lack of intensive contact in the early period before the ancestors of Southern Athapaskan and eastern Eskimo populations dispersed. This possibility would be consistent with the general dichotomy between the Eskimo maritime and Athapaskan inland patterns.

In more recent times, the fur trade intensified contact between Athapaskans and Eskimos. Their relationships varied over the years from ambivalence to active hostility.[21] Hearne's (1911:184) late eighteenth-century account of the events at Bloody Falls near the mouth of the Coppermine River, Northwest Territories, suggests something of the tone of the interaction. Hearne's Athapaskan companions traveled far out of their way expressly to attack and kill the people at an Inuit encampment, destroying their tools and weapons and keeping only the copper implements. Even in recent times, encounters between Inuit and Chipewyan caribou hunters have been tense and occasionally have involved exchanges of gunfire on the barren grounds west of Hudson Bay.[22]

On the other hand, the nineteenth-century fur trade also led to friendlier and more regularized contact in parts of Alaska, when trade fairs were held at the mouth of the Yukon River (VanStone 1974:94).[23] Eskimos, Athapaskans, and even Chukchi from Siberia took part, with Koyukon and Ingalik Athapaskans acting as middlemen trading with groups of the interior. During this era native Siberian trade items found their way hundreds of miles up the Yukon River (VanStone 1974:94).[24]

Despite these instances of peaceful interaction, though, in the absence of any overall mechanism to mediate disputes among these groups, responses to friction by direct hostile action was always a possibility. Intergroup relations throughout the Arctic and Subarctic and within the Eskimo and Athapaskan populations themselves tended to be uneasy and often volatile (see Ackerman and Ackerman 1973; Osgood 1937:109). The tone of these relationships might help to account for why the overt cultural influences between them have tended to center on technology rather than other aspects of culture.

The fur trade directly affected groups of the western Subarctic much later than it did Algonkian and Siouan-speaking peoples to the east. But by the end of the eighteenth century, segments of the southeasternmost Athapaskan population, particularly the Chipewyan, were deeply engaged. Some of the Chipewyan, in fact, had acquired manufactured trade implements by the early 1700s, apparently without any direct contact with European traders (A. Ray 1974:59).[25] Such commodities might very well have stimulated their motivation to continue and intensify their involvement in the trade.

The Chipewyan and some of the other eastern Athapaskan had developed patterns long before to exploit the caribou herds of the barren grounds. With the establishment of Prince of Wales's Fort, a major trading post at the mouth of the Churchill River on the western shore of Hudson Bay, the Chipewyan expanded their territory to control access to the fort from the north and west. In the process they replaced, or possibly displaced, Eskimo groups along the shore and pushed back the territory used by the Cree and Assiniboine, who had engaged in the trade earlier (Gillespie 1975; J. Smith and Burch 1979; Yerbury 1980).

The Athapaskan frontier facing these non-Athapaskan groups tended to be a scene of conflict, just as in the North. Because of the sparseness of the population, the boundary was unstable and rather permeable. There are many traditional accounts of small Cree raiding parties penetrating hundreds of miles into Athapaskan territory, sometimes as far as the Kaska at the watershed between the Arctic and Pacific drainages (Honigmann 1964:92). The tradition of the *nakani* (bad man) of the forest might have been amplified by the danger of Cree surprise attacks and the kidnapping of women during the fur trade days (E. Basso 1978). For the Athapaskan peoples who were engaged in the early fur trade, then, an initial effect probably was to increase intergroup conflict and the dangers of attack. But there were more far-reaching effects as well. The fur trade constituted an important shift in their food quest.

The Chipewyan and other eastern Athapaskan peoples had been accustomed to operating in small, flexible aggregates which moved freely to exploit wild foods in harsh regions. This way of life required them to make the most of any sporadic opportunities that arose to secure large amounts of food at the few times of the year when it became available. The major caribou drives that Hearne witnessed are an example of this strategy.

This life-style meant developing and maintaining an intricate knowledge of the region and the habits of the animals and using this knowledge either to be in strategic places at the proper time or to cover extensive territory to locate wandering game. In a sense these capacities were "preadapted" to the fur trade. They lent themselves easily to that enterprise, since the quest for either meat or hides meant seeking out faunal resources that were dispersed over an expansive territory.

The time they invested in seeking furs, though, was time they lost for securing food. When they traded pelts for food and other items, the hides sometimes became the primary, but indirect, means of providing sustenance, and a life-and-death dependency on the trade developed very quickly in some areas. Even in the late eighteenth century, Hearne (1911:124) mused with some ambivalence about the contrasts he perceived between the "Northern Indians" of his acquaintance who were directly involved in the fur trade and the more remote groups still farther north, who continued to hunt the caribou and remained well fed, healthy, independent, and in his opinion, far better off. Hearne's observation seems especially ironic considering his role as Hudson's Bay Company agent in attempting to draw these people into the trade.

Moreover, the Athapaskan speakers who were deeply involved in the trade did not enjoy a stable situation. Because of the demands of the trade, the population of fur-bearing animals within range of the posts was soon depleted. Consequently, groups nearest the post shifted their role from trappers to middlemen, traveling farther into the vast tracts of the interior regions with trade goods to exchange with more distant peoples for furs and transporting the hides back to the fort.

Hearne (1911:316) describes his travels with such a group in the course of his mission to expand the sphere of the trade. These Chipewyan traders underwent remarkable hardships, traveling on foot through areas that, according to Hearne, were so vast and barren that starvation was a genuine danger in crossing them. The Chipewyan defended their monopoly with vigor, nonetheless, guarding their role of middlemen and endeavoring to prevent interior groups such as the Dogrib from trading directly with the post. For many of the Northern Athapaskan population, this shift in the subsistence focus from meat to furs, and eventually to transport, had far-reaching consequences, and it very quickly set off changes that came to affect the status and role of women in some of the groups.

The growing distance between the sources of furs and the trading outlet presented problems of transportation far greater in the western Subarctic than they were farther to the east, where waterways allowed easier transportation by canoe. In Athapaskan territory, foot travel was the only means of moving goods. Dogsleds were not part of the traditional repertoire, and they would have been useless during the warmer time of the year in any case. Over much of the territory, the broken terrain strewn with large boulders would have made such travel almost impossible even in winter (Hearne 1911: 63). Dogs would have required food, which was almost always in short supply. Instead, human carriers transported the hides, and for the most part these carriers were women.

In earlier times the custom had been for women to pack and carry domestic goods and supplies when the group moved. As people traveled from one campsite to another in the course of the food quest, the women and children would take a direct route with the equipment, while the men took a more circuitous course with weapons ready in case of a chance encounter with game and perhaps to scout ahead for the presence of other people who might well have been hostile (Osgood 1936:112). The traditional pattern had developed as a system of complementary functions to maximize the chances of survival.

As the fur trade became established, the distances that had to be traversed became greater, and women, because of the precedent pattern, fell into the role of overland carriers of furs. Hearne's eighteenth-century Chipewyan companion Matonabbee was explicit about this, telling Hearne that it was impossible to travel any distance over the barren ground without women, since men who carried such burdens would not be free to hunt. Coincident with this modification of women's economic role among these groups, their status, by any standard criterion, dropped considerably. They had little decision-making power even over their own lives, and an early explorer referred to them as "poor wretches" (Jenness 1956:22).

A similar phenomenon occurred among the Kutchin for a limited period in the mid-nineteenth century, when several writers described the status of women as deplorably low. One observer claimed that

Kutchin women at this time purposely allowed their infant daughters to die in order to spare them the misery of growing up to be women (Hardisty 1867:312; Jenness 1956:22). This practice coincided with a period when many of the Kutchin also were engaged in the fur trade, with long overland journeys between the sources of furs and the trading post at Old Fort Good Hope on the lower Mackenzie River. Yet observers of the Kutchin before and after this period emphatically deny that women were oppressed.

It seems most likely that all of these observations of the Kutchin are essentially accurate and that, just as among the Chipewyan, changes caused by the fur trade can account for the disparity. The earliest observations of the Kutchin probably reflect a social system that was relatively undisrupted. By the same token, more recent accounts from the twentieth century depict a time when fur trading posts had multiplied and reduced the necessity to travel overland for extreme distances, while dogsled transport had become an established practice. In the mid-nineteenth century, Kutchin dogs were "miserable creatures no larger than foxes," incapable of playing any major part in transportation (Jones 1867:324). Eventually, though, dogsleds became far more important, and women resumed their traditional status in the society (Perry 1979:99–118). Among most other Northern Athapaskan groups, the fur trade did not produce a similar combination of effects, and little or no evidence exists that women held the oppressed status they did among the Chipewyan and Kutchin during those periods (Honigmann 1964:44, 133, 162; Jenness 1972:391; Osgood 1936:131).

There is no doubt that the fur trade drew some parts of the Athapaskan population away from their traditional subsistence patterns and that, ironically, many of their preexisting strategies and characteristics facilitated this process. Mobility, small-group autonomy, and other traits that turned out to be useful in the fur trade had developed far earlier within the traditional food quest itself. Initially these changes were merely shifts in an older pattern, but eventually they proved to be momentous choices with far-reaching repercussions. In some ways they were irreversible.

Many Athapaskan social systems were able to adapt and readjust, as in the restoration of higher status among Kutchin women. Tragically, though, devastating epidemics of smallpox and other diseases swept these populations in the early years of the fur trade, touched off by a growing intensity of contact with outsiders. In some large areas of Northern Athapaskan territory, as many as 90 percent of the people died as a result. Probably we can never appreciate the horrors of these decades, and the changes that took place in the face of such human loss must have far surpassed any change caused directly by the economic implications of the fur trade itself.

In traditional times furs had never been especially sought-after.[26] But in the generations after the early phase of the trade, fur trapping for the market, particularly through the Hudson's Bay Company, has remained a predominant economic activity among the Northern Athapaskan peoples. There is some reason to feel that this enterprise is on the decline,[27] but it continues to provide an important supplement to the food quest for people who have been compelled for some time now to exist in a world dominated by a cash economy. Fur trapping has acquired the standing of a traditional activity, and it has come into conflict recently with oil and gas interests based in the metropolitan areas to the south. But in many regions, hunting and fishing still provide a major portion of the food consumed. The quantity of wild foods, calculated in terms of the dollar value of meat, is impressive.[28]

The people continue to respond to alterations in their circumstances. The Dene Nation, a political association organized to represent Northern Athapaskan peoples, has emerged from a tradition in which small-group autonomy in the past precluded the development of overreaching political structures (Price 1978:257–259). Through political organizations that have developed to represent native interests, peoples of the North have succeeded in exerting some effective pressure on the national governments of Canada and, to a lesser degree, the United States to enhance the possibility of their cultural survival. This phenomenon seems to be a manifestation of a tendency to adapt and maintain the continuity, through change, of an ancient unbroken existence.

Pacific Coast Athapaskan

Cultural features that occur throughout the western Subarctic provide a good starting point for a comparison of the major Athapaskan groupings. On the Pacific Coast well to the south, a distinctive cluster of Athapaskan-speaking peoples have been separated from their former relatives in the Subarctic for many centuries. Not surprisingly, their cultures are different in many respects from those of other Athapaskans. But what they continue to have in common with Northern Athapaskans and the Apache is especially interesting.

The Athapaskan-speaking peoples of the Pacific Coast occupy sections of northern California and southern Oregon. At least two different Athapaskan languages are spoken in this area (Dyen and Aberle 1974:158)[29] (see Appendix A), but there is no doubt about

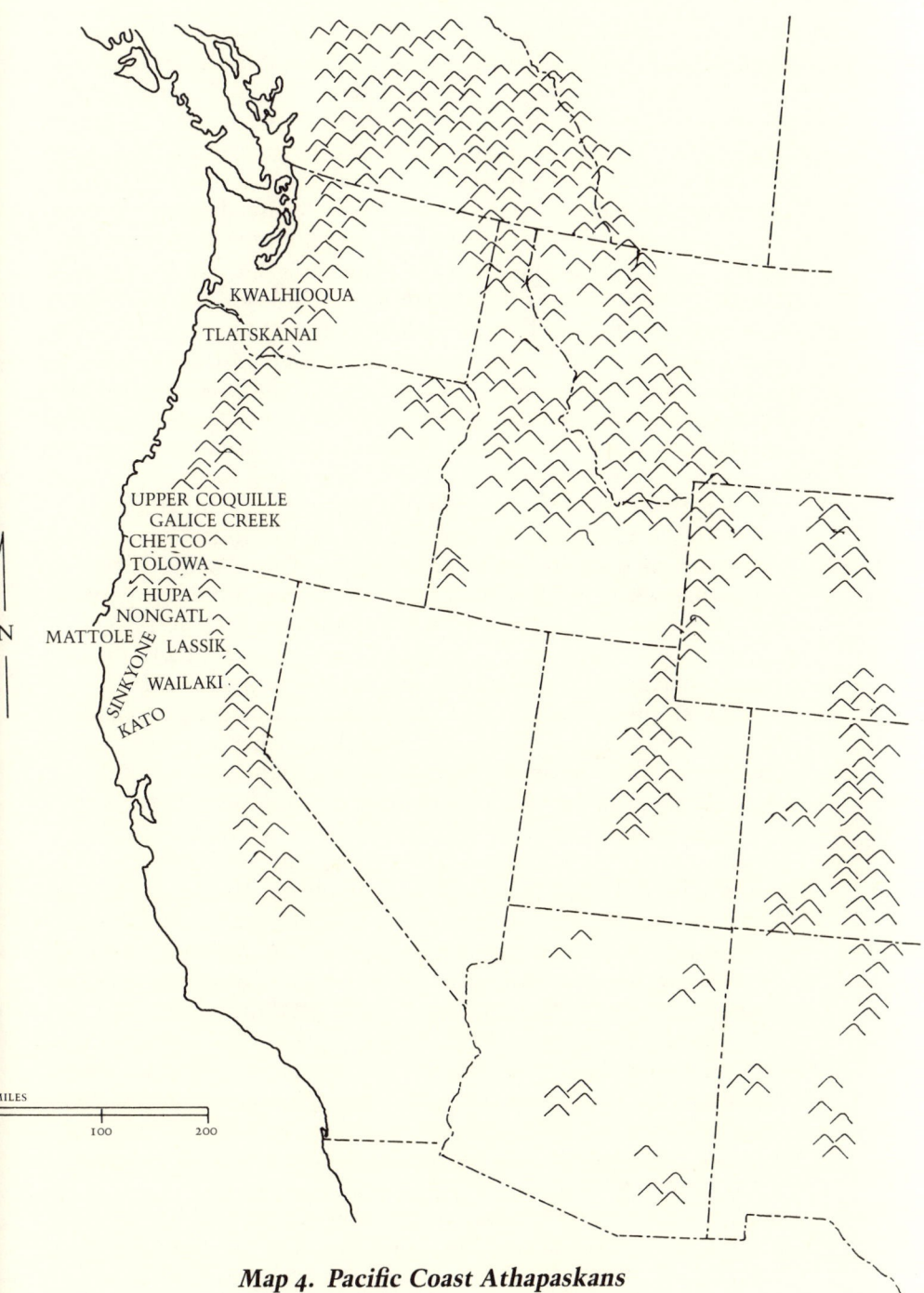

KWALHIOQUA

TLATSKANAI

UPPER COQUILLE
GALICE CREEK
CHETCO
TOLOWA
HUPA
NONGATL
MATTOLE   SINKYONE   LASSIK
WAILAKI
KATO

N

MILES

100   200

Map 4. Pacific Coast Athapaskans

their close relationship and common origins. Despite instances of population mergers and language transfer,[30] most of these people are the descendants of a single early migration to the Pacific from the Subarctic. Jorgensen (1980:71) notes that the Athapaskan speakers of the Pacific Coast "were surely the last language group to penetrate the Northwest Coast and were sandwiched in among speakers of Penutian, Hokan, and Algonkian who were already there."

The California cluster includes local populations known as Kato, Wailaki, Lassik, Sinkyone, Mattole, Nongatl, Whilkut, Hupa, and Chilula. To the north on the Oregon Coast, Tolowa, Chetco, Lower Rogue, and upper Coquille divisions form a separate, internally contiguous population. A bit inland from this cluster are the Applegate and Galice Creek aggregates, which appear to have been culturally similar to the others (see map, Dyen and Aberle 1974:8). It is probably valid to consider all of these Pacific Coast Athapaskans a single population. Most of the cultural variation among them arises from the differing influences of neighboring non-Athapaskan groups, particularly those to the south along the central California coast.

The influence of the earlier inhabitants of the Pacific Coast on these Athapaskan peoples is most evident in technology, particularly food-getting equipment of various kinds, and the activities associated with subsistence. Throughout the region peoples of various linguistic backgrounds shared much the same material culture,[31] and Athapaskans on the Pacific Coast were practically indistinguishable from their neighbors in that regard (Kroeber 1925:5). There seems to have been a general homogeneity in equipment, methods, and materials used throughout that region (Gould 1978:130).

This part of native North America enjoyed a rich natural food supply with a variety of resources. The region supported dense populations which had no need to resort to agriculture. Marine mammals, fish, inland game, and plant foods not only allowed people to maintain themselves in stable groups but to develop elaborate concepts of wealth interwoven with ideas of differential status and prestige. Athapaskan peoples who came into the coastal area from the Subarctic adapted their own older patterns to this new context. Like their neighbors, the Pacific Coast Athapaskans established stable residential villages. But they continued to follow seasonal rounds in their quest for wild food which included deer, acorns, and sea mammals, and they incorporated the sea lion into their cognitive framework as "ocean deer" (Drucker 1937:231).

Many of the coastal Athapaskan groups came to organize relationships on the basis of patrilineal descent. Most of the neighboring non-Athapaskan societies in the region also have patrilineal descent with patrilocal residence patterns, although some had bilateral organization with a patrilineal bias. Some Athapaskan groups on the Pacific Coast became so strongly patrilineal that the preferential choice of marriage for a man was his mother's brother's daughter, on the grounds that a cousin on the mother's side was far more remote than cousins on the father's (Drucker 1937:247). This stands in striking contrast to the matrilineal emphasis of Athapaskan groups, and it raises some questions. What was there about the Pacific Coast that can account for this development? Was it simply a matter of the influence of surrounding groups, or were additional factors involved?

The population along the Pacific Coast is denser than in the interior regions of the Subarctic, and patrilineal descent might have some special adaptive advantages in thickly settled areas with unevenly distributed resources (Dyen and Aberle 1974:192). On the Pacific Coast, food sources do tend to be concentrated unevenly, and despite their overall quantity, they are often accessible only at fixed points. The rivers, for example, are reliable sources of seasonally migrating fish, a major food resource. But river mouths and other key fishing spots provide extremely localized points of access, even to the extent of allowing local groups to establish a disproportionate control over their use. It is possible to intercept vast quantities of fish at the beginning of their upstream migrations when they are in prime condition.

To avert that problem, defining rights to local resources and specifying lines of distribution can be crucial. On the Pacific Coast, patrilineal descent and patrilocal residence added structure to the system. Patrilineal descent with residence among the husband's people specifies the individual's affiliation in a fairly absolute sense, which can be an effective way to maintain local holdings of territory, resources, and property that can be inherited through males who live together.

In the Subarctic interior, this practice would have hampered people's ability to respond to vagaries in the food supply. In the sparser regions of the western Subarctic from which the Athapaskans migrated, food sources were mobile and at times, either concentrated or thinly scattered. The patterns of residence and relationships allowed a far wider degree of flexibility and options, which had the advantage of making it easier for the population to redistribute itself in response to far less predictable resources.

In the Subarctic, matrilineal descent with matrilocal residence allowed greater maneuverability because it spread related males throughout the territory, to reside with their wives' people and hunt for them. Matrilineal descent did not anchor local groups to bounded territories, even though they might return to the same base camps to cover the same broad region year after year. For Northern Athapaskan peoples east of the Cordillera, where it was necessary to cover even larger territories to subsist, bilateral kinship allowed even wider options because the individual could affiliate with a range of relatives on either the mother's or the father's side. That system allowed still more capacity for sensitive response to irregular resources. But on the Pacific Coast, the patrilineal and patrilocal system, entailing more absolute social and economic prescription, solved problems there that did not exist in the interior.

On the other hand, these distinctively coastal features overlay traces of the older Athapaskan cultural stratum. Some writers have referred to the Athapaskan-speaking groups having "simpler" versions of widespread coastal patterns, which could reflect their having been borrowed. The Athapaskan speakers were inland hunting peoples who arrived in a rich coastal area that had been occupied for tens of centuries by villagers who had developed and refined methods of exploiting the local food resources long before. In adapting to this niche, the Athapaskan speakers borrowed many of these proven subsistence techniques from the earlier occupants, and in the process they acquired other cultural features as well.

The concept of wealth, for example, served among other things as a device for regulating social relationships. Coastal peoples employed it to solve disputes, bind marriages, define rights and status, and to some extent, provide a medium for interaction with some degree of behavioral predictability among the diverse populations of the Pacific Coast who lived in close conjunction with one another (Barnett 1937:158; Driver 1939).

Considering the pervasive emphasis on wealth in this area, it is not surprising that bridewealth payments should have become an important part of marriage among coastal Athapaskans. On the other hand, a secondary type of marriage continued to exist as well. Among the Tolowa, Hupa, and other groups, this type was sometimes referred to as "half marriage." With this arrangement, the groom would perform bride service by working for the parents of his wife for an agreed-upon length of time in lieu of bridewealth payments (Nomland 1935:160, 1938:104; Gould 1978:131; Wallace 1978:167). Such a pattern, of course, was the usual pattern throughout the Subarctic, and temporarily, at least, it involved matrilocal residence. It appears that this older form survived among coastal Athapaskan peoples despite the shift to marriage payments and patrilocality, as a less prestigious alternative and an echo of the past.

The inland hunting background of these coastal Athapaskan peoples not only was reflected in their reference to the economically important sea lion as "ocean deer," but in subtler ways (Drucker 1937:231). Despite the emphasis on wealth and status that pervaded the region, status concerns among the Tolowa were not "constantly present in the everyday lives of the people." Like other Athapaskan speakers, these Pacific Coast people maintained a wide-ranging food quest without any particular specialization, utilizing a "wide margin" of subsistence. Although an emphasis on individual property predominated in the region, the Sinkyone perceived of land ownership in collective terms and exploited their food resources communally. The Tolowa distributed food freely within the village (Drucker 1937:231, 235).

It is worth noting, too, that even though the Sinkyone had villages throughout their territory, they did not conceive of them as permanent social entities or political units, but as geographic locations (Nomland 1935:151; Kobrinsky 1977:203). These perspectives reflect a more nomadic, egalitarian social organization of a sort that typifies small, freely ranging hunting groups. In the Subarctic the salient clusters of people tended to be seasonal base camps at key localities, rather than villages. They were not continuously occupied. Communal access to resources is far more feasible in the Subarctic than an emphasis on private ownership and differential wealth.

This blending of patterns on the Pacific Coast shows up in many other aspects of life. Athapaskan practices and attitudes associated with death, including the destruction of property, continued in some forms on the Pacific Coast (Gould 1978:134; Wallace 1978:167), but these practices came into conflict with the greater array of property and the importance attached to it. Some groups resolved the problem by ritually purifying such major items as canoes and paddles after the death of their owners, making it possible for them to be recovered and inherited by the survivors. In other cases people gave away important items of property to their intended heirs before death, thereby avoiding the need to destroy the property.

In the same vein, the plank houses in this area were far more substantial than most Athapaskan dwellings in the Subarctic interior or in the Southwest, and to destroy or abandon them would have entailed great sacrifice for the survivors. Moreover, since the crucial food sources in the coastal area tended to be fixed in particular localities, to evacuate a site whenever a death occurred would have made life much more difficult. Consequently, in many of these groups, a ritual to purify the house and the place of death eliminated the need for those measures.

Unlike non-Athapaskan peoples of the Pacific Coast who buried their dead next to the dwelling, the Athapaskan speakers usually took the remains some distance away from the dwellings (Elsasser 1978:186). They also continued the practice of avoiding the name of the deceased. Among the Sinkyone this lasted for five years (Nomland 1935:163; DuBois 1932:252). Among the Tolowa and other groups, relatives of the dead could exact a fine—a distinctively Pacific Coast embellishment—if people violated this restriction in their presence (Gould 1978:133; Dubois 1932:252). Many groups, though, ritually purified the names of deceased relatives after a lapse of time and gave them to children (Drucker 1937:253), a practice that both eliminated restrictions on their utterance and allowed the names to be passed on as a means of emphasizing relationships of descent (Gould 1978:133).

The custom of removing the body from an opening other than the normal doorway was another continuation of Subarctic patterns. In the 1930s a Tolowa woman stated that "the Indians are afraid of the dead. They must not be taken out of the regular door. That is the way the living go out" (DuBois 1932:133). In general, the concern with maintaining a separation between the living and the dead continued. Several of these groups considered it dangerous to cry for the deceased after dark (Nomland 1938:103). In Sinkyone belief, owls and doves were "transformed persons who mourned their deceased and hence were not eaten" (Nomland 1935:263).

Female puberty was a matter of ritual concern, as it was in many of the surrounding groups. But once again, the practices of Pacific Coast Athapaskan speakers were consistent with Northern Athapaskan patterns in important ways. Generally the young woman's eyes were shaded or covered during her seclusion. Among the Tolowa she wore a feather visor to restrict her vision and was not allowed to "look around" for ten days (Drucker 1937:263). In other groups her hair was combed down over her eyes for the same reason, and she was forbidden to look at the sky (Nomland 1938:99).

Consequences for the violation of these strictures reveal an interesting shift from the Northern Athapaskan pattern. Throughout the Subarctic, Athapaskan peoples felt that a young woman's gaze during her seclusion could project harmful influence from herself to others. It could ruin hunting luck, cause a boy to be killed on a hunt, offend animals, and so on. On the Pacific Coast, Athapaskan peoples almost uniformly believed that the effects of her gaze were harmful to the young woman herself. A Sinkyone woman in seclusion who gazed at the sky, for example, could become blind (Nomland 1935: 162). If a young Bear River woman in seclusion should "look piercingly at anyone or into the distance" she, too, might develop poor eyesight or go blind (Nomland 1938:99).

These ideas imply a reflexive rather than a projective emphasis. It seems that a redirection of the dangerous power of femaleness coincided with the change from matrilineal descent and matrilocal residence to patrilineal descent, patrilocal residence, and male inheritance of property. To some extent the dangers of this power seem to have shifted away from men and become an added vulnerability of women.

The primary concern of female seclusion, though, was to ensure the young woman's good health and long life. She could not drink cold water or eat fresh meat. She used special scratching sticks or an abalone shell scratcher, in the case of the Tolowa, because if she were to touch herself directly, her hair would fall out or sores would develop (DuBois 1932:250).

Other concepts of power in some of these groups are reminiscent of those held among Athapaskan peoples in the Subarctic. Among the Sinkyone, "all things animate and inanimate had souls" (Nomland 1935:169). As to the Tolowa, "one receives the impression that every outcrop of rock, every trickle of water, every little clearing in the brush had power for good or evil, or figured in some event in mythological times" (Drucker 1937:228).

The Pacific Athapaskan case is an important source of insight into processes of culture change. It provides some clear instances of cultural blending, but more than that, it presents an example of what happened to a people who left a region of sparse resources and entered a richer region with a dense, more sedentary population.

There may be no way to detect how or why this segment of the earlier Athapaskan population found its way to the Pacific Coast. The rich food resources of the area must have been a major inducement. No clear archaeological record of Pacific Coast Athapaskan cultures predates A.D. 1000, and this is consistent with the supposition that Athapaskan speakers migrated into the area more recently than their neighbors.

Language provides some hints about the relationship between the Pacific Coast populations and other Athapaskan speakers. The simple fact that language changes over time is crucial. When a population speaking a single language separates into two or more segments, the resulting groups will develop different speech patterns.

For a while, they will continue to retain words in common that sound very much alike and that mean about the same thing. Linguists refer to these as cognate words. In general, the more recently two or more populations have separated, the more cognates they are likely to retain in common.

Calculations based on the percentage of cognate words among the Athapaskan languages indicate that the dialects of the Pacific Coast group are all about equal in the extent to which they differ from each of the other Athapaskan languages. This suggests that the Pacific Coast Athapaskans shared a common history until after they departed from the parent population and began to diverge among themselves.

With regard to the relationship of Pacific Coast dialect to other Athapaskan languages, as a group they differ most from Tanaina in southern Alaska. They show a somewhat lesser degree of divergence from other Alaskan languages such as Ahtna, Koyukon-Tanana, and Ingalik.[32] Pacific Coast Athapaskan appears to be more closely related to Canadian and Southern Athapaskan than to the Alaskan languages. By the same token, it seems to be about equally distant from both Apache and Canadian Athapaskan.

What does this mean? It could be that the Pacific Coast contingent separated from the northern population after splits among some of the Alaskan languages already had occurred, but before there was much further differentiation. It suggests, for example, that the Pacific Coast Athapaskans already had separated from the rest long before the ancestors of the Apache left the Canadian groups (Hoijer 1971).

Glottochronology is a method of calculating the time that has passed since languages known to share a common past have separated. It is based on the idea that, even though languages can change at different rates for a variety of reasons, some words tend to be more resistant than others to outside influences. Examples of this are personal pronouns or kinship terms. Such words, it has been argued, constitute a "core vocabulary" that is relatively conservative and changes at a slow and constant rate. If that is true, and if we knew just what that rate of change has been, then by counting how many of these "core vocabulary" words they still share as cognate words, we ought to be able to get some idea of how long ago they split.

As it happens, most researchers have discounted glottochronology as a valid means of determining the time of language separations. For one thing, linguists now recognize that languages do not seem to change at a predictable rate, even with regard to their "core vocabularies." This is a fairly decisive blow to the fundamental concept. But with that in mind, and for what it may be worth, glottochronology indicated that the Pacific Coast Athapaskan languages and dialects began to diverge some time in the first millennium A.D.

We cannot consider this reliable, but it does seem plausible. We must also keep in mind that as far as language differentiation is concerned, things are not so neat as a simple branching model of genetic divergence might suggest. Most Athapaskan languages and dialects have not been isolated but have continued to influence one another over the centuries. They have shared linguistic innovations, creating new similarities that have nothing to do with past relationships. On the other hand, profound differences exist between some Athapaskan languages in adjacent territories. Similarity between geographically continuous populations within the three major Athapaskan linguistic divisions has different significance from similarities among those that have been separated for centuries.

Apache

In many ways the region inhabited by Southern Athapaskan speakers is far more varied and cosmopolitan than those occupied by the other two Athapaskan divisions. Aside from the general aridity of the Southwest, the territories of Apache peoples encompass high-altitude slopes and grassy plateaus, expanses of the southern Plains, jagged, precipitous mountains, cool upland pine forests, and the hot broken dry country of the northern part of the Sonoran Desert, cut by arroyos and scattered with mesas and low mountains.

When the Proto-Apache arrived in the Southwest several centuries ago, their culture had much in common with Athapaskan cultures of the Canadian Subarctic milieu from which it sprang. The people moved into an area that already had been occupied for well over a thousand years by sedentary agricultural peoples. The western and Rio Grande Pueblo communities in the northern part of the region and the Pima, Papago, and others farther to the south had long traditions that reverberated from the ancient complex civilizations of Mexico.

On their migration to the Southwest, the Proto-Apache probably had encountered other nomads with different cultural origins. Some of these peoples, no doubt, had roots in the ancient desert traditions of the arid west. Uto-Aztecan speakers who came out of the Great Basin became an important element in the political sphere of the Southwest, and there were other nomadic groups to the south. The

Suma of early historic accounts, for example, may have been Yuman speakers, although they have long since disappeared, and their identity is uncertain.

As the Apache found their way southward, they encountered still another profoundly different cultural tradition. Spaniards with a culture enriched by the Renaissance of southern Europe, whose own traditions had incorporated some of the culture of the Islamic peoples who had invaded and occupied their own territory in Europe centuries before, had begun to establish inroads from deep in Mexico. In the following centuries, the long history of interaction among these peoples and their descendants was to have significant and far-reaching effects on all of them.

Throughout most of the historic period, Apachean peoples maintained their mobility and possession of their territory, and in small groups, they remained autonomous without developing cumbersome, overarching political structures. The differentiation that took place among them in the Southwest was mostly a matter of a developing cultural diversity that grew as local groups gravitated into various geographic zones. But in their strategies of opportunism in the food quest and their general receptivity to innovation, their ancient culture base continued to impel their lives.

At various periods of history the Western Apache, Navajo, and Jicarilla adopted agriculture, to some degree.[33] By the 1700s, in fact, most of the Apache supplemented their food supply with small garden plots here and there throughout their territories. The Navajo in particular, and the Jicarilla to a lesser extent, adopted an array of Puebloan features along with agriculture, including even the use of masonry or adobe dwellings in Pueblo styles at certain periods and locales (J. Gunnerson 1969; D. Gunnerson 1974; Opler 1945; Opler and Bittle 1961).[34] All of these Apache groups in the Southwest adopted the Pueblo pattern of masked dancers who represented benevolent deities in ceremonies. Navajo ceremonials show especially strong Puebloan influences. The Navajo sheltered refugees during the Pueblo Revolt against the Spanish in the 1680s. A long history of mutual visiting and the incorporation of contingents from Pueblo communities into the Navajo population reinforced this association.[35]

The tenor of relations between Apache and other peoples in the Southwest was variable and often volatile. The Navajo term for corn (enemy food), staple food of the region, suggests the ambiguity of the Apachean role in the Southwest. To these scattered families of hunters and foragers, the large supplies of surplus food stored in the sedentary farming communities represented an additional resource to be tapped. Apache mobility and other patterns they had developed in their earlier experiences in the North lent themselves easily to raiding for subsistence. This adaptation to accommodate crops cultivated by other peoples into the food quest was a change that eventually would have profound political implications. On the other hand, the earliest relationships with sedentary peoples were marked more by trade than hostility. Only after the Apache had lived in the Southwest for several generations, in the wake of Spanish slave raids, did they commit themselves heavily to raiding.

But below these changes, fundamental Athapaskan patterns persisted. Ancient practices and attitudes associated with concepts about life and death continued to be important aspects of Apachean culture. After death, in accordance with custom, the Apache removed the body through a hole in the wall and abandoned or destroyed the dwelling. They destroyed the property of the deceased or left it at the grave and avoided mentioning the names of their dead (Opler 1965).

Just as in the Subarctic and the Pacific Coast, these practices kept the living separated from the dead. And like their ancestors in the Subarctic, the Apache believed in a two-component soul, one aspect of which was malevolent and remained near the body or grave after death. In the early twentieth century, a Kiowa Apache maintained that the ghost sounded like static in the air near the body, "like a radio" (McAllister 1955:162). It was especially dangerous to close relatives. As in the North, the Apache associated the other component of the soul with wind, air, and breath. In Navajo belief this component translates as an "in-standing wind soul" that enters a person's body at the time of birth and leaves it at death (Witherspoon 1977:29–30; McNeley 1981). According to Gary Witherspoon (1977: 205), there is an emphatic association in Navajo thought between life and air. "When one dies, the evil remains behind with the physical body and thus it must be avoided." Opler (1945:123) writes that "according to Lipan Apache doctrine, a small whirlwind enters the human body and provides the vitalizing 'wind inside that keeps you alive.'"

The fundamental Athapaskan concern with femaleness and female puberty underwent considerable elaboration in the Southwest. But although the Apache continued to associate some dangers with it, for the most part the concept of femaleness as a reified quality acquired far more positive connotations. In the Apache groups, a totally benevolent anthropomorphic deity whose name is translated variously as Changing Woman or White Painted Woman came to personify femaleness (K. Basso 1966).

The different ratio of plant to animal foods in the Southwest, compared to the Subarctic, and hence the greater importance of plants in the food supply in the Southwest, may have contributed to this. Women in the Subarctic were not able to contribute a great deal directly to the bulk of the food supply, since plant foods in that region are scarce. A symbolic dissociation of women from hunting weapons reinforced the sexual division of labor in the North, and meat acquired through hunting by males constituted the major portion of the diet. Although women were responsible for the butchering, transportation, and preparation of game and participated in major game drives, in many ways these vital functions were secondary to the hunting and killing of game.

In the Southwest the quantity and variety of wild plant foods is far greater (Castetter and Opler 1936). Such resources as mescal, piñon nuts, mesquite beans, cactus and other fruits, in addition to acorns, which were an important staple, were gathered mainly by women and constituted a major proportion of the diet (Perry 1977). Hunting continued, but the relative importance of plant to animal foods in the array of available resources differed dramatically from their proportions in the Subarctic setting (Opler 1972).

Some researchers have argued on the basis of broad comparative studies that a significant contribution by women to subsistence has strong implications for their status.[36] The causal relationship here is debatable, but in the Apache case, it does seem indisputable that as wild plant foods increased in importance, there was a positive shift in the connotations of femaleness as well.

Apache groups downplayed female seclusion at menstruation in favor of more public and positive recognition of femaleness. Ceremonial recognition of female puberty became a distinctly celebrative occasion. Nonetheless, in the preparatory phase of the Chiricahua Apache puberty ceremony, the young woman stayed in a special shelter under the supervision of an older woman. She was supposed to eat little, stay inside, and not "go out in the brush much." The older woman advised her "how to drink water through the tube . . . how to scratch herself with the stick . . . that she must not scratch herself with her nails, because, if she does, it will leave scars, and that she must not touch water with her lips but must use the tube for eight days or it will rain " (Opler 1941a:92, 93). The drinking tube and scratching sticks were important in the Western Apache female puberty ceremony as well.

There continued to be a sense of danger associated with menstruation (Opler 1941a:81, 154, 1969:26; Dyk 1966:13−14; and Goodwin, quoted in Opler 1973:27). And it was dangerous for men to be at the scene of childbirth. A Chiricahua Apache man said that "men don't come to a birth because there are so many women around, and a man would feel funny." Men's association with such an event could cause them to suffer "painful swelling of the joints" (Opler 1941a:7).

The Apache concept of power investing all objects and beings is reminiscent of the North and the Pacific Coast as well. In Western Apache belief, "Power, in its *di yih* meaning, is a supernatural force which man may obtain under certain conditions from all phenomena of the Apache universe. . . . When used properly, *di yih* serves as a vital tool not only as an aid to the individual in his day-to-day existence, but also as a safeguard against the very source from which it is derived. To ward off lightning, one needs lightning power; to kill bear, bear power; to cure snake sickness, snake power" (K. Basso 1966:150).

Despite various cultural innovations and adaptations to the unique settings in which the three major populations of Athapaskan-speaking peoples found themselves, many aspects of their common cultural heritage have persisted. The perpetuation of ancient practices and concepts have counterbalanced a propensity for cultural innovation and a receptivity to external influence. Shifts in the food quest have been closely implicated in many changes that have occurred in other aspects of culture.

The following pages will present evidence for the earliest phase of the Athapaskan presence in North America in an attempt to capture a sense of the Proto-Athapaskan cultural setting. Reconstruction of as much of Proto-Athapaskan culture as possible will be a starting point for the later dispersion and segmentation of the Athapaskan population.

CHAPTER 3

Subarctic Beginnings

It is entirely arbitrary, in a sense, to posit a prehistoric "beginning" for Athapaskan culture in the Subarctic. Culture is a continuous process of decision, choice, remembering, and learning that ultimately derives from a murky inception deep in the recesses of human history. The concept that any cultural system had a beginning point in recent millennia is inherently inaccurate.

In the case of Proto-Athapaskan peoples, their earliest cultural phase in North America was an Asian tradition with far deeper roots in the Eastern Hemisphere. Yet their initial presence in the Western Hemisphere, perhaps not a great distance across the strait from the scene of their former domain, does provide a convenient marker. We can perceive it as a time when the ancestral population shared some degree of cultural unity that was a basis for many of the common features that appear in the Athapaskan cultures of historic times. Perhaps it can provide a rare glimpse of native American cultural traditions fresh from an Asian milieu.

We have something approaching consensus that the origins of native American cultures lie in Asia. More specifically, we can assume that most, and probably all, of these populations spent some time in northeastern Siberia, which is the geographic corridor from the Old World to the west coast of Alaska. Beyond this general agreement, new evidence continuously feeds debate. One of the oldest aspects of the debate involves the time and complexity of the migration to North America. When did humans first make the crossing? How long did the communication between North America and Siberia continue? Were there a few major waves of migration or many, over a long span of time?

With regard to the last question, the evidence seems decisively tipped toward the "multiple wave" alternative. Research in native American gene frequencies, for example, supports the hypothesis that major contingents of the North American population spring from different Asian base populations. If so, they probably left Asia at different times.[1]

Actually, there is not much reason to suppose otherwise. There has been a tendency in popular thought to see the Bering Strait as an absolute barrier. The implication has been that when major glaciers melted at the end of the Pleistocene and freed vast quantities of water, causing ocean levels to rise and flood the land connecting Alaska with Siberia, mutual access between the continents ended. This was not the case.

Eskimo trade fairs in Alaska, involving Siberian Chukchi from across the Bering Strait, were common in the nineteenth century. The strait can be rough and dangerous to cross, but with the intervening Diomede Islands, the distance over water is not enough to prevent communication among people whose routine subsistence activities often involved far more dangerous ventures. In recent times people have often crossed the strait on foot while it was frozen over. Around the turn of the century, the Oblate priest and missionary A.G. Morice (1914:144) wrote that "a sheet of water the shores of which can be seen with the naked eye by anyone standing on either of them can be no serious impediment to intercourse."

Archaeology provides ample evidence that cultural influence was transmitted across the Bering Strait long after the land bridge was flooded (Jenness 1972:244).[2] It makes a good deal of sense, in fact, to visualize cultures of this part of the world as a North Pacific cultural sphere, ranging from the Kamchatka Peninsula on the Asian coast, through the Aleutians, to the Pacific Coast of North America (Laughlin 1980; Fitzhugh and Crowell 1988; Gurvich 1988:17–21). The end of the Pleistocene and the inundation of the Bering land bridge did not isolate the continents. Confronted with evidence of routine interaction between Alaska and Siberia throughout history, we have no reason to assume that migration to North America from Asia ended ten thousand years ago.

The Evidence of Language

Researchers often have suggested that Athapaskan peoples were among the latest of the native American population to enter North America. Their geographic location at the upper end of the migration corridor into the rest of the continent is compatible with this idea, and linguistic evidence lends further support.[3]

We noted earlier that the greatest differences among Athapaskan languages occur in Alaska. In some cases the languages spoken there by Athapaskan peoples in adjacent territories are more different from one another than other Athapaskan languages that are separated by thousands of miles. Linguists have taken this kind of distribution to indicate a center of early dispersion. This surmise is based on the inference that the region where related languages are most different from one another is likely to be the place where they have been separate for the longest time, where the earliest splits occurred. The deepest division among all Athapaskan languages is the separation of Tanaina in southern Alaska from all the rest.[4]

Calculations based on glottochronology, which we must treat with caution, place the time of this primary separation at somewhat over 2,000 years ago (Krauss 1973b:953). Some researchers have argued flatly that glottochronology does not work and should be thrown out altogether (Donohue 1977:86). Since the glottochronological method of dating has raised such serious questions, these dates are mentioned here only as possibilities. They cannot stand by themselves. The linguist Michael Krauss (1973b:953) calculates the date at 2,400 +/- 500 years, which means that if the method were valid, the split could have taken place at any time between 1,900 and 2,900 years in the past.

This issue arose in the last chapter with regard to the Pacific Coast Athapaskan divergence, and at this point it is worth assessing this linguistic evidence more fully. It is important to keep in mind the long and continuous mutual influence among speakers of these languages and dialects. Clearly a simple "tree" model of their past relationships is not adequate, insofar as it implies a series of clean segmentations from a parent language, with further branching among dialects and an absence of significant contact after these partings. As Krauss points out, it is more accurate to describe Athapaskan languages as large dialect chains whose speakers have continued to influence one another long after they have split (Krauss and Golla 1981:69; Krauss 1979). A particular linguistic innovation that occurs in one area might spread among certain adjacent dialects, but another innovation might show up in an entirely different pattern. If several of these innovations are mapped and the maps are superimposed, the result looks rather chaotic. The influences of dialects and languages on one another, reflected in the spread of innovations among them, display a variety of patterns and directions. All of this means that any hope of gauging the precise degrees of linguistic differences among the dialects and languages in the three major Athapaskan regions probably is overly optimistic (Krauss and Golla 1981:70, 71).

On the other hand, there is no doubt that as a general principle, languages that share a common origin do tend to become more and more different from one another as long as they are separated. In a sense, the fact that mutual influence has pervaded among languages throughout the western Subarctic raises other questions about the sharp distinctions that do occur among adjacent languages. These abrupt language boundaries are all the more interesting and suggestive.

The conventional criterion to distinguish languages from dialects is that dialects are mutually intelligible, while languages are not. In operation, this distinction is not precise and involves a certain amount of judgment. But since speakers of two related dialects are more likely to communicate with each other than are speakers of two different languages, we might reasonably expect that dialects are more likely than languages to influence one another through the spread of innovations. The bilingualism that occurs throughout the region, however, complicates things further.

The degrees of difference among languages spoken by populations who have been separated for a long time also have something to tell us. Apache, for example, constitutes a dialect chain within itself with a fair amount of mutual influence among the dialects. But for centuries, at least, Apache has not been part of a greater dialect chain with Pacific Coast or Canadian Athapaskan. Although we cannot depend on glottochronology for any precise dates and reconstructions, we still can gain valuable insights from it. As it happens, the time spans for Athapaskan splits that glottochronology offers seem fairly compatible with the archaeological and ethnographic evidence.[5]

Many Athapaskan languages and dialects probably have not survived into historic times. This means that an Athapaskan language even more divergent than Tanaina might once have existed. If so, this would imply a still earlier breakup of Proto-Athapaskan (Krauss 1979:806–807). But we do have some control over the maximum age of such a split because Athapaskan languages as a group have a common relationship with a non-Athapaskan language of the Subarctic known as Eyak, which was spoken on the Pacific Coast. On the basis of Eyak's similarities with Athapaskan, the two now constitute a larger family known as Eyak-Athapaskan. Glottochronology, for what it may be worth, indicates that Eyak and Athapaskan diverged roughly 3,400 years ago. Perhaps a more surprising and useful insight, though, is that there is no evidence that Eyak and Athapaskan influenced each other after the split. Eyak is no closer to the neighboring Athapaskan language Ahtna than it is to Navajo (Krauss 1973b:953; Krauss and Golla 1981:68).

We can bracket the Proto-Athapaskan phase, then, between the divergence of Eyak from Athapaskan at the early end and the divergence of Tanaina from the rest of Athapaskan. Provisionally, we can define this phase roughly between 3,400 and 2,000 years ago. Eyak gives us extraordinarily valuable clues to the Athapaskan past. Its ancient relationship, combined with the apparent lack of interaction between Eyak and Athapaskan groups in subsequent centuries, affords a unique basis for comparison. The cultural similarities among Eyak and Athapaskan speakers are of special interest in our attempt to illuminate something of Proto-Athapaskan culture.

Until a few years ago, linguists grouped Eyak-Athapaskan with Haida and Tlingit in a still larger category known as Na-Dene. Haida and Tlingit are spoken to the south of Eyak on the Pacific Coast, from Alaska to the Queen Charlotte Islands off the coast of British Columbia. Robert Levine (1979) has challenged this assertion of past relationships among Tlingit, Haida, and Eyak-Athapaskan. Many linguists now feel that whatever similarities exist among these languages result from their having been adjacent to one another for long periods of time, rather than their deriving from any common origins. Krauss agrees with the exclusion of Haida from Na-Dene, but he implies that the case of Tlingit remains uncertain. He and Victor Golla (1981) note that "the close similarities between Tlingit and Eyak-Athapaskan verb morphology, in particular, clearly require a historical explanation." Still more recently, Joseph Greenberg (1987) has reexamined the general Na-Dene issue and pointed out that if Levine's stringent standards were applied to Indo-European, they would exclude many relationships that are now accepted by consensus (Krauss 1979; Krauss and Golla 1981 : 67).[6] It appears that the inclusion of Haida within Na-Dene must remain a question at the moment.

The evidence from physical anthropology is interesting in the context of this debate. Biological evidence of past relationships suggests a high probability of genetic affinity among speakers of Haida, Tlingit, and other Na-Dene populations. The similarities in gene frequencies among them are much higher, in fact, than they are between any of them and "Arctic-Siberian" (Eskimo/Aleut/Chukchi) population samples, despite their geographic nearness to these other groups.[7] In the wake of all of this evidence, we are left to ponder the fact that although linguistic opinion for a time drifted away from the old idea of a Na-Dene phylum, other evidence seems to support the idea that the speakers of Eyak-Athapaskan, Tlingit, and Haida languages might, indeed, have shared a common past in one way or another.

Whatever the case, though, their common past would have been far earlier than the Proto-Athapaskan phase that concerns us here. The question it poses is interesting, but hardly crucial for the issue at hand. If we care to turn once again to glottochronology, the divergence between Tlingit and Eyak-Athapaskan would have been roughly 5,000 years ago and that between Haida and the rest still earlier (Krauss 1973:952–953). If these groups did share a common origin, it would be far more ancient than the Proto-Athapaskan divergence. Still, perhaps we can indulge briefly in sorting out the evidence available to date and can contemplate some possibilities.

What Can We Make of the Evidence?
A Speculative Discussion

The geographic distribution of Haida, Tlingit, Eyak, and Northern Athapaskan populations raises some interesting issues. There is no evidence that any of them arrived in their present location from the south (cf. Dumond 1969). There is little solid evidence, for that matter, to establish the length of time Athapaskans have occupied their historic territory. Most researchers would agree, though, that whenever it may have happened, they spread into their historic territories from some place in Alaska.

If we consider the linguistic principle that the deepest language divisions often mark the earliest center of dispersal, then the location of both Eyak and Athapaskan speakers in southern Alaska near the coast, with Tlingit immediately to the south, is suggestive. Tanaina, the most divergent of Athapaskan languages, is spoken just to the north of Eyak. Most of these groups have shifted their boundaries in historic times, but there is no reason to think that any recent, major, long-distance migrations have taken place in that area.

If we posit that this region is the homeland of the Tlingit, Haida, and Proto-Eyak-Athapaskan population, the depth of language differentiation implies a very lengthy presence of these peoples in southern Alaska. We might call this the "in situ model" of differentiation. On the other hand, there is no clear evidence that Athapaskan peoples were in the western Subarctic until the first millennium A.D. This does not prove anything. The fact that no one has found earlier evidence does not mean that no one will, and indeed, it might exist even if no one ever finds it. But on the other hand, there is no compelling reason to assume that Athapaskan speakers were present before they appear in the archaeological record.

If we compare the glottochronological estimates of the time of the

Eyak-Athapaskan divergence with the earliest clear archaeological evidence of Athapaskans, they differ about 1,500 years. This is just about the length of time that has passed since the occupation of the earliest known Athapaskan sites. Even if these glottochronological dates turn out to be wildly inaccurate, the degree of language difference among Eyak and Athapaskan leaves no doubt that they have been separated for a long time. The length of separation that these differences imply is difficult to account for within the time span that the archaeological record provides.

There is another possibility, though. Suppose we set aside the assumption that all of these language splits took place on the American side of the Bering Strait. The strait could have been crossed at any time during the past 10,000 years, and it often was. Some of the early language splits could just as well have taken place on the Asian side. Over the course of thousands of years, small groups of people could have departed from the Siberian base population and, after the crossing, found their way south along the Pacific Coast.

The relatively mild temperatures and rich food supply make the coastal region attractive. Even during the Pleistocene, the coastline would have provided an inviting avenue for migration south from the Bering Sea region (see also Fladmark 1979). If we can entertain this notion as a possibility, then it is easy to visualize numerous small populations over a lengthy period of time finding their way to settle along the coast of Alaska. The Proto-Eyak could have been just such a contingent, ending up on the coast north of the Tlingit almost in the manner of beads dropping down a string. We might refer to this as the "migration model."

The "in situ model" would require a split between Eyak and Athapaskan in southern Alaska, with the Proto-Athapaskan population separating a few thousand years ago and eventually spreading farther inland. The "migration model" would have the Proto-Athapaskans remaining within the Siberian population when the Eyak departed. The Proto-Athapaskans could have followed roughly the same route, leading them to end up adjacent to their linguistic relatives, the Eyak. This would have been followed by a series of language divergences within Athapaskan itself.

In either case these peoples would be among the more recent arrivals from Asia. Both models incorporate a base in southern Alaska from which Athapaskan populations spread toward their historic distribution. If Athapaskan speakers do share origins with other peoples in southern Alaska, the "migration model," involving separations in Asia and later migrations across the strait, has some advantages over the idea that all divergences took place within North

America. It accounts more easily for the deep splits that exist among languages spoken by people who live in adjacent territories. It also points to ecological factors, such as the availability of a rich food supply on the Pacific Coast, to account for the route and final destination of these populations.

By the time the Proto-Athapaskan migrations could have taken place, most of the Pacific coastline south of the Alaska Peninsula was occupied and would have been unavailable to newcomers without some displacement of the previous inhabitants. But the territories of the Tanaina and Ahtna at the northern end of this zone, reaching into the interior from Cook Inlet just north of the Eyak and the Copper River delta, still provide a fairly rich food supply and a climate much milder than it was farther inland. If Proto-Athapaskans ended up there at the top of the "string" soon after their arrival in North America, a later spread inland through the mountains to the north, west, and south would account for the early linguistic splits.

Considering Tanaina and Ahtna territories from this perspective, the position of Tanaina is especially suggestive. Tanaina is the language consistently most remote from all others—as distant from its neighbors in Alaska as it is from Apache.

The language divisions and distributions in this part of Alaska are consistent with the idea that some descendants of the Proto-Eyak-Athapaskan population continued to occupy the same general region, while others expanded and migrated inland away from the coast. This process would have to result in increasing language divergence as the population spread and scattered. People tend to lose track of one another as distances between local groupings become more remote.

We should remember that few people took part in these processes compared to the numbers of historic Athapaskan speakers. Human populations many times throughout history have demonstrated their capacity to expand rapidly under the proper conditions. In this context, with people pursuing a hunting and gathering existence in a subarctic region, it is unlikely that any large, dense populations could have been involved. Each of the contingents leaving Siberia might have amounted to no more than a few hundred people. By the same token, the split between Tanaina and the other Proto-Athapaskans could have involved only a few small groups of people who ventured beyond their home territory and expanded later over generations, undergoing further segmentation in the following centuries. Even now, for example, the Tanaina number only a few hundred people, although they may have comprised several thousand early in the historic period.

Whenever these departures from Siberia occurred, the motivations that spurred them in the first place probably will always be inaccessible to us. But communication and the exchange of ideas within the North Pacific cultural sphere have gone on for thousands of years. The search for richer food sources, perhaps even based on tales of those who had been there and returned, would have been reasonable incentives.

The estimated time of the split between Eyak and Athapaskan appears to correlate roughly with a major climatic change. About 3,500 years ago, there seems to have been a rather sudden return to cold, wet conditions after about 3,000 years of relatively warm and dry weather known as the Hypsithermal.[8] Such a change would have required some readjustments on the part of people who relied on a natural food supply. Suggestive as these developments are, though, their possible connections with population movements are obscure.

We also are confronted with an unfortunate lack of information about Siberian base population from which these departures would have occurred. The complexity of Siberian prehistory has been explored and illuminated to some extent in recent years, but there is far more that we would like to know.

Some researchers have concluded that genetic data indicate that Athapaskan-speaking peoples share a very ancient common past with Eskimo and Aleut peoples. They estimate the time of this common population base at 11,000 years ago or more (Szathmary and Ossenberg 1978). This date would not be inconsistent with the sequential migration model discussed earlier. It could accommodate proto-Eskimo peoples having separated from a general Siberian parent population at a very early time, around the end of the Pleistocene. At this early period we can reincorporate the Bering land bridge into the scheme and consider western Alaska and northeastern Siberia as a single, contiguous region. There is some evidence that Proto-Eskimo-Aleut populations were present in the Aleutians by at least 8,000 years ago, which lends further support to their early presence in mainland North America (Laughlin 1980).

Whatever these remote relationships might have been, though, there are other reasons to suspect that the arrival of Proto-Athapaskans in North America was relatively recent compared to other native American groups. Linguists agree, generally, that even the maximal differentiation among Athapaskan languages is shallow compared to differences within other native American language families. If the estimated time span of 2,000 years is inaccurate, there is little doubt, at least, that the splits are comparatively recent.

A long occupancy of Proto-Athapaskans in one locality, if we accept the "in situ" model, would mean that the language remained undifferentiated in the Subarctic for a millennium or so and then suddenly developed a propensity for branching. It seems more plausible, as an alternative, that the earliest linguistic divergence within Athapaskan, between Tanaina and the rest, occurred not too long after their arrival and initiated a process of diversification that has continued into the present.

Whatever more ancient relationships of Eyak and Athapaskan ancestors may have had with other populations, and whatever the sequence of events that led them to the western Subarctic, their antecedents lie somewhere in Asia. And as we have noted earlier, communication between the North American Subarctic and northern Siberia continued long after the major migrations took place. With that in mind, we might examine the northern Athapaskan population from the perspective of this wider context.

The Wider Ethnographic Context

Many cultural features occur broadly across the Northern Hemisphere. Some of these may be the result of a rapid and extensive spread of ideas. Others, no doubt, represent continuities from more ancient cultural strata.[9] A special ideological concern with the bear, for example, shows up throughout northern Asia and North America (Hallowell 1926). Conical tepee-style dwellings, braided hairstyles, and many other features associated with native American cultures occur in Siberia as well. These parallels have been noted by generations of scholars (e.g., Bogoras 1902; Morice 1914; Hatt 1916; Lowie 1923; Hallowell 1926; Davidson 1937; Boas 1910, 1940:344; Lamont 1946:124; Gurvich 1979).[10]

Some aspects of Athapaskan cultures reminiscent of Siberian patterns may reflect an early Asian cultural milieu from which they derived, or they may result from later intercultural influences around the North Pacific sphere (Bogoras 1902; Levin and Potapov 1964). Throughout native Siberia, for example, many peoples held the concept that the human soul has multiple components (Dupre 1974). Altaian peoples thought that the soul consists of six parts, while the Chukchi believed that various components of the soul were associated with particular parts of the body (Czaplicka 1914:260, 281). The Samoyedic-speaking Nentsi, whose historic territory was thousands of miles to the west of the Bering Strait, believed that the human spirit consisted of "the intellect" or conscious mind, the "soul-life," and the "shadow-soul." The shadow-soul was the aspect of the soul "accompanying a man beside himself." The Nentsi referred to the soul-life, which was associated with air, by a term that also meant "breath" or "vapor rising from the bodies of men and animals in winter" (Czaplicka 1934:176). The loss of one's shadow caused death in a short time, and fainting was a brief, temporary loss of the shadow.

These Samoyedic-speaking peoples considered the shadow-soul dangerous. It lingered near the body after death or around the grave and sometimes attempted to take the shadows of living relatives. People took numerous measures to keep the shadow of the deceased away from the living. After the death they burned or otherwise destroyed the house and abandoned the site. They left the property of the deceased at the grave and damaged it in some way, and for years afterward, relatives never mentioned the name of the deceased (Montefiore 1895:406; Prokof'yeva 1964:565), since "the name of the dead is strictly tabued" (Czaplicka 1934:176). Throughout eastern Siberia it was a common practice to remove the body from the dwelling through a window, smoke hole, or some opening other than the doorway.

The beliefs and practices of other Siberian peoples differed considerably from the Nentsi pattern. M. A. Czaplicka states that the Koryak of eastern Siberia "draw no very sharp line of distinction between life and death" (Czaplicka 1914:281). Among the Kamchadals the corpse was dragged out to be eaten by dogs. The Yukagir constructed platforms to allow exposure to the elements but also distributed parts of the body to close relatives, who could keep them as amulets (Czaplicka 1914:145, 157). The Chukchi cut the throat of the deceased and covered the body with reindeer meat to ensure its disposal by carnivores. They examined the internal organs for evidence of the cause of death, and in a custom perhaps analogous to that of the Yukagir, distributed small pieces of fur from the clothing of the deceased to the relatives. Such practices were quite incompatible with the Samoyedic Nentsi beliefs that a lingering shadow made any contact with the body dangerous.

Samoyedic and other Siberian peoples perceived a sense of danger associated with femaleness as well, which was manifest in a variety of prohibitions. Nentsi women were not allowed to occupy the area of the dwelling opposite the doorway, which was considered the "sacred" or "clean" part of the house, or to walk around the outside of the dwelling. Women were prohibited from stepping over hunting weapons and the ropes or harnesses associated with reindeer herding. After childbirth, smoke purified the dwelling in which the birth had occurred (Prokof' yeva 1964:565; Hajdu 1963; Czaplicka 1914:226; Montefiore 1895:406). The close parallels with northern Athapaskan practices are obvious. Athapaskan cultures clearly developed from a broader Asian context, but these populations have a history of their own in the Subarctic. The archaeological evidence provides some record of this, but it leaves many questions unanswered and raises still others.

The Archaeological Evidence

Many researchers have assumed a long occupancy of Athapaskan speakers in North America, but the archaeological evidence to support this is far from conclusive. William Workman (1978) has conducted studies with some important implications for this issue in the southwestern region of the Yukon Territory. The evidence available so far in that area lends itself to a number of interpretations. Workman suggests that in the Aishihik-Kluane region, not far from the Pacific Coast in the southwestern corner of the Yukon, there was cultural continuity between what he calls the Taye Lake phase, beginning around 3000 B.C., through the subsequent Aishihik and Bennett phases, which are dated respectively from A.D. 400 to 1800 and from 1800 to the present.

There is a clear historic continuity from the Aishihik phase, beginning at A.D. 400, to the modern Athapaskan-speaking Tutchone who presently inhabit the area. If this continuity extends more deeply into the past from the beginning of the Taye Lake phase, it would imply that there was a Proto-Eyak-Athapaskan occupation in the region for about 5,000 years. On the other hand, if the linguistic estimate of Eyak-Athapaskan language separation is at all accurate, this would mean that the ancestors of these peoples began to occupy the area more than a millennium before the Eyak and Athapaskan languages split.

As Workman (1978:68–69) points out, by 3,000 years ago, or roughly 1300 to 1400 B.C., the climate of the region was changing. For about 3,000 years before that, the area had been relatively dry as a local manifestation of the Hypsithermal. During that warm episode, the region was predominantly grassland, and bison (*Bison bison athabaskae*) were a major food source for the local populace. But then around 3,300 years ago the climate changed rather abruptly toward a colder, wetter "neoglacial" phase. Bison no longer lived in the area, as grasslands gave way to the conifer forests that characterize the region today. The appearance of peat soils in the archaeological record reflects this change (Workman 1978:367). These drastic alterations in the environment would have had tremendous repercussions for people who had been hunting grassland animals.

The older Taye Lake phase is separated from the Aishihik phase by a layer of volcanic ash resulting from an eruption about A.D. 400. The residue from this eruption serves as a somewhat arbitrary before and after boundary marker between time periods. The change in the weather, with its broader environmental impacts, had been under way for well over 1,000 years when the layer of white ash fell in A.D. 400, but in the archaeological record the ash provides a convenient, if coincidental, marker. It delineates a rather imprecise boundary between the two types of environmental conditions.

The sequence of living patterns evident at the site raises an important question. Does it reflect continuity of a population faced with changing conditions who altered their strategies in response? Or did the earlier population depart, to be succeeded by a new group? The evidence for the transition from the Taye Lake to Aishihik phases leaves plenty of room for debate.

The argument for continuity of population depends on certain artifact forms that recur in different levels of the site. The evidence consists of bone implements, a notched point, stone wedges and boulder spalls, endscrapers, flake blade cores, and blunted discoids (Workman 1978:367). On closer consideration, though, this evidence turns out to be rather ambiguous. Bone implements, for example, do occur at different levels at the site, but they show a variety of forms. The type of barbed bone projectile points usually associated with Athapaskan peoples appears only above the layer of ash or just beneath it. These recent levels also hold a bird bone tube, resembling the drinking tube used in Athapaskan female seclusion practices.

The bone implements of the earlier Taye Lake phase are different. There are some smooth bone awls and slotted hafts that could have held rows of the small stone flakes known as microblades. But microblades have not usually been associated with Athapaskan peoples, and there are no barbed bone projectile points. Moreover, the Aishihik endscrapers are of quite a different style from their counterparts in the earlier Taye Lake phase (Workman 1978: 367, 1977b:48).

Other artifacts at the site, such as hammered copper implements and the small projectile points with contracting bases known as the Kavik type, are broadly reminiscent of the type used by Athapaskan peoples, but they occur in the Aishihik phase, not in the earlier Taye Lake (Workman 1978: 367). By no means, then, does the evidence establish clearly and firmly a 5,000-year continuity of the population in the Aishihik-Kluane area of the southwestern Yukon Territory.

Following the Taye Lake phase, the local population's food-getting strategies changed to a more scattered, mobile occupation of the area by smaller groups (Workman 1978:367–368). One possible explanation for this would be that it represents an adjustment of the same population's subsistence from grassland to spruce forest conditions. But the change in pattern could just as easily have resulted from the earlier Taye Lake inhabitants, who had more focused and specialized food-getting patterns, departing the region, to be replaced by Proto-Athapaskan people. If so, these new arrivals probably would have shared many of the technological patterns current at that time throughout the Subarctic cultural sphere, but they also brought a unique tradition of their own into the area.

There is intriguing evidence here, in fact, to support the possibility that Proto-Athapaskans spread from southern Alaska near the coastline into the Aishihik-Kluane area and other parts of the interior. Workman, who excavated the Yukon site, states that there is strong archaeological evidence to tie the Aishihik phase in the southwest Yukon Territory to the Pacific Coast. "Traits shared between the Aishihik Phase and the Yakutat-Angoon areas include a series of elaborate and nearly identical copper implements, ground adzes, abraided cobbles, blunt-ground slate pieces, boulder spalls, tabular schist bifaces and, in a general way, certain bone implements" (Workman 1978:419).[11]

Yakutat Bay lies adjacent to the historic territory of the Eyak. Although past relationships between these two regions are far from clear, we might expect to find such a distribution of cultural features if the Aishihik phase represented an incursion of Proto-Athapaskan peoples into the region from an earlier habitat near the coast. This particular case seems to add more weight to the idea that the Athapaskan speakers are recent arrivals in the western Subarctic.

Workman and others have suggested that the volcanic eruption of A.D. 300–400 provoked subsequent Athapaskan migrations away from the southern Yukon. The geographic distribution of the Kavik type of stone projectile point extends from the southern Yukon northward toward the Brooks Range. This corresponds roughly to the historic distribution of the Tutchone, Han, and Kutchin, who speak closely related dialects, from south to north (Derry 1975). The distribution of Kavik points would be compatible with a migration out of the southern Yukon region, where the eruption occurred, toward the north. The boundary between Kutchin at the far northern end of the chain and Koyukon, across the Yukon River, is "perhaps the most abrupt linguistic boundary within Athapaskan" (Krauss and Golla 1981:73). This is what we could expect at the leading edge of a migration.

There were similar movements of people along the mountains to the southeast as well.[12] But all of these processes have to do with a time after Athapaskan speakers were present in the Subarctic. Their initial arrival remains a mystery. Yet when we survey the evidence throughout the region, a pattern emerges. Across the entire western Subarctic, prehistoric remains that we can clearly associate with Athapaskan peoples do not date earlier than the first millennium A.D. A site called Onion Portage in northern Alaska, for example, contains evidence of a long sequence of development associated with Paleo-eskimo traditions. Suddenly this is interrupted at around A.D. 400 by the appearance of an entirely different culture type called the Itkillik complex. The Itkillik, who have been identified provisionally as Athapaskan (Anderson 1970),[13] soon disappear, and Eskimo occupancy of the site resumes and continues to present times.

Kavik-type points occur at Anaktuvuk Pass in northern Alaska, suggesting an Athapaskan presence, but they are undated. Similar points appear throughout Alaska in the first millennium A.D. They show up in the northern Yukon Territory near the Alaskan border at the Klo-Kut site, where there may have been a continuous Kutchin occupation for up to 1,500 years (Morlan 1972), but this would not make them older than the middle of the first millennium A.D. In central Alaska the Minchumina site reflects an Eskimo-to-Athapaskan transition as early as A.D. 200–800, which still is within the same time range (Holmes 1971 : 106).

Some have suggested that a Subarctic "Athapaskan Tradition" began at around 1000 B.C., based on the Healy Lake site in east-central Alaska (Cook 1969). But even at that site, no clear, identifiable Athapaskan affinities occur until more recent levels, and some researchers have questioned assertions of cultural continuity there (Workman 1978 : 424).[14] At least one researcher sees a break in continuity there around A.D. 1000 and states that "only after an interruption is it possible to pick up early Athapaskan technology" (Bacon 1977 : 5).

Some archaeologists have suggested Athapaskan continuities with the much earlier Tuktu and Denali traditions, but strong evidence for this is lacking as well. Farther to the east in the Mackenzie district, the Spence River complex, a possible candidate for Athapaskan associations, is associated with small side-notched points and appears around A.D. 500 (A. Clark 1977 : 125).

Also to the east of the Cordillera in the Great Slave Lake region, William Noble (1977, 1981) has posited an Athapaskan cultural continuity from the Taltheilei Shale Complex, beginning around 600 B.C., to the historic period when the Athapaskan-speaking Chipewyan inhabited the area. An Athapaskan presence east of the Cordillera this early would challenge the model of an Athapaskan dispersion from southern Alaska in the first few centuries A.D. Once again, though, continuity in the archaeological record is not entirely clear and has been questioned by other researchers (Donohue 1977 : 88). The Taltheilei Shale Complex has some antiquity in this area. The earlier phases of this complex are associated with stemmed projectile points and date from 600 B.C. to A.D. 200–400. Much later, from A.D. 900 to 1100, the Narrows phase appears in the region. The Narrows phase is associated with a different type of unstemmed point, with "ears" at the basal corners.

Points of the Narrows phase occur in the region of Great Slave Lake, Artillery Lake, and Lake Athabasca, and an association between the Narrows phase and historic Athapaskan speakers seems plausible. The problem is to link the Narrows phase with the earlier manifestations of the Taltheilei Shale Complex. One archaeologist posits a phase referred to as the "Unnamed Gap" to link them. The connection between the early Taltheilei Shale Complex phases and the Narrows phase across the "Unnamed Gap" of roughly half a millennium, though, seems tenuous.

Among the early phases of the Taltheilei complex the Windy Point phase occurs just before this gap, spanning the period from A.D. 400 to A.D. 900, after which the Narrows phase appears. The Windy Point phase has a more restricted distribution than the phases preceding it. But following the gap of five centuries or so, after the Narrows phase appears around A.D. 900, its distribution increases (Noble 1977 : 68). Gordon suggests that the territorial contraction of the Windy Point phase of the Taltheilei reflects a tendency toward regionalization (Gordon 1977 : 74). But an alternative explanation would be that such a pattern of shrinking distribution, followed by a lengthy hiatus and then the appearance and subsequent spread of different forms, could reflect a gradual reduction and departure of an earlier population followed by the arrival of a new one.

The small notched points and bone and copper tools that occur in that region are characteristic of Athapaskan sites in other places. But they appear late, from A.D. 800 to 1750 (Gordon 1977 : 75). Once again, evidence for two and a half millennia of Athapaskan occupation in the Chipewyan region is open to differing interpretations.

The archaeologist Anne Shinkwin's (1977, 1979) thorough analysis of the archaeological data in Alaska leads her to conclude that there is not sufficient evidence to justify the idea of an "Athapaskan Tradition" any earlier than the first millennium A.D. When one surveys the published research in the area, the dates of the earliest clear Athapaskan affinities hover within the first millennium with rather striking consistency.

Glen Bacon (1977:9) also argues that Athapaskans arrived late in Alaska. He notes that there is no clear basis for deriving either the Athapaskan or recent Thule (Eskimo) traditions from the preceding Denali or Arctic Small Tool traditions. He points out that the sudden appearance of the Thule around A.D 500 roughly corresponds in time to the "finale of the Denali tradition, which after a brief hiatus was replaced by a technology identical in many respects to the early historic Alaskan Athapaskan technology." Bacon suggests that the appearance of the Thule tradition could have been associated with a change in Bering ice conditions and that these regional climatic changes could also have been associated with the Athapaskan appearance.

In central Alaska at the Minchumina site, there appears to have been a major technological change at around A.D. 1000. The evidence leads Charles Holmes (1977:15) to suggest a fairly rapid spread of Athapaskans into Alaska "from a nearby staging area at a relatively late period." He goes on to observe that "this rapid a dispersal and diversification does not seem to be substantiated by linguistic studies but it would provide a reason for the change we have noted in material culture after about A.D. 1000."

But Holmes' suggestion would not contradict linguistic conclusions unless the original center of Athapaskan dispersion was assumed to be in central Alaska, as some have suggested (Krauss 1973a), rather than southern Alaska. The earliest archaeological evidence of an Athapaskan presence there is later than the linguistic evidence of divergence would demand that it should be if central Alaska is the original Athapaskan homeland. On the other hand, if the Athapaskan population expanded from southern rather than central Alaska from an area near the coast toward the interior, with the earliest departures occurring in the region somewhere between Cook Inlet and Yakutat—and if the population then expanded inland toward Minchumina and other central Alaskan locales—then Holmes' model fits quite nicely. We must note once again, though, that the archaeological evidence for Athapaskan prehistory in southern Alaska is very scanty (Reger 1977).[15]

James Dixon (1985:53) sees the "Athapaskan Tradition" in Alaska as having lasted from 1500 to 100 years ago, characterized by a "deemphasis on stonework" and an "increased use of organic materials" such as bone. He concludes that "the archaeological record suggests replacement of the Late Denali complex by the Athapaskan Tradition in interior Alaska sometime shortly before 1500 B.P. [before present]. . . . The replacement was complete in all parts of the interior by 1000 B.P. . . . Several archaeological assemblages after 1000 B.P. can be traced through the direct historic approach and linked to recent Athapaskan groups" (1985:61).

Although it may never be possible to rule out absolutely an Athapaskan presence in the Subarctic before the first millenium A.D., the archaeological evidence gives no reason to assume it. In the words of Shinkwin (1977), during earlier periods Athapaskans "are not visible in the archaeological record."

The Proto-Athapaskan Setting

Wherever Athapaskan-speaking peoples may have been in the first millenium B.C., by the first few centuries A.D. they were in the western Subarctic of North America. In other parts of the North American continent, Maya temple centers were being renovated and expanded. In the Southwest, village farmers had begun to construct large permanent buildings of stone and adobe. In the Ohio River Valley, a cosmopolitan society was constructing huge earthen mounds and attracting trade goods from as far away as the Gulf of Mexico. Across the Atlantic, Rome had begun to expand its empire, and village peoples occupied the forests of Europe. To the east across the Eurasian steppes, nomads dominated the vast area between the Black Sea and China, while farther north, reindeer hunters survived where the taiga gave way to barren ground. These peoples hunted reindeer far into northeastern Siberia until the land ended at the Bering Sea. To the east across the strait lay the western Subarctic of North America. What was it like?

Two thousand years ago the climate of this region was not appreciably different from present conditions (Holmes 1977:106). Away from the coast in the mountainous terrain of the interior, conifer forests had long since completed their domination of the region and replaced the grasslands of the Hypsithermal period. Then, as now, the Pacific coastline caught the effects of the Japanese Current flowing up from the South Pacific with its warm, moist air blown eastward by the prevailing winds and trapped by the Cordillera running south along the coast. These moderating influences had less effect in the interior beyond the mountains.

Subarctic conifer forests hold a sparse food supply compared with many other kinds of ecosystems. Caribou would have been the primary source of protein for people living there. To the west of the Bering Strait in eastern Siberia, reindeer, the Old World equivalent of the caribou, were the staple of hunters who later became herders. Moose were available to the south and in various parts of the Subarctic at different times in the past.

Woods buffalo were more common during this period. In historic times they grazed as far north as Great Slave Lake. On the Pacific side of the Cordillera, salmon would have been an important staple, perhaps in some cases supporting more sedentary communities. Vegetable foods, because of their scarcity, could only have been a relatively minor part of the diet. On both sides of the Bering Strait away from the coast, the combination of salmon and reindeer, or caribou, provided the bases for the food quest.

From the Alaska Peninsula north and westward into the Aleutian Islands, the coast itself was occupied by increasingly specialized maritime peoples. By two thousand years ago, Proto-Eskimo and Aleut peoples had long since developed a successful style of life based on sea mammals along the west coast of Alaska (Laughlin 1980). The increasingly specialized Eskimo coastal adaptation with its maritime focus was soon to develop into the Thule tradition, which eventually would spread eastward across the Arctic to Greenland. The Athapaskan food quest, by contrast, developed in a mountainous, forested context with an emphasis on multiple but scattered food sources. The nature and context of this food quest affected the fundamental character of Proto-Athapaskan culture, which became, in turn, the basis for the further diversification of Athapaskan peoples.

CHAPTER 4

Proto-Athapaskan Culture

The Proto-Athapaskan Locale

Southern Alaska near historic Tanaina territory or the regions occupied by the Eyak and Ahtna may have been the earliest North American homeland of Proto-Athapaskans. Archaeological evidence does not corroborate a lengthy occupation of Tanaina around Cook Inlet, but the prehistory of this area is far from certain, and a lack of positive evidence to confirm a group's presence is far from conclusive proof of their absence.

The area around Cook Inlet in Alaska, historic territory of the Tanaina, may be the richest of any locale Northern Athapaskans occupied. The depth of the Tanaina language split from the rest of Athapaskan suggests that the earliest population expansions were in this general area of southern Alaska, probably inland away from the coast. The similarities between artifacts found in the Yakutat region to the south near the Pacific Coast and those found within historic Tutchone territory in the interior are suggestive.

Such movements of people would not necessarily have involved a departure from a coastal maritime-focused subsistence quest. In the first place, there is no evidence that any Athapaskan group has ever specialized in maritime resources. Not even the Tanaina, despite their access to the coast, developed any significant maritime pattern but utilized inland food sources extensively. If we can make assumptions based on what we know about Athapaskan groups who continued to operate more recently in the same region, the Proto-Athapaskans must have been relatively unspecialized in their subsistence patterns and have maintained a flexible strategy, remaining opportunistic enough to exploit whatever became available. This in turn would demand a capacity for easy dispersal, probably involving periodic returns to base camps or villages in favored locations. The overall population size would depend on the richness and reliability of the total food supply.

Not only does the ethnographic record of historic Athapaskan peoples suggest an inland focus for Proto-Athapaskan groups, but the absence of mutual linguistic borrowing in the Inuit or Athapaskan dialects of populations that left the Alaskan region at an early time lends further support (Krauss 1979: 184–185). It seems likely that when the easternmost carriers of the Eskimoan Thule tradition spread along the Arctic Coast from western Alaska, the Proto-Athapaskan population occupied a different zone. There is, of course, the noted Athapaskan linguistic conservatism to consider. But since the Athapaskan contingent who were later to become Apache eventually migrated farther to the south than any of the rest of the Athapaskan population, they might well have come from the southernmost portion of the territory. This would mean that even if Eskimo peoples did occupy much of the coast of Alaska during the period of early Athapaskan expansion, the Proto-Apachean section of that population might not have been exposed to them.

By A.D. 1, Eskimoan peoples had been exploiting the coastal niche successfully for a long time (Laughlin 1979:174). There are a few archaeological sites within historic Eskimo territory containing Eskimo materials interspersed at different levels with artifacts that are probably Athapaskan, but for the most part these sites are in marginal zones near the tree line, which has fluctuated through time. It appears that in some cases, at least, the occupation levels at these sites were separated by periods of abandonment.[1] In general, Athapaskan activities seem to have had a consistent inland focus with very little association with coastal areas or overlap with the maritime Eskimo populations.

The Social Framework

What was Proto-Athapaskan social organization like? Subsistence possibilities in Alaska included salmon, plentiful enough in coastal areas occupied by the Tlingit to allow large groups of people to cluster during large portions of the year. Caribou would also have been important, perhaps even more than would salmon. Caribou could be hunted in a number of ways, but with their propensity to herd, one of the most successful techniques would have been to use game drives which call for the collective efforts of sizable aggregates of people. On the other hand, caribou are extremely mobile, and in mountainous regions they tend to move to different altitudes at different times of the year. Hence, hunters' mobility, as well as their capacity to gather in large numbers for certain purposes, would have been a key aspect of the subsistence pattern.

These considerations imply local populations able to exploit a diverse range of terrain by maintaining a capacity to coalesce for certain purposes and disperse when the situation demanded it, without losing the interpersonal ties that would allow them to regroup easily once again in larger aggregates when it was necessary or desirable. The situation demands an ability to cover vast territories, allowing ad hoc responses to unexpected opportunities or shortages in the food supply and permitting the population to redistribute itself continually in response to short-term fluctuations.

Isidore Dyen and David F. Aberle (1974) reconstructed the Proto-Athapaskan kinship system through a painstaking comparison of Athapaskan kin terms. They concluded that the Proto-Athapaskan population had an Iroquois type of cousin terminology. This type of system groups the children of the mother's sisters and those of the father's brothers into a single category that also includes one's own brothers and sisters.

Usually kinship terms of this sort occur in societies that have unilineal descent groups such as clans or lineages. In such a system, one is automatically born into a category based on descent, either through the mother's or the father's line, according to the rule stressed in that particular social organization. This produces unambiguous lines of relationship. An Iroquois type of kin terminology usually develops in such systems because it distinguishes the cousins who are likely to belong to one's own descent group from those who cannot belong to it. The children of one's mother's brothers or one's father's sisters cannot possibly belong to one's own clan. The children of one's mother's sisters and father's brothers can.

In many societies throughout the world, the cross-parallel cousin distinctions that define an Iroquois type of cousin terminology designate membership in sociocentric, sharply bounded corporate groups: that is, groups that have social and political reality as entities beyond the ties that unite their individual members. This is the case in some of the Pacific-drainage Athapaskan groups who have named clans and moieties. But Iroquois cousin terms need not necessarily be associated with such corporate groups. In some cases these terms can be associated with a pattern in which the definition of interpersonal relationships predominates over group membership.

To take the matrilineal, matrilocal systems of many Athapaskan groups as an example, at the individual level such terms identify those people with whom one is likely to share close relationships through women. These people would certainly include the mother's sister's children, and they might include the father's brother's children as well if he married one of the sisters of the mother.

By the same token, this type of kinship terminology also identifies those to whom one does *not* have a close relationship through women. Ties to the father's sister's children and to the mother's brother's children are interrupted by links through an intervening male.

From a distributional analysis of social organization among the historic Athapaskan-speaking peoples, Dyen and Aberle (1974) argue that Proto-Athapaskan social organization was unilineal, involving a matrilineal principle of descent with matrilocal residence. The principle of relationship, in other words, was through the mother's line, and after marriage the couple normally resided with the wife's relatives. Other researchers have come to the same conclusions (Hosley 1980; Bishop and Krech 1980).[2]

According to one standard anthropological viewpoint, this kind of social organization might be surprising in a population that subsisted through hunting and gathering. As Dyen and Aberle (1974: 379–380) point out, though, matrilineal descent and matrilocal residence are compatible with this type of subsistence if the food supply allows the maintenance of groups large enough to permit marriage within the local population without violation of incest rules. The concept of "local" in this setting has a very broad geographic sense, though, given the sparseness and mobility of the population. Marriage ties would extend among small, scattered aggregates who operated over hundreds and perhaps thousands of square miles of territory.

Cross-cultural data bear out the tendency for matrilineal, matrilocal systems to be associated with patterns of marriage within the local population. It is worth pointing out that whatever the antiquity of such a system might have been in the western Subarctic, many Northern Athapaskan groups in historic times did maintain systems of matrilineal descent and matrilocal residence in the same ecological context.[3] This in itself should dispel any doubts about this type of organization's feasibility in the western Subarctic.

On balance, the evidence indicates that the use of Iroquois cousin terms in the Proto-Athapaskan context was more the result of a stress on descent through females as a fundamental criterion of relationships among individuals than an indication of any highly structured system of corporate unilineal descent groups. The principle of relationship through females, manifest in a variety of ways in Athapaskan social organizations, is harmonious with a matrilocal residence pattern, and we can see this residence pattern, in turn, as a response to the conditions of subsistence in the western Subarctic. These entailed a high degree of male absenteeism and a heightened importance of women as the basis for social coherence.

In this situation regional populations large enough to include a number of intermarrying lineages or clans would have to have allowed smaller, scattered aggregates to move freely over considerable territory. Ties of descent and marriage could have functioned to maintain social coherence over a broad area and to provide some interpersonal predictability of behavior, making it easier for these populations to come together periodically at regular base camps or other favored sites.

From the perspective of genetics, Christopher Meiklejohn's (1977: 108) work provides some interesting insights in this regard. Through computer simulation, he concludes that "totally isolated populations have to have above ca. 475 persons to survive over any appreciable number of generations." In the western Subarctic, the local resource base would rarely have allowed coresidential groupings that large to exist for very long in any locality. Since Proto-Athapaskan aggregates would have tended to be much smaller than Meiklejohn's figure of 475, they could not have existed as isolates. Broader regional ties among these small mobile groups would have been necessary to incorporate a sufficient number of people.

With this in mind, it is interesting that in his study of the Kaska, Roger McDonnell (1984) notes that in some cases, local groups observed at one period seemed to have "disappeared" years later. He attributes the ephemeral nature of Kaska social groupings to an ideological system that places a high value on fluidity and free movement. But the Kaska example is also rather suggestive from the perspective of Meiklejohn's discussion of population maintenance. Given the need for population clusters to remain small and to move freely, Meiklejohn questions whether any distinct, lasting groups could exist "beyond those ephemerally observable at one point in time" throughout the Athapaskan region. He concludes that "the Athapaskan population in time can therefore be treated as a single functioning biological unit with changing internal structure of a fleeting nature" (1977: 109).

On the other hand, some writers have suggested that an archaic "three-clan" system, or some type of triadic descent group structure, characterized early Athapaskan social organization. Such a division existed among the lower Tanana, Koyukon, and Chandalar and Yukon Kutchin (McKennan 1969: 107). Referring to Southern Athapaskans, Grenville Goodwin (1969: 102) writes that "many western Apache clans claim relationship to, or direct descent from, what may be called three archaic clans. . . . curiously enough, these archaic clans are either attributed to or are Navajo clans." He also states that the western Apache "read clans into the three Chiricahua bands, asserting that these are clans like their own" (Goodwin 1969: 105). We can only view this as a possibility, though. If the Proto-Athapaskans had matrilineal descent groups, they may very well have had three rather than some other number, but it seems unlikely that this can ever be confirmed.

But it may be erroneous in any case to view Proto-Athapaskan descent groups as corporate entities that subsumed and defined individual relationships, particularly in light of Meiklejohn's conclusions. McDonnell (1984:53) notes that Kaska moiety membership was "largely a distinction that functioned in the interpretation of relations that emerged independently of it." In the same vein, Louise Lamphere (1977:94) sees Navajo clan ties in the Southwest as links conceived in terms of a social field of personal bonds among individuals, rather than as membership in bounded social units. She describes these as "ties of matrifiliation, not matrilineal descent," with the key relationship between mother and child, particularly mother and daughter. The extension of shared maternal bonds among siblings appears more significant than membership in one or another corporate group (1977:81).

These examples manifest an Athapaskan cultural characteristic that some writers have called "individualism." But rather than an isolating atomism, it involves networks of highly personalized and well-defined ties among individuals that in some cases may appear as collective designations expressed in terms of descent groups. Often the social categories that reflect these ties seem to be the collective effect of such personal linkages rather than their cause. The individual significance of matrilineal ties seems more fundamental than their resultant collective categories.

Based on what we can gather from patterns that characterize Athapaskan-speaking groups throughout North America, and from inferences based on the conditions of the western Subarctic, we probably can best describe Proto-Athapaskan social organization as a system of small, flexible aggregates built upon personalized ties. A major basis for these ties was relationship through women, whether by descent or marriage, rather than through membership in sociocentric corporate groups.

In the mountains and forests of southern Alaska, the easy mobility necessary for rapid exploitation of far-flung and often uncertain food sources was not totally unstructured. A tendency toward matrilocal residence and the expectation of bride service have tempered population movements in these regions. Mother-in-law avoidance is typical among Eyak and Athapaskan peoples in the Subarctic as well as the Southwest. This, of course, is meaningful only in situations in which the husband and his wife's mother are likely to come into contact (see Appendix C).[4]

Among Northern Athapaskan peoples in historic times, the subsistence pattern required the lengthy absence of males from base camps, as hunters covered hundreds of square miles in the search for game. In such circumstances women with their young children formed the most stable component of the residential cluster. With matrilocal residence these women would tend to be mothers, daughters, and sisters, and children of the group would be related to one another through ties linking their mothers. This situation is consistent with an organizational theme or concept that defines the most fundamental interpersonal relationships through women.

The distribution of data on historic Athapaskan populations shows an interesting consistency at the personal level in the patterning of interaction among people with the same mother. In the case of Eyak and a substantial proportion of Northern and Southern Athapaskan-speaking groups, siblings of the opposite sex were expected to show extreme reticence and respect in one another's presence or to avoid each other altogether (see Appendix C). This pattern occurs in all three major Athapaskan groupings, as well as among the Eyak. We probably can attribute it to Proto-Athapaskan culture as well.

In most societies with principles of unilineal descent, this criterion affects marriage choice. Marriage with a parallel cousin is prohibited in all Athapaskan groups, since the children of two brothers or two sisters are considered to be in the same line of descent. This rule has the effect of producing either de facto or de jure descent group exogamy, whether the effective categories involved happen to be lineages, clans, or moieties. This marriage rule prohibiting marriage within each group has the effect of producing links between them. Consequently, marriages tend to have some political impact, and typically they are arranged by close kin of the couple. Arranged marriages were the common pattern among the Chiricahua, the Western Apache, and other Apachean divisions, as well as the Eyak, the Tanaina, and most of the other Athapaskan groups in the Subarctic (Opler 1941a:154–156; Goodwin 1969:316; Osgood 1937: 164). (Appendix C documents the nearly universal distribution of these features among Athapaskan-speaking peoples.) Bride service expectations show up among almost all of the northern groups and were implicit in the matrilocal pattern of the Apache (Honigmann 1964:131; Osgood 1936:145, 147, 1937:164). (See Appendix C for the distribution of this pattern.)

Some of these observations give us a start in discerning aspects of

Proto-Athapaskan culture, and we can add other features to this basic framework. At this point we have some sense of the time, place, and general conditions in which the Proto-Athapaskan population existed and the major aspects of their social organization. To go farther and build upon this framework, it will be necessary to rely more heavily on ethnographic reconstruction. Evidence from archaeology, linguistics, and history provide considerable insight, but further reconstruction, based on ethnographic comparisons of the diverse and scattered Athapaskan cultures of the historic period, can shed more light on some of the more elusive aspects of the culture base.

The Rationale of Ethnographic Reconstruction

A traditional school of thought within anthropology would reject ethnographic reconstruction out of hand on the grounds that without written records or other "tangible" evidence, any depiction of the past is bound to be based on speculation. This view implies assumptions about the accuracy of written accounts that few historians would accept as a general premise, although that is another issue.

If "speculation" means making assertions based on inadequate data or jumping to unwarranted conclusions, then it certainly should have no place in anthropology. But if a major aspect of learning amounts to proceeding from the known to the unknown, it behooves us to go beyond observed "facts" and use them to glean whatever they can tell us about those things we cannot observe directly, but which we would very much like to understand. Some of what we can observe about people in the present can help us to understand something interesting and important about the processes that have affected them in the past.

Despite the absence of written records earlier than a few generations ago, in the Athapaskan case the evidence we do have, and which has burgeoned in the last few decades, points to certain conclusions about what has gone before. Because so much of this discussion of the Athapaskan experience depends on ethnographic reconstruction, it is necessary at this point to discuss the approach that was used. It is essential that the evidence supporting the conclusions and the reasoning that led to the espousal of certain interpretations over others be open and accessible to allow an assessment of the soundness of the reconstruction and the basis on which it was developed.

Any culture involves continuities from the past that may range in time depth from a single generation or less to more open-ended antiquity. When two or more populations diverge from a single parent group, their cultures are likely to retain some features of their common heritage—perhaps as modified versions of older forms. Moreover, groups that share such a common heritage may each retain versions of some of the same cultural features. By comparing these modified forms of older features—winnowing out what is constant from what is not and assessing what is left—sometimes we can roughly, at least, discern the older underlying patterns. Comparison of these shared derivations may reveal something of the ancient common culture base.

A basic problem is to detect such continuities through ethnographic comparison. Ultimately the resolution of this issue must lean to some extent on judgment in assessing probability and plausibility. Comparison of a small number of features within a single language family does not lend itself easily to the quantitative statistical methods that have been used so effectively in broader comparative studies involving the distribution of hundreds of discrete variables among scores of cultures (e.g., Driver 1966; Jorgensen 1980). The approach here owes more to Fred Eggan's (1954) "controlled comparison" and borrows a great deal from linguistic reconstruction (see also Vansina 1973). We can avoid pitfalls in the procedure only through a cautious approach to the data.

The parallels here between linguistic and ethnographic reconstruction are significant, but they are limited in important ways. In diachronic linguistics, cognate words, which are similar in both sound and meaning in two or more languages, can serve as a basis for inference about past forms. With caution this principle can also be used as a model for comparing extralinguistic cultural phenomena such as ceremonial patterns, details of social organization, or religious beliefs.

In any case for words to qualify as cognates or for sociocultural similarities to be valid, they must share resemblances not merely in form (or sound, in the case of language), but in meaning within their appropriate contexts—whether speech, social life, or ideology. We can use both linguistic and sociocultural similarities among groups known to share a common past as a basis for inferring something about that past. Beyond these parallels in method, though, some important differences emerge.

Similarities in sound and meaning invest cognate words with far greater power than other sociocultural similarities to indicate past relationships. The significance of cognate words rests on the wide range of possible sounds that occur in languages and the arbitrary attachment of meaning to these sounds. A purely coincidental correspondence of both sound and meaning among numerous words in two or more languages would be so improbable that we can all but dismiss it at the outset. The discovery of a large number of cognates in two languages, therefore, is sufficient in itself to indicate some sort of past relationship among the ancestors of the populations who speak these languages, and this evidence can often go much of the way toward distinguishing whether that relationship was a matter of common origins, or merely of contact.

This is not the case when we compare other sociocultural phenomena. The number of ways in which people organize and carry out their lives is far from infinite. As varied as the human experience is, it has enough common features to have produced many similar ways of behaving and interpreting events. Many similarities appear among populations who have no common heritage more recent than the ancient evolutionary stratum shared by all human beings. As a result the cross-cultural similarities that we can observe in most sociocultural phenomena, unlike those in language, do not in themselves indicate much of anything about past relationships. They provide a starting point, but they barely take us off the mark. They merely suggest a place to look.

At best, ethnographic reconstruction is limited to the gleaning of all-too-meager bits and pieces. In many cases patterns of behavior and belief once shared among a population who later diverged may change so much that eventually they are no longer detectable as similarities. Such patterns are lost as a possible basis for reconstruction. Without discernible similarity, we cannot identify them as variations on a single pattern for comparison. A comparable problem exists in diachronic linguistics when words that do in fact share a common origin in an earlier protolanguage come to differ so much over the course of time that their relationship as cognates no longer is detectable. They become unavailable for the purposes of reconstruction.

This loss of potential data decreases the scope of comparison. Nonetheless, where we can assume that *some* form of a particular aspect of culture did exist in the earlier population, the forms that exist in descendant populations can be helpful. All known human populations use some means of categorizing kin, for example, and all have some concepts about the nature of death. In this case all Athapaskan groups in recent times have shared beliefs about various aspects of life that we can reasonably assume occupied the thoughts of their ancestors as well. It can be useful to examine the distribution of versions of these beliefs manifest among related populations. Even if no particular form predominates among them, if one form is significantly more frequent than its alternatives, or if we can clearly attribute the alternatives to factors other than retention from an older common base, we might discern something of the earlier pattern.

It is important to keep in mind that what we are referring to here is not the persistence of patterns or features with an independent reality of their own, as if cultural entities of some sort had managed to survive over generations and divide into mutant forms among various populations. Nor, when we refer to a feature or pattern spreading through diffusion, is there an implication that anything "moves" from one group to another unless physical objects actually change hands. It is rather the case that individuals have emulated certain ways of behaving in one group as a result of their exposure to people in another.

The phenomenon we are concerned with here involves people choosing to act in a particular way and interpreting their experiences through one or another intellectual framework. The issue is to understand why people in various populations chose to act in much the same way in certain circumstances, why they interpreted things according to similar concepts, and what this can tell us about the choices and interpretations their ancestors made in the past. This, in turn, can reveal something about the processes of change.

Viewed at "ground level," it is clear that such collective behavior is inherently volatile. People can and often do make choices that are different from those they made in the past. Older ways of doing things and the rationales for doing them are constantly being forgotten, modified, and replaced. On the other hand, although people make the choices they do for myriad reasons, many of these reasons lead to consistency. Among the factors that enter into their choices is the knowledge available to them (whether this knowledge is "accurate" or not). This can include the "received wisdom" of tradition to which one has access as a member of any continuing population and the conclusions one derives from idiosyncratic personal experience.

Conventional knowledge might exert a preponderant influence on choice, while novel information, perhaps resulting from contact with other populations whose collective historical experience is different, can result in departures from the kinds of choices made previously. Beliefs and opinions about the probable effectiveness of choices perceived as alternatives are also involved. These, with the knowledge available and to some extent based on it, are closely associated with peoples' interpretations of choices that have been made in the past.

Normative considerations that reflect shared beliefs also affect peoples' interpretations of past choices and their consequences as well as their perceptions of the immediate situation in which they make decisions. Not only available knowledge but constraints regarding the social acceptability of certain alternatives restrict the range of likely individual choices.

Even though wealth accumulation might receive collective approval, for example, certain ways of acquiring wealth, such as theft, may be condemned. If an ecological change affects a population's food supply, a species that could otherwise be available to eat might be unacceptable because of beliefs that rule it out as food. Choices of action in a society where risk takers are admired may differ considerably from those made in a group where such gambles are considered irresponsible or foolish. Concepts of right and wrong, prestige, propriety, and other factors that exist in the minds of individuals may have powerful effects on choices. The choice maker's perception of the situation itself is bound to be molded by all of these factors and, in itself, will be a crucial aspect of the choices made.

How does this bear on the strategy for reconstruction? The task is to judge whether people in related populations made similar choices because these people continue to share versions of a body of knowledge, traditional wisdom, normative expectations, or cosmological orientations derived from an ancient common historical experience, or whether they have made such choices for other reasons—perhaps because of mutual influence or the effects of contact with other populations, through coincidence, or because many rational people in their situations would do the same thing.

The Treatment of Cultural Features

When evident cultural similarities occur among populations that we know share a common past, we can begin the search for an explanation by recognizing two possibilities. The first is that these observed similarities in each group result from the perpetuation of patterns of behavior or belief that were characteristic of the ancestral population and hence reflect something of that common culture base. The second is that they do not.

We can dismiss the peripheral issue of whether the phenomena that appear to be similar are, in fact, comparable or analogous, since the possibility that they are not is subsumed by the second alternative: that they do not represent retention from a common pattern.

But to address the first alternative: if similar phenomena occurring among related populations do reflect something of their shared culture base, then we must allow two further possibilities. If the ancestral population shared a fairly homogeneous culture, then the appearance of these similar phenomena in descendant populations might be a consequence of each having perpetuated the belief or practice without interruption since their departure from that common base. If, on the other hand, the culture of the ancestral population was heterogeneous with regard to that aspect, then only one of the descendant groups might have perpetuated the pattern and subsequently introduced it to the other(s). In similar fashion, if several populations had formerly shared a cultural feature and some had subsequently lost it, one might have reintroduced it to the other later.

A number of considerations bear on these possibilities. All of the alternatives involve the perpetuation of a feature from the culture of the ancestral population. Hence, these alternative possibilities do not threaten the validity of the reconstruction in that sense, but they do introduce methodological problems. For the purpose of reconstruction, a comparison of detailed similarities among features with a single origin that two or more populations have perpetuated independently is far more useful than a comparison of patterns that have been borrowed recently.

To some extent we can sidestep this problem by assessing the probability that the populations involved might have influenced one another since their divergence. For this purpose we must consider several factors. One involves the simple factor of the time and space that have separated them. Throughout the western Subarctic where the Athapaskan population has a broad, continuous distribution, there is no doubt that there has been extensive contact and mutual influence. But between this population and the Pacific Coast Athapaskans, and between either of these and the Apache, there is no reason to suspect any recent contact. This is especially so between the extremes within these distributions: Apache and Tanaina, for example, and Apache and Eyak to an even greater extent.

A second consideration involves other cultural influences that might have accompanied features that could have been diffused between these groups. If a ritual pattern has diffused from one population to another group some distance away, one might expect to find other evidence of influence as well. We might also expect to find the diffused feature occurring in intervening populations who do *not* share this common past. If there is no evidence of recent contact between these distant related groups, and the similarities do not occur in intervening regions, then the case for mutual retention rather than diffusion is stronger.

Similarity is a concept that can be viewed in terms of gradation. At one level, broad similarities abound among the populations of the world. A general "fear of death" and concerns with female puberty, for example, are widespread throughout western North America. But it is more useful for these purposes to deal with such phenomena at a level of greater detail. Many societies in a particular part of the world might share certain general characteristics, but detailed correspondences between patterns that occur in widely separated, related groups can afford more useful insights, particularly if these patterns are *more similar* to each other than they are to comparable patterns in geographically intervening populations.

Rather than attempting to interpret the frequency and distribution of single, discrete "traits," as many studies have in the past, it will be more useful here to deal with sociocultural similarities in terms of "clusters" of phenomena that are interrelated or complementary in some way. To shed light on Proto-Athapaskan cultural forms, it is not sufficient simply to break down these cultural phenomena into a list of specific traits, map their distribution, and score the frequency of occurrence. We can gain more insight if we view them together as coherent but multifaceted aspects of an entire cultural system, as they occur in their normal, "living" context. If we pay attention to interrelationships among these features that give them significance in their "natural" milieu, their distinctiveness as Athapaskan patterns is more apparent.

For example, the use of scratching sticks by young women during the time of their first menstruation is so widespread throughout western North America that the occurrence of this feature in any particular population is almost meaningless for the purposes of reconstruction. On the other hand, in the Athapaskan case, cultural features associated with female puberty occur together in what appears to be a distinctive cluster of beliefs and practices. These in turn reflect something of the nature of interpersonal relationships, especially with regard to those between male and female.

Among Athapaskan peoples such a cluster of features touches on social aspects discussed earlier that stress the relationship of individuals through women as an organizational theme, manifest in various forms of matrilineal groupings and institutionalized bonds, which in turn seem to be associated with matrilocal residence patterns. These aspects of Athapaskan culture verge on a conceptual realm that includes a sense of femaleness as a power to be treated with some ambivalence, expressed in the array of practices associated with menstruation and childbirth. The cognitive treatment of femaleness also is consistent with more general Athapaskan concepts of the transcendental nature of qualities or "powers" that provide an intellectual framework for these beliefs. Such a framework gives structure to the Athapaskan concern for maintaining male-female differences associated with the division of labor, which is strongly reflected in the array of restrictions pertaining to women and hunting weapons. (See Appendix C for the distribution of these features among Eyak and Athapaskan groups.)

Taken as a whole, this cluster of features represents a complex, specifically Athapaskan view of the nature of interpersonal relationships whose consequences reach into other aspects of culture. The issue of women and hunting, for example, blends into another cluster of cultural features having to do with the relationship of human beings to the rest of "nature." (See Appendix E for the distribution of these features.) There is a high degree of consistency within such clusters of features among Athapaskan peoples that suggest an internal compatibility among those concepts and practices.

The Method of Ethnographic Reconstruction

If perceived similarities among related groups are *not* the result of retention from a common protoculture, then one of two possibilities must account for their presence. They may have developed independently, either as a result of similar processes in the fashion of "convergent" or "parallel" evolution, or coincidentally in some other way; or they may have an interdependent basis as a result of cross-cultural influences. To rule out both of these is to eliminate the possibility that they are not the result of retention. This would leave the other possibility—that they are—as the only alternative.

The method of reconstruction used here incorporates these considerations, but they are not sufficient. While in some cases it is possible to *eliminate* certain cultural features through clear evidence that recent diffusion has occurred, it is far more difficult to show conclusively that diffusion can be ruled out.

The method of reconstruction used here is applied to features that have survived elimination after we have assessed the likelihood that they could have been diffused. After this preliminary consideration, the fundamental procedure is to consider the distribution of cultural features among all sufficiently documented Athapaskan and Eyak populations. Quite simply, assessment of the likelihood that shared features represent retention from Proto-Athapaskan culture is based on the frequency of their occurrence among widely separated historic Athapaskan populations. This method employs principles used by David Aberle (1974) in his reconstruction of the kinship systems of several ancestral native American populations.

In attempting to deduce the kinship systems of earlier populations, Aberle begins with the assumption that whatever the former pattern of descent may have been in a particular case, it was based on rules that are known in the present. He divides the possible variations into four basic alternatives: patrilineal, matrilineal, both, and neither (bilateral or ambilateral). Essentially, the method is to determine which ancestral form would have required the fewest changes in order to result in the distribution that exists among the descendant groups.

As an example, if 80 percent of the groups within a particular language family have matrilineal descent, a few have patrilineal descent, and one or two are bilateral, then we can consider matrilineal descent most likely to have been a feature of the earlier population. To put it another way, if the ancestral population were anything but matrilineal, we would have to assume a larger number of changes in the past in order to account for the present situation.

As Aberle points out, the definition of the groups involved in this calculation is crucial. Whether one chooses to treat half a dozen adjacent groups who speak closely related dialects as six cases or one case could well have a major effect on the results. And again, it is necessary to assess the likelihood that extraneous factors such as the influence of other populations might account for the distribution of these forms.

Fundamentally, the procedure employed here involved four phases. Given the understanding that Athapaskan-speaking groups share a common past, we can (1) note evident similarities among the cultures of these populations; (2) explore the possibility of accounting for the observed phenomena through explanations other than retention and eliminate features attributable to any of these from further consideration; (3) note the distribution of remaining cultural similarities among the major Athapaskan population groupings; and (4) apply the principle of "least required change" to the remaining clusters of features in order to discern patterns of the earlier culture base.

Because of the ambiguities of linguistic and cultural boundaries among populations and the certainty of continued mutual influence within each of the divisions, the most useful groupings for the analysis of distributional data are Eyak and the three major divisions: Northern Athapaskan, Pacific Coast Athapaskan, and Apache. On the other hand, the distribution of cultural phenomena within each division is of interest as well. With this consideration, clusters of features discussed in the text are compiled for Eyak and thirty-one Athapaskan populations in Appendices C, D, and E. Appendix A discusses the reasons for decisions to employ the Athapaskan groupings used here.

Application of the Method

It is possible that many features occurring widely among both Athapaskan and non-Athapaskan groups predate the Proto-Athapaskan base. They may constitute retention from a still older cultural stratum, and the distribution of such features may be extremely widespread far beyond the Athapaskan sphere. Harold Driver (1941:60) has suggested, for example, that certain "universal" elements of female puberty observances that occur sporadically in the Old World as well as in western North America may have been associated with the very earliest migrations to the continent. Ideological concerns with the bear might be comparably ancient (Hallowell 1926).

If we can identify such features, it does not matter that they occur beyond Athapaskan cultures unless there is reason to suspect that they diffused to Athapaskan-speaking groups after their mutual divergence. These features that other populations share constitute aspects of the Proto-Athapaskan base as legitimate as those unique to Proto-Athapaskan culture. Moreover, even though such ancient patterns in a general sense may have been widespread, in many cases the Athapaskan versions have distinctive characteristics.

In drawing on the Athapaskan and Eyak ethnographic data, similarities between Tanaina and Apachean cultures deserve special attention. Although the population sizes of these groups are vastly different, they are comparable in the sense that each represents a single Athapaskan language. Not only do they constitute extremes within the geographic range of Athapaskan speakers and represent adaptations to very different ecological circumstances, but since Tanaina is the most divergent language within Athapaskan—almost as different from its neighboring Alaskan languages as it is from Apache[5]—this comparison provides one of the deepest possible separations in time as well as in space. As such, it helps minimize the probability that factors other than a common heritage can account for similarities.

By the same token, comparisons between Apache and Eyak may be even more valuable, since they transcend the Athapaskan sphere altogether. The Eyak language is as different from its nearest Athapaskan neighbors as it is from Apache, and Eyak territory on the north Pacific coast is practically as remote from the Apache as the Tanaina (Krauss and Golla 1981). Since the divergence of Eyak from Athapaskan preceded the Proto-Athapaskan phase, the cultural similarities between Eyak and Apache offer especially interesting possibilities for discerning retention.

Proto-Athapaskan Culture

We have already discussed in some detail many of the cultural features common to Athapaskan groups. Fuller documentation appears in Appendices C, D, and E. On the basis of this evidence, we can posit that one attribute of Proto-Athapaskan ideology was a belief that the soul consisted of two component aspects, one of which was associated with wind, breath, or air.

The Tanaina concepts of "body, breath, and shadow-spirit" (Osgood 1937:69) and the Ingalik beliefs that the individual was "made up of three constituent elements—the body, the shadow (*yeg*), and the 'speech'" associated with breath (Osgood 1959:107) are strikingly similar to the Navajo distinction between the "in-standing wind soul" and the evil essence remaining near the body after death (Witherspoon 1977:29–30). Other Apachean versions have been mentioned earlier, and the pattern occurs on the Pacific Coast as well (Barnett 1937:184). Kai Birket-Smith and Frederica de Laguna (1938:231–232) note that "the Eyak may have had a vague notion of two souls," and an Eyak informant in the 1930s associated the "mind" aspect of the soul with breath: "'The mind is just like the wind.'"

Based on the distribution of these ideas among Athapaskan groups, we can infer some features of Proto-Athapaskan belief. The evil component of the soul lingered near the grave and constituted a threat to the survivors. Death itself resulted from the departure of the "shadow." We also can establish some of the patterns of behavior associated with these beliefs. To cope with this threat, the survivors rid themselves not only of the body but the property, dwelling, and name of the deceased. Beliefs about threatening aspects of the soul, with a range of associated patterns, occur in other parts of North America, but the detailed congruence of these beliefs and practices among the Pacific Coast Athapaskan, Apachean, Northern Athapaskan, and Eyak populations seems reasonably attributed to a shared culture base.

On the other hand, belief in reincarnation is widespread among Northern Athapaskan groups, but this concept was not particularly important and perhaps not even present in most groups of the Pacific

Coast or the Southwest. Thus, it is not possible to tell whether such a concept is a Proto-Athapaskan derivation lost in the course of migrations, a later introduction from Siberia, or an innovation in the northern region. Beliefs of this sort do occur on both sides of the Bering Strait, and they may represent a later spread of ideas. Because of this uncertainty, we cannot attribute a concept of reincarnation with any confidence to Proto-Athapaskan ideology. (See Appendix D for the distribution of these patterns.)

The general Athapaskan concept of capricious or unpredictable power associated with all animate and inanimate objects, though, is an identifiable Proto-Athapaskan retention. Ethnographic comparisons indicate that the Proto-Athapaskan cognitive system involved reification of what in Euro-american thought would be considered abstract qualities of objects, animals, or people and the attribution of spiritual essence, not necessarily good or evil, to most objects and beings.

In a sense these qualities were transcendent and were independent of the concrete object with which they were associated. They could be present or absent to varying degrees. Although they were not necessarily good or bad, generally they were powerful and hence dangerous when excessive. "Femaleness," for example, not only was associated with women as persons but was a quality that could nullify the effectiveness of hunting weapons or weaken men.

This cognitive stance is implicit in the Apachean concept that lightning can cause harm by striking nearby even if it does no apparent physical damage, or that wood struck by lightning has a special, potentially dangerous power (Opler 1969:25; K. Basso 1970:35–36). It is also manifest in the idea that the bear can cause illness through its odor or by having waded through a stream from which a person drinks. Still more clearly, perhaps, it can be seen in the Chiricahua Apache belief that a person can contract bear sickness by dreaming about a bear or simply by fearing it (Opler 1941a:224–225).

In the Tanaina context, Cornelius Osgood (1937:169) equates this belief with Robert Marett's classic concept of animatism. It involves the attribution to all natural objects of a "power" that can affect human beings positively or negatively. Such an ideological feature occurs among other Northern Athapaskan groups as well. In Koyukon belief all objects have power that can affect humans in a whimsical fashion (A. Clark 1970:80). Osgood (1936:154) writes of the Peel River Kutchin that "they regard the world in which they live as made up of forms which have more living aspect to them." Gladys Nomland (1935:169) notes that among the Sinkyone of the Pacific Coast, "all things animate and inanimate had souls."

Although this manner of interpreting reality is not unique to Athapaskan cultures in its general characteristics, it is, nonetheless, ubiquitous among them with striking and detailed conformity between the Subarctic and the Southwest, and it also occurs among Athapaskan groups of the Pacific Coast. The attribution of extra-somatic power to all or most objects and things, a reified essence or quality, a power that is not considered good or bad in any inherent sense but unpredictable and potentially dangerous, is most likely an ancient continuity from the Proto-Athapaskan cultural stratum. In the great majority of Athapaskan populations in all areas, moreover, human communication and contact with such powers occurred through dreams. (See Appendix E.)

We can also attribute concepts of the power of femaleness with its associated practices of menstrual seclusion to Proto-Athapaskan culture. The use of scratching sticks and the drinking tube, dated archaeologically to early in the first millennium A.D. in the southern Yukon, also are ancient aspects of this complex.

Further comparison fills out the picture a bit more. The human gaze had special significance in many historic Athapaskan cultures. Among both the Ingalik and the Western Apache, it was rude and to some extent even threatening for a person to stare directly into the eyes of another. In most versions of female puberty observances, the young woman's vision was restricted by a hood or visor or by having her hair brushed over her face, or in some cases, merely by the stipulation that she must not gaze over the woods or into the distance.

Among Athapaskan groups throughout the North, the young woman's gaze could cause harm by ruining a hunter's luck, offending game animals, or causing a young hunter to be killed. On the Pacific Coast, for a young woman in seclusion to stare off into the distance or at the sky could be harmful to her, causing sore eyes or even blindness. Young Western Apache women undergoing the puberty ceremony were expected to keep their eyes lowered to the ground in front of them (K. Basso 1966:149).[6] Many of the Apache groups believed that if a young woman looked at the sky during this time it could cause excessive rainfall. Despite the aridity of the Southwest, this apparently was considered a serious misfortune (Driver 1941:32–33). Far to the north, the Eyak also believed that a young woman who looked up at the sky could cause bad weather (de Laguna 1937:74). This concern seems distinct and frequent enough among distantly separated Athapaskan peoples to be a reflection of an earlier Proto-Athapaskan trait.

We can see other fairly specific aspects of the general concern with femaleness in the dissociation of men from the scene of childbirth. On the Pacific Coast in the Bear River group, men were said to be "afraid" of babies (Nomland 1938:102). Among the Tanaina, "men are strictly excluded from the immediate vicinity" of the birth (Osgood 1937:160). A similar pattern applied to the Apache. Eyak men were expected to leave the house during childbirth (de Laguna 1937:160). This pattern is extremely widespread throughout the world and probably is very old. It almost certainly predates the Proto-Athapaskan phase. Whatever its ultimate origins may have been, though, it was also a part of Proto-Athapaskan life. (See Appendix C for distribution.)

A special dread associated with the owl also seems to be a fundamental Athapaskan feature. Among the Tanaina as well as the Apache, the owl was a harbinger of death. In historic times the Tanaina sometimes ate owls, but they were a source of fear because of their ability to speak and to foretell tragic events, sometimes announcing that "something is going to happen" (Townsend 1963:217; Osgood 1937:175; Nomland 1935:169). Among the Sinkyone on the Pacific Coast, all kinds of birds were eaten except the owl and dove, which were "transformed persons who mourned their relatives" (Nomland 1935:152). The Tolowa excluded owls as a food source (Drucker 1937:232). As elsewhere, the horror of owls among Apache groups derived from their cognitive association with death. In this case ghosts often took the form of owls (Opler 1941a:230).[7] The Chiricahua Apache believed that owls spoke in the Chiricahua dialect, and among the Western Apache, owls sometimes identified themselves as dead relatives. (See Appendix D for the distribution of this belief.)

Most Athapaskan peoples viewed dogs and such similar animals as wolves, coyotes, and foxes with considerable ambivalence.[8] The Chiricahua Apache felt that dogs should not be allowed in a camp where there were infants because a dog might bark at a child and frighten it, and "the fright will go inside that child and make it sick. So they don't like dogs very much" (Opler 1941a:4). The Eyak also viewed dogs with misgivings, and there was great reluctance to kill them (de Laguna 1937:70). Among the Kutchin, a dog that cried in its sleep was killed because "the cries show he doesn't like people and will cause bad luck" (Osgood 1936:155). The Tanaina "will not kill or eat one of them" (Osgood 1937:37). On the Pacific Coast, the Sinkyone treated dogs well because they were transformed humans (Nomland 1935:151). The Tolowa valued good hunting dogs, but regarded them with suspicion because of their power for supernatural evil (Drucker 1937:240).

With regard to attitudes about dogs in earlier times, a Chiricahua

Apache stated that "the dog was classed with the coyote, wolf and fox. We felt that all of them could cause you trouble. We wouldn't touch the skin of a dead dog" (Opler 1941a:226).[9] Much the same feeling seems to prevail in the Western Apache community of San Carlos. In 1963 a six-year-old girl had a small puppy that one day sickened and died. In response to condolences, she looked genuinely puzzled and pointed out that "it was only a dog, you know." Although dogs are present in most Western Apache households, people generally viewed the Euro-American practice of petting dogs with distaste. When a large dog died in 1970, it lay untouched for more than a day until a visiting anthropologist disposed of it.

It seems likely that in part, attitudes toward dogs may derive from their similarities to wolves. Most Athapaskan peoples did not eat wolves, and some peoples in the Subarctic felt that the wolf had once been human (Osgood 1959:67). More than this, though, the attitude toward dogs might also stem from the dog's anomalous position in the context of a hunting life-style as the only animal that is neither wild nor potential game. It is a nonhuman creature associated, nonetheless, with human society.[10] As the dog straddles both the human and nonhuman realms, its status in Athapaskan thought seems to have been unique in many ways, and as such, it was subject to considerable ambivalence.

In food-producing societies where domesticated animals occupy a more substantial and integrated role, the status of dogs may be less paradoxical. But in the early Athapaskan context in which survival depended overwhelmingly on the quest for wild animal foods, the anomalous position of the dog may have been more conspicuous and, hence, given more significance. Dogs in the Proto-Athapaskan phase probably were not especially numerous. But the wide distribution of this attitude suggests that it was an aspect of the Proto-Athapaskan ideology and must have been generated by some familiarity with them.

Based on the distribution of these clusters of features among the total range of Eyak and Athapaskan populations, we can establish their derivation from Proto-Athapaskan culture with some confidence. There are a few others we could consider as possibilities because they occur in widely separated contexts, but they are more tentative because their occurrence among Athapaskan peoples is less frequent.

Whistling, for example, was associated with a sense of dread in all three major Athapaskan divisions. The Apache in the Southwest associated whistling at night with ghosts (Opler 1941a:231). Among the Kutchin of the Subarctic, wandering dead souls called *djin kuo* were "sometimes heard whistling around graves" (Osgood 1936:154). In many other Northern Athapaskan groups, including the Tanaina and the Fort Nelson Slave, whistling in the woods at night was believed to be a trait of the *nakani* (Osgood 1937:172; Honigmann 1946:80). Among the Tolowa of the Pacific Coast, whistling was a characteristic of "wood devils" or, in the Chetco group, "Indian devils" (Drucker 1937:268, 275).

Athapaskan peoples widely considered fear itself to be capable of causing harm. People of the Chetco group on the Pacific Coast believed that fear resulted in soul loss, which would cause a person to become thin and weak (Drucker 1937:275). Among the Chiricahua Apache, "the words of an owl can cause sickness through fright" (Opler 1941a:232). According to a Chiricahua informant, "when you get scared you get sick" (Opler 1941a:231). The Ingalik of Alaska saw fear, particularly the terror caused by the sight of supernatural beings, as a source of potentially fatal illness (Osgood 1959:67).

We might attribute some aspects of material culture to Proto-Athapaskan culture as well. A device variously called a "bull roarer" or a "buzz toy" occurs in all three Athapaskan areas. Usually consisting of a flat piece of wood perhaps a foot long attached to a cord, it was whirled rapidly through the air to produce a buzzing or humming sound. On the Pacific Coast, such a device occurred only among the Kato and Sinkyone (Driver 1939). In the Subarctic it occurred among the Ingalik and the Tanaina, where formerly it was used only by shamans (Osgood 1959:108, 1937:175, 178). The Western Apache "clown" *gaan* dancer "The Gray One" (*łibaahu*) still whirls it in the female puberty ceremony. This device is extremely ancient and has a sporadic distribution throughout the world, and its appearance among these Athapaskan groups suggests that it might also have been an aspect of Proto-Athapaskan culture.

Many Athapaskan peoples used the sweat bath, as did other societies throughout western North America. In many native American cultures, the sweat bath had religious connotations and was important in ceremonial practices, but generally this was not the case among most Athapaskan peoples. With a few exceptions, Athapaskan sweat baths appear to have served purposes that were therapeutic, secular, and recreational for relaxation and sociability. But considering the general concern with health and long life among Athapaskan peoples, the distinction between the secular and the religious is not always clear. Preparation for curing ceremonies often involve sweat baths, for example. On the Pacific Coast, sweat lodges among non-Athapaskan groups served important ceremonial functions, but for Athapaskan peoples in that region the primary ritual use of sweat baths was in such ceremonies as first-salmon rituals or "deer singing" that were borrowed from surrounding non-Athapaskan cultures (Drucker 1937:232). The Western Apache sweat bath is important in preparation for the female puberty ceremony, but people in San Carlos generally asserted that the main use of the sweat bath is for good health and a sense of well-being.

By sifting through these multiple sources of evidence, we can reconstruct an image of Proto-Athapaskan culture on an ecological framework, enhanced through ethnographic comparison, to include aspects of ideology as well as social organization. This can serve as a conceptual starting point in considering later divergences of Athapaskan peoples and the concomitant processes of cultural differentiation.

What can we conclude? It appears that the Proto-Athapaskan population operated in a multizoned, mountainous environment in southern Alaska. They may have had some access to the sea coast, but their subsistence focus was primarily inland, utilizing caribou as well as salmon. At certain fixed locales, rich food sources are available in this region on a seasonal basis. On the other hand, the overall sparseness of the subarctic food supply and the seasonality and mobility of large game make it necessary for resident hunters to move a great deal to take advantage of scattered resources.

Proto-Athapaskan hunters had to be able to disperse periodically in small groups over a vast territory to take advantage of diffuse and unpredictable food sources. Yet they had to retain a capacity to come together at times, coalescing into larger aggregates to exploit the opportunities of salmon runs or caribou migrations. Game drive techniques for caribou require a substantial number of people. Writers have described historic Athapaskan groups of central Alaska as "upland big game hunters who adapted their seasonal round to include an emphasis on fishing in those environs where fish were abundant." Caribou drive structures and fishing spots in the territory of a single group were often more than fifty miles apart (Hosley 1980:13).

The Proto-Athapaskan population maintained a flexible social organization through networks of kinship ties among people who were essentially autonomous and free ranging in their day-to-day activities. These kinship bonds, including both "blood" ties based on a matrilineal principle of relationship and affinal bonds maintained by marriage, constituted abstract social networks that did nothing to inhibit the free movement of individuals necessary for certain phases of the food quest. These bonds served as a basis for their coming together periodically at base camps.

The mobility demanded by the subsistence base and the gender-based division of labor among most Athapaskan peoples implies that men were absent much of the time. This, in turn, is compatible with a tendency toward matrilocal residence. Although in historic times Athapaskan peoples often moved their entire households to different camps, men were engaged far more directly and frequently in hunting, which took them away from the domestic sphere for significant lengths of time.

The institution of bride service, involving matrilocal residence for at least one or a few years, tends to reinforce kinship ties on the wife's side. Bride service appears to have some advantages in such a setting because it extends the territory with which a man becomes familiar, thereby, presumably, increasing his potential hunting effectiveness. Bride service also is highly compatible with the definition of interpersonal ties in terms of relationships through women.

Populations who exploit many of the same resources within broad regions tend to be endogamous. Marriages in this case would be especially frequent among people of different lines of descent who shared particular locales or even seasonal base camps. In the past such camps may have served as social reference points, as they did in more recent times, functioning as grounds for a sense of common identity among the populations associated with them.

Regarding the issue of matrilocal and matrilineal patterns in prehistoric Athapaskan culture, Charles Bishop and Shepard Krech (1980:39) argue that "matriorganization is highly adaptive both in fostering internal sociopolitical cohesion at the level of the microband . . . and in aiding mobile, alternatively aggregating and fissioning bands to exploit resources that vary by region, season and year." On the other hand, the subsistence capacity of the Subarctic required that small groups of people be widely spaced much of the time. Regional intermarrying populations would have to be spaced over a wide territory.

In Proto-Athapaskan times, no doubt, the number of persons per square mile of this mountainous terrain was slight, just as it is today compared with other areas of North America. A strategy of dispersal and free movement to exploit wide-ranging, sparse food resources would have inhibited the development of overarching political structures. Most peaceful interactions among individuals would tend to be on the basis of individual kinship ties. Conversely, conflicts of interest or disputes are liable to occur sooner or later among individuals who lack any defined kin ties with one another, or among small groups whose encounters are occasional and unpredictable. In the absence of any overall mediating mechanisms to resolve such episodes, open hostility would be a chronic possibility. The only ready means available to settle disputes would be direct action by the people involved. Fighting is one alternative. Retreat is another.

The net result of this would be a tendency for aggregates without links of apparent, remembered relationships to avoid one another. This strengthened regional endogamy among those small clusters of descent groups who shared base villages or resource sites. Repeated marriages among them would maintain ties to keep them all within a sphere of mutual familiarity and affinity.

With an increase in the population, eventually the ecological need for spacing social clusters would make strangers of the more distant groups. A spread of Athapaskan-speaking peoples farther into the interior would coincide with a decrease in close interaction among groups more remote from one another, fostering linguistic divergence through reduced communication.

In many ways the reconstructed system of beliefs associated with this social and ecological framework is reminiscent of Siberian patterns, and it might even reflect a widespread Asian cultural stratum associated with nomadic reindeer hunting. The Proto-Athapaskan people saw life or power in all beings and objects, with the potential to hurt or assist humans. Their contact and communication with these powers occurred through dreams. The spiritual aspect of their universe, like the physical realm with which it was so finely interwoven, was unpredictable and varied; always posing danger, but providing the occasional bounty as well.

Among the essences of reality that they had to deal with, the quality of femaleness created anxiety, partly because of its power to affect the tenuous luck on which hunting, and hence survival, depended. The people coped with this uncontrollable aspect of life through numerous measures. Many of them effected an emphatic dissociation between women and the paraphernalia of hunting. Women underwent seclusion and other measures of avoidance during times when the strength and consequent dangers of femaleness were most intense. Femaleness was a theme in the structure of interpersonal ties. Descent through women, which matrilocal residence reinforced, provided a sense of interpersonal cohesion. Siblings of the opposite sex, on the other hand, avoided treating each other with familiarity, and a married man had to show his wife's mother the greatest respect.

The Proto-Athapaskans believed that their spiritual essence was multifaceted. Associated with each person was a shadow whose permanent detachment from the body was equated with death, but which could linger nearby afterward to cause harm. The other spiritual component was associated with the breath or air that entered the body at birth and departed at the end of life. To deal with the dangers of the shadow and the universal human dilemma of mortality, to widen the margin between death and the living, they rid themselves of the property, the dwellings, the name, and, if it were possible, thoughts of the deceased. They believed that the owl spoke to them in their language, telling them of tragic events yet to happen. Malevolent beings may have whistled in the forest at night outside their camps. They perceived a special power in the human gaze, and they regarded the dog as an uncertain ally.

They probably used sweat lodges for enjoyment and physical well-being, no doubt savoring its moist heat as a relief from the bitter, dry cold of the Subarctic. They tried to avoid the debilitating power of fear, which could cause a sickness of its own. In their ceremonies they used the ancient bull roarer.

This glimpse provides a bit fuller picture of the Proto-Athapaskan condition. A few relatively minor details, such as the attitude toward dogs or owls, appear to stand out in disproportionate relief. For whatever reason, disparate Athapaskan groups separated from one another over vast distances of time and space retained and perpetuated these features. Why these aspects of culture should have been passed down over so many generations, surviving the elimination process of shifting circumstances and cultural segmentation, is an interesting question in itself.

We could surmise more about Proto-Athapaskan culture. Certainly there were shamans, specialists in dealing with the supernatural, practitioners with special virtuosity in dealing with the many powers that affected human life. Proto-Athapaskan shamanistic patterns probably were consistent with those occurring throughout the Northern Hemisphere on both sides of the Bering Strait, but in this aspect of life the diversity among historic Athapaskan groups confounds the search for similarities as clear-cut as those of other cultural features.

An expansionist tendency may have been inherent in this early Athapaskan base. The nature of the food quest created a need to take advantage of a variety of food sources and to maintain a capacity to respond to unpredictable opportunities. This called for a social strategy that enhanced small-group and individual autonomy, flexibility, and easy movement. The nonspecialized, mountain-oriented food quest opened the way for the spread of the population throughout the Cordillera. The geography of the Subarctic involves mountainous terrain and conifer forest, consistent in its diversity through most of the Alaskan interior and southeastward toward the Rockies; consequently, Athapaskan groups could spread over vast distances while remaining roughly within the same ecological setting.

As the Proto-Athapaskans expanded toward the interior and segmented into distinct regional aggregates, mountains were the corridor of their movement and the medium of their existence, rather than a barrier. It might be accurate to perceive the Proto-Athapaskans as progressively filling a niche to which they were particularly well adapted as they spread through the Cordillera, moving into new areas that required no major changes at first in the ways to which they had been accustomed for dealing with the problems of survival. The following pages will follow the divergences and segmentation of Athapaskan groups in more detail.

CHAPTER 5

The Early Divergences

The remarkable expansion of Athapaskan peoples throughout large tracts of western North America was as much a pattern of consistency as abrupt change, particularly in its earliest phases. The people had developed strategies that were successful in a type of environment that stretched ahead of them for thousands of miles. We can examine in more detail the nature of their expansion now and the beginning of the process of differentiation that eventually led to the San Carlos community in Arizona.

The present distribution of Athapaskan-speaking peoples gives the impression of vast numbers. The Navajo, in fact, presently are one of the most numerous of all native American peoples, with an estimated 150,000. Yet in the earlier phases, the Athapaskan population was far smaller. The Navajo are a striking example of the capacity of a population to increase dramatically over a short period of time. Just over a century ago, they numbered approximately 10,000, less than a tenth of their present population.

The environmental constraints of the Subarctic in the Proto-Athapaskan phase would have dictated a population size far smaller than the number of modern Athapaskan peoples. The present population of the Tanaina, for example, is approximately 900, although they may have numbered 3,000 or so before Russian contact in the late eighteenth century (Krauss 1979:850). We should remember, too, that these people are no longer under the constraints of relying totally on wild foods for their subsistence. There seems to be a general tendency among human populations to expand when the food supply allows it. The availability of additional territory exploitable through subsistence strategies already in use might have set off both migrations and an expansion of the population.

The inland mountainous regions may have been a positive attraction, but they might also have been the only avenue of expansion possible. On the sea coast, people with refined, well-developed styles of life already adapted to that environment had occupied that zone for a long time. It is unlikely that generalized hunters with sparse, mobile populations could have supplanted these coastal inhabitants on a large enough scale to take over that niche. In early historic times, the Tanaina held their own in territory adjacent to the Koniaq and Chugash Eskimo, and at one point even joined them in an alliance against Russian fur traders, but there is no evidence that the Tanaina ever really contested these groups successfully for their territories.

Let us suppose that the Proto-Athapaskan phase began when Eyak diverged from Athapaskan perhaps some time in the second millennium B.C. Suppose further that the first divergences within Athapaskan occurred a bit over 2,000 years ago, involving a dispersal of the population. Proto-Athapaskans may not have been established in southern Alaska very long before they began to spread into the interior, and the Athapaskan expansion inland could have been rapid. The other possibility is that there had been a lengthy, relatively stable Proto-Eyak-Athapaskan occupancy in the North American Subarctic, followed by what then would have been a rather abrupt population increase and dispersion. An early and continuous spread throughout the mountainous corridors of the Subarctic is at least as plausible as the alternative. This implies a relatively recent migration from Asia.

Initial Expansions in Alaska

As we noted earlier, clear archaeological evidence for Athapaskans in Alaska appears in the first few centuries A.D. If the evidence for language divergence means anything, this would have been a few generations after the first major split occurred among Athapaskan languages. This suggests a scenario in which Athapaskan groups first spread into the interior of Alaska during the earlier phases of their presence in the western Subarctic, after which they moved deeper into the Yukon Territory and through the Cordillera to the south.

Artifacts associated with Athapaskans in the southwestern Yukon Territory, dated early in the first millennium A.D., appear almost identical to materials on the Pacific Coast in south Alaska near Yakutat Bay. These occur in the Yukon Territory in the Aishihik phase, which shows a cultural continuity to the present Athapaskan inhabitants of the area. In the nineteenth century, Eyak territory ranged from Yakutat to Controller Bay (Workman 1978:419; Krauss and Golla 1981:68). Both archaeological and linguistic evidence support the idea of an Athapaskan expansion away from the coastal region into the mountainous corridors inland.

The Tanana Valley of central Alaska is a bit puzzling because the archaeological evidence shows a continuance of an older, conservative microblade tool tradition long after it had disappeared elsewhere. Since microblades have not been associated with Athapaskans, this suggests that earlier occupants may have continued to live there for some time even though Athapaskans were present in other parts of Alaska and the Yukon. Eventually Athapaskan speakers did occupy that area, but perhaps that occurred after they had already spread to the regions surrounding the central Alaskan plateau.

Whatever pattern the migration may have taken, the Athapaskan spread into Alaska involved further linguistic diversification that led eventually to the historic Alaskan languages Ingalik, Tanana, Ahtna, and Koyukon,[1] all of which are separated now by deep divisions, and the Canadian Athapaskan languages and dialects. The degree of differentiation among them reflects the precipitation of various groups into scattered territories.

The Pacific Coast Athapaskan Separation

The Pacific Coast Athapaskan groups departed from the North soon after this early phase. Collectively these languages are more closely related to Canadian Athapaskan than they are to the other major Northern Athapaskan groups, but they also appear to be about equally distant from all of Canadian and Southern Athapaskan groups. On the other hand, they are more distant from both Canadian and Apache than these two are from each other.

It is possible that the Pacific group were part of an early vanguard toward the south in the migration down the Cordillera, although archaeological evidence for this is scant. We only know for certain that they did make the odyssey from the north to the California-Oregon coast, by whatever route. There are two major possibilities. One would be that they took a direct route from the inland Subarctic. In that case they would have passed through the Frazer River Plateau and perhaps even spent some time in that general plateau region, coming into contact with Salishan peoples who probably were long-time inhabitants in that area (Jorgensen 1980:74).[2] But archaeological evidence does not support the idea of an Athapaskan presence in the Frazer River Plateau before the thirteenth century A.D. James Helmer (1977:96) states that "the spread of Athapaskan-speaking Carrier and Chilcotin into the Interior Plateau must be considered a relatively recent phenomenon." Athapaskans were not present in the Chilcotin area of British Columbia until at least A.D. 1200 and probably arrived after the area had been abandoned by its previous inhabitants (Wilmeth 1975, 1978, 1977:101).

Another possibility would be more consistent with the Athapaskan mountain orientation. In northern British Columbia, the Cordillera divides into the Rockies, which stretch to the southeast, and the Coast Ranges to the west, like two prongs of a fork running south to surround the Plateau region. A likely route southward for the ancestors of the Pacific Coast Athapaskans would have been to follow the western Coast Ranges into the Cascades, rather than to have left the mountainous ecosystem, for which they had developed successful strategies, and cross the Plateau to get to the Pacific Coast. The Cascade route would have led them to their present territories.

Canadian and Apache

The spread and diversification of Canadian dialects and further divisions in the Alaskan interior followed the initial break from Tanaina. The archaeological evidence at the Klo-Kut site near the Brooks Range in the Yukon Territory indicates that the Kutchin have occupied their present territory for as long as 1,500 years (Morlan 1972). There are deep differences among the various Kutchin dialects, which we might expect of a population that inhabited their region for such a length of time.

Kutchin is closely related to Han, Tutchone, and to a lesser degree, perhaps, Tanana (Dyen and Aberle 1974:14; Krauss and Golla 1981:74). The territories of these populations extend in an unbroken continuum from the northwest Yukon Territory back toward the Pacific region, where lower Tanana territory adjoins the region in which Ahtna was spoken and at one point nearly touches the territory of the Tanaina. A likely explanation for this distribution would be that it results from a northward population spread from the coastal area toward the Brooks Range, following an initial split near the Proto-Athapaskan territory in southern Alaska. This scheme also is compatible with archaeological distribution of the Kavik point, which has been associated with early Kutchin sites, and it fits the time frame of the major volcanic eruption and ash fall near the coast in A.D. 200–400. The phenomena associated with this event could easily have stimulated some population movement.[3]

Another major contingent of Canadian Athapaskan speakers spread southward along the Rocky Mountain system. This movement may have been fairly rapid, since the internal differentiation among dialects of this branch of Athapaskan does not seem especially deep, despite the multitude of dialects. The diversification process is not very advanced.[4] Once again the mountain ranges acted as a corridor, in this case toward the south. To the people moving into these ranges, the continuity in their food quest probably was more salient than the changes in their geographic location.

Apache is most closely related to the southern dialects of Canadian Athapaskan, particularly Chipewyan and Sarsi. By the eighteenth century, the Apache's southward movement had propelled them as far as the Sierra Madres of Mexico. They may have derived from the southernmost section of the expanding Canadian Athapaskan populace. Perhaps as early as the first few centuries A.D., the Canadian Athapaskans were scattered thinly among the Subarctic mountain ranges, with an increasing tendency toward diversification among local and regional aggregates because of their geographic spacing. At the same time, their mobility and the dynamic, fluid nature of their social organization would have made the total isolation of any groups unlikely. Sporadic contact, whether friendly or hostile, prevailed over wide regions.

The mountains extending southward from the western Subarctic acted as a corridor for Athapaskan migration and eventually led them thousands of miles to the south, deep into the Sierra Madres of Mexico, before their population movements were halted in the nineteenth century. As the Proto-Apache people followed this mountainous ecological zone southward, it was only within the present millennium that they became separated once and for all from their northern relatives.

Perhaps events in the twentieth century will lead to a reestablishment of contact. But during the centuries following their departure, the Apache underwent a series of collective experiences and changes quite different from those of the Subarctic Athapaskans. Among the Northern Athapaskan population, certain cultural developments, including the refined snowshoe and perhaps the bow and arrow, may have given impetus to their movement eastward from the Subarctic Cordillera into the taiga. Once there, some of them became "edge of the woods people," exploiting the huge caribou herds of the barren grounds to the east. Continued passage of time allowed further changes among this population, and differentiation, including a change from matrilineal to bilateral organization, followed the extreme scattering of the population over their sparse territory.

The events of a later history, particularly those associated with the fur trade, stimulated population movements back toward the north. We can see a result of this in the Hare dialect of Canadian

Athapaskan, which now is spoken in a territory adjacent to that of the Kutchin, even though the two are different enough to constitute separate languages.[5] Hare is far more closely related to Chipewyan, Slave, and Dogrib in the south, from which it differs only at the level of dialect.[6] To some extent, then, the historic distribution of many Athapaskan languages of the Arctic drainage results from political and economic pressures of the fur trade era. In the case of the Hare, this involved a northward migration that culminated at last in their coming to settle adjacent to their distant relatives, the Kutchin.

Secondary Movements

There is reason to think that long before the fur trade era, some time in the first millennium A.D., an earlier northward contraction of the Athapaskan population took place. We could view it as a temporary reversal of their spread to the south, perhaps in response to changing climatic conditions. Chapter 6 will deal more fully with the evidence for this, but its repercussions extended far to the north, possibly even as far as the west coast of Alaska.

In the course of their initial expansion, local Athapaskan groupings needed to maintain a significant degree of spacing among themselves. The wild food resources imposed constraints on the ways in which the people could distribute themselves over the terrain, and the earliest divisions among Athapaskan dialects took place under these conditions. As communication tapered off, mutually unintelligible languages developed among increasingly separated parts of the population.

The deep divergences among the Athapaskan languages of Alaska raise some questions, since many of them are spoken in adjacent territories. Usually, throughout the northern Athapaskan region this closeness has led to languages and dialects influencing one another and maintaining similarities, rather than becoming radically different. To be sure, the sparse population densities would have kept the various local aggregates far more remote from one another than their distribution on a map would suggest. On the other hand, it also is possible that a warming trend, which began in the first millennium A.D., might have brought about some compression of the population. This would have forced together groups that once had been more thinly dispersed. The crucial factor in this would have been the northward contraction in the range of such key subarctic fauna as caribou as a result of warming conditions.

As the population had expanded toward the south, their numbers would have increased as they came to occupy more territory, whether as cause of this population spread or an effect of it. A northward contraction later would have caused problems of territorial crowding as a chain reaction over an appreciable distance.

On the Alaska coast at this time, in the first millennium A.D., events among the Eskimo population could have been affected by such a phenomenon. The major Eskimo linguistic division is between Inupiaq, spoken from western Alaska eastward to Greenland, and Yupik, whose distribution includes the Bering Sea coast and the Alaska Peninsula as well as the Pacific Coast south of Cook Inlet, St. Lawrence Island in the Bering Sea, and the coast of the Chukchi Peninsula in Siberia.

The width of Eskimo territory inland from the sea varies considerably. In most areas it is restricted to the coastal regions, ending roughly at the tree line. From the Northwest Territories of Canada to the west along the Alaska coast, it circumscribes regions occupied by Athapaskan peoples. Eskimo territory reaches its thinnest point at Norton Sound on the west coast of Alaska, where in early historic times it was pinched between the sea and the traditional lands of the Koyukon.[7] This is the point, near Unalakleet, where the linguistic break between Yupik and Inupiaq occurs (Krauss 1973a:819).

This linguistic division could have come about in a number of ways. Some researchers have suggested that both Yupik and Inupiaq language variants stem from dialects that originated some distance apart and spread toward each other along the coast, eventually meeting at Norton Sound (Krauss 1979:808). Another possibility, though, is that communication among the Eskimo population in one locality was interrupted long enough for language differentiation to have occurred. This seems more consistent with the known spread of the Thule Eskimo tradition from west to east out of Alaska.

Glottochronology would set the date of the Yupik-Inupiaq split about 1,500 years ago, in the middle of the first millennium A.D. (Krauss 1973a:819). Athapaskan population shifts from the south could have resulted in a push to the coast at that vulnerable point near Unalakleet, followed by an occupancy long enough to have caused a linguistic division in the Eskimo population.

There is little doubt that Athapaskan speakers were in the Alaskan interior at the time of this linguistic split, and it is possible that at some point around 1,500 years ago some of them managed to push through to the coast. In his ethnography of the Tanaina, Cornelius Osgood (1937) refers to their chronic disputes with Eskimo groups over possession of the "valuable sea-coast" (see also Yerbury 1976). There have been other instances of Athapaskan peoples taking over small sections of coastline that had been occupied by Eskimo groups. Perhaps one of the best documented cases was associated with the early fur trade, when Chipewyans pushed east to the coast of Hudson Bay near the mouth of the Churchill River to secure a favored location with regard to the fur trade routes.

Episodes of this type from recent periods underscore the possibility that such things may have happened at an earlier time as well. There is reason to think that much of the hostility noted between Eskimo and Athapaskan groups was aggravated and perhaps even created by the fur trade (Yerbury 1980; J. Smith and Burch 1979). Whatever the case, an Athapaskan push from the interior to the coast at Norton Sound is not inconsistent with known patterns of intergroup relationships, despite the overall association of Athapaskan-speaking peoples with inland settings rather than maritime zones.

We have noted, too, that the division between American and Siberian Yupik is almost as great as that between Yupik and Inupiaq (Hammerich 1960). This suggests that a contingent of the Eskimo population departed for the Siberian coast not too long after the split of Yupik from Inupiaq. In general, a variety of evidence indicates that there was a good deal of population movement and realignment during this period. A brief Athapaskan interruption of the Eskimo sequence at Onion Portage in northern Alaska, dated roughly at A.D. 400−800, also is consistent with the suggestion of an early Athapaskan push from the south. It was during this relatively warm period, too, that early manifestations of the Thule tradition, which shows a direct continuity with historic Eskimo cultures, developed in the Bering Sea region and eventually spread westward along the Arctic Coast to Greenland.[8]

The relationships among these northern events and the hypothetical shift of the Athapaskan population during the warming trend of the first millennium A.D. is far from certain, but combined evidence, including the correspondences of estimated dates from archaeology and linguistics, lends some support to the model.

There is little reason to doubt that the primary Athapaskan subsistence focus was always more toward inland game than maritime food sources, with inland fishing of major importance in some cases as well. On both sides of the Bering Strait, inland peoples have had a long association with reindeer and their North American counterpart, caribou, first as hunters in Asia and later as herders. As important as this animal was, though, it can be overemphasized, since in a broader perspective, the most striking feature of Athapaskan subsistence is the lack of specialization. Groups that inhabited areas in which caribou were plentiful spent most of their hunting energies on these animals when they were available, but in other places and at other times of the year they relied on foods ranging from fish to mountain goats.

The optimum strategy for Athapaskan peoples would have been an emphasis on general adaptability. It was a matter of keeping options open rather than an overcommitment to a particular resource that might entail dependence and greater vulnerability to fluctuations in supply. At times certain Athapaskan groups tended to focus on one game species or another, but this was largely a matter of making the most of the best food source available at the moment. Consequently, the apparent emphasis on caribou in many groups was due as much to the availability of these animals, sometimes in staggering numbers, as it was to any deep-seated cultural commitment to them.

This subsistence flexibility does not explain precisely why Athapaskans might have pushed or been pushed to the coast at that time. But such a flux would have been consistent with the opportunism of the Athapaskan food quest. If pressure on resources in the interior was great enough to cause stress in populations near the coastal margin, then a shift toward maritime food sources would be a likely response. But that would require access to the sea. Other data fill out this picture considerably and suggest a broader context for such an episode. To begin to put the pieces together, though, we shall have to direct our attention much farther south along the continental divide to what is now the Montana-Wyoming region.

One result of the warming trend in the first millennium A.D. seems to have been that part of the southernmost segment of the population, the Proto-Apache, remained in the southern region while other sections of the population withdrew northward. The eventual separation of Northern from Southern Athapaskans probably was not a matter of Proto-Apache striking out for the Southwest suddenly and inexplicably. More likely it was a matter of maintaining a consistent strategy in their food quest, continuing a way of life that had long been established in the Proto-Athapaskan phase and which had led them down the mountain corridor in the first place.

As conditions changed, this pursuit eventually left the Proto-Apache separated from their northern relatives. The conditions of their environment continued to alter, and their quest for food finally led them even farther south along the mountain corridor to the threshold of the arid, agricultural Southwest. In the following chapter this phase of the Athapaskan southward movement will be examined in more detail.

CHAPTER 6

In the Mountain Corridor

Migrations and population segmentations are human events that imply motivation. So far we have considered what the lives of Proto-Athapaskan peoples were like before the northern and southern sections of the population became separated. The assumption of a mixed hunting and fishing subsistence base, in which caribou played a significant part, is based on the ethnographic record of Athapaskan groups who continue to live throughout the western Subarctic. Most likely, Canadian Athapaskans initially spread from Alaska southward along the Cordillera (Dyen and Aberle 1974:276), and groups from the Arctic drainage side moved eastward only after the refined snowshoe gave them the mobility they needed to exploit the barren ground caribou herds more effectively (Davidson 1937).

James VanStone (1974:7) observes that "northern Athapaskans can best be understood as basically a mountain people who have, in some cases, moved out of the cordilleran area" (see also Perry 1980). To begin to understand why they diverged, we need to focus more attention on the mountainous section of the continent where the population ancestral to both Northern and Southern Athapaskans last shared a common domain.

The Role of Caribou in the Athapaskan Food Quest

The vast numbers of caribou that sometimes congregate for migration have led many observers to assume that they constitute a reliable, almost unlimited food supply for the hunters who utilize them. But Ernest Burch (1972:356) points out that "human populations largely dependent on caribou will be faced with a major resource crisis at least every two or three generations." Although the movements of hunting groups may be finely attuned to those of caribou, it is not possible for humans to "follow the herds" physically in any literal sense (Burch 1972:346, 351). The animals travel much too rapidly over rugged terrain for humans to be able to keep pace with them over any length of time.

The most feasible ways for people to hunt these animals would involve either intercepting them at certain points on their migrations or locating them while they are not moving, stalking them to make a kill. In either case this would have been an occasional, perhaps even seasonal harvest rather than a reliable resource to be judiciously tapped whenever people felt the need. As Burch (1972:351) expresses it, "Far from following the animals and killing only when supplies are needed, hunters have to wait until the prey appears and then try to make a major kill that will provision them for some time."

Contrary to general belief, moreover, caribou herds do not necessarily follow the same migration routes year after year, although the terrain may channel their movements through certain mountain passes. At various seasons they might be present in a number of different ecological settings and altitudes within their general range. These factors, combined with the wild fluctuations in numbers that characterize many other Subarctic species as well, introduce a high degree of chance and uncertainty into caribou hunting. People who hunted caribou on a regular basis would certainly have been in the habit of exploiting a wide variety of other food sources. When we look at the Athapaskan subsistence pattern from this perspective, it is clear that their essential strategy has been to minimize risk by maximizing the variety of food sources they can obtain when necessary.

Early Athapaskan peoples no doubt used a number of hunting techniques for caribou, but the most productive of these must have been the game drive system known from the historic period. Using this technique late in the summer, people could provide themselves with a good supply of meat and skins to help carry them through the colder months. The rugged terrain of the Cordillera merging with the Rocky Mountains to the south provides not only caribou but species ranging from trout to mountain goats. Buffalo once grazed as far north as Great Slave Lake (D. Gunnerson 1974:140). These animals could be tapped as an additional resource by people able to utilize the variety of zones and food sources afforded by major mountain ranges and who had learned to be at the right place at the proper time. For those with that capacity, the mountains would have been a source of refuge and sustenance rather than an obstacle—a base from which they could take advantage of several possibilities.

Despite this broad range of alternatives, caribou must have been the major focus of attention for most of these groups. As large and plentiful game animals, they were one of the most sought-after species wherever they occurred and probably even attracted people into areas where they could be hunted. These considerations can provide useful insights for fleshing out the circumstances by which the northern-southern divergence came about.

There is every reason to think that, as Athapaskans spread from southern Alaska through the Cordillera, they expanded into areas in which similar conditions—a mountainous setting with caribou and a general range of other familiar fauna—offered them a good chance of getting food. Over time these groups would have tended to fill in zones where the ecological setting was fairly consistent with what they had known before. To a great extent their distribution would have tended to become congruent with the distribution of mountain caribou.

In the first few centuries A.D., when Athapaskans may still have been recently arrived in North America and in the process of spreading, conditions were colder than they are at present. The range of game species was somewhat different as well. Even in the early twentieth century, caribou (*Rangifer tarandas montana*) were recorded as far south as Elk City, Idaho, which is well south of the present Canadian border (Hall and Kelson 1958 : 1020). It is virtually certain that during a period of colder conditions, the range of caribou and other typically subarctic fauna in the mountains would have extended still farther to the south.

As Athapaskan speakers first made their way down the mountain ranges that extend through the continent, there probably was little about the natural setting to stop or discourage their expansion until they reached areas where the range of familiar game species tapered off. At that time this range was well within what is now the United States. This southward spread would have required nothing more than a continuance of their established pattern. Perhaps only a few generations after their arrival in North America, the Athapaskan diaspora took them farther south along the mountain chain than the present Northern Athapaskan territory.

Archaeological Evidence

The archaeological evidence for this southward spread is suggestive, but not conclusive. A number of cultural changes from southern Alberta through northern Colorado occurred during this period, but as is often the case, any links between prehistoric remains and living peoples are highly tentative. Some researchers have suggested that Athapaskans were present in the Wyoming region since the Altithermal period, which would date to perhaps 7,000 years ago (G. Wright

1978:135). But the bulk of evidence considered so far indicates that the Athapaskan arrival was much more recent and that Proto-Athapaskans may not have entered North America until long after that time. The data from Mummy Cave, one of the richest sites in this part of the continent, make it clear that there was no stable, continuous occupancy in that region over such a lengthy span of time.

Mummy Cave in the Absaroka Range of northwestern Wyoming contains deep deposits that represent a sequence of occupation extending over almost 10,000 years (Wedel, Husted, and Moss 1968; Wedel 1978:196–198). Level 38 of this site, dated at A.D. 1580+/−90 years and coinciding with the Shoshonean occupancy of the region, contains small side-notched points. At this time the Apache had left the region for the southwest and were no longer a part of the local picture. Farther down, in level 36, dated at A.D. 720+/−110 years, are small corner-notched forms. They are similar in shape and size to those found in other Wyoming and Colorado sites, and they have the proper age to have been associated with Athapaskans.

Below these levels is a variety of point types. As the authors of the published report put it, "It is abundantly clear that during 9000 years or more the cave was occupied, abandoned, and reoccupied many times, probably by people coming into the locality from widely different locations, but all of whom tended to adjust their life-ways to a mountain-adapted economy" (Wedel 1978:184).

To the north at the end of the Canadian Cordillera, there is provocative evidence of a break in continuity in the archaeological record beginning in the first century A.D., with the appearance of a different hunting style that involved driving herds of buffalo over cliffs. This technique is associated with a distinctive type of notched stone point and other features that constitute what is known as the Besant complex.[1]

One of the richest sites from this period is the Old Woman's Buffalo Jump in southern Alberta, where, as H. M. Wormington and Richard Forbis (1965:132) note, "In all details the situation must have been so perfect for the driving of buffalo that the site was used continuously for a period of approximately 1,500 years, beginning about the time of Christ." The use of buffalo jumps may be a modification of older drive techniques, making it possible to hunt these large dangerous animals in regions where not enough wood was available to build drive enclosures (Wormington and Forbis 1965:193).[2]

Although a general association of Athapaskan-speaking peoples with the Besant remains a possibility, a number of factors make many of the Besant sites appear decidedly un-Athapaskan. For one thing, they are distributed throughout the northern Plains as far east as the Dakotas, where they are dated as early as A.D. 1 (Reeves 1983:93). Even in Alaska no clear evidence of Athapaskan peoples occurs until several centuries later. The Besant sites also are associated with burial mounds with log-covered pits and grave goods, unlike anything Athapaskan-speaking peoples are known to have created. In general, the Besant seems to be a predominantly Plains-oriented culture.

In sum, the Besant dates are too early for the postulated Athapaskan move south; the geographic distribution extends too far to the east into the prairies; and such cultural features as burial mounds seem distinctly non-Athapaskan. Nonetheless, the Besant merits attention as an example of important cultural changes that affected that region. The extensiveness of the Besant distribution suggests that it may not have been coterminous with a particular ethnic population, but might instead represent technological innovations and hunting techniques that were particularly effective in that ecological zone. Whatever their origins, these could have been adopted by various unrelated groups. Certainly the nineteenth-century spread of the horse-based buffalo-hunting complex in the same region provides an instructive example.

Even though many Besant sites were associated with some of the wrong cultural features and the wrong places at the wrong times to indicate a close association with Athapaskans, the Besant complex persisted for several centuries, and there is no reason to suppose that Athapaskan speakers would not have been influenced by the Besant if they were in the region. In light of their demonstrated receptivity to cultural innovation elsewhere, including the Northwest Coast, California, and the Southwest, a cultural aloofness to successful hunting techniques would seem to be distinctly out of character. It would be misleading to assume that Athapaskans in this area would have used a particular uniform point type and stuck with it exclusively over many centuries. We might recall the nineteenth-century Navajo group that used several types of stone points at the same time. In the archaeological record of this part of the continent, technology appears to be linked more reliably to ecological zones than to linguistic divisions (Donohue 1975:89). If Apache in the historic period used a variety of point types, there is no reason to think that Athapaskans would have been less receptive to innovation in the first millennium A.D. than they were in the second. If the technological style of the Besant extended beyond ethnic boundaries, it may have involved Athapaskans.

But changes in the Besant complex over time are suggestive as well. Lower levels at the Old Woman's Buffalo Jump site contain

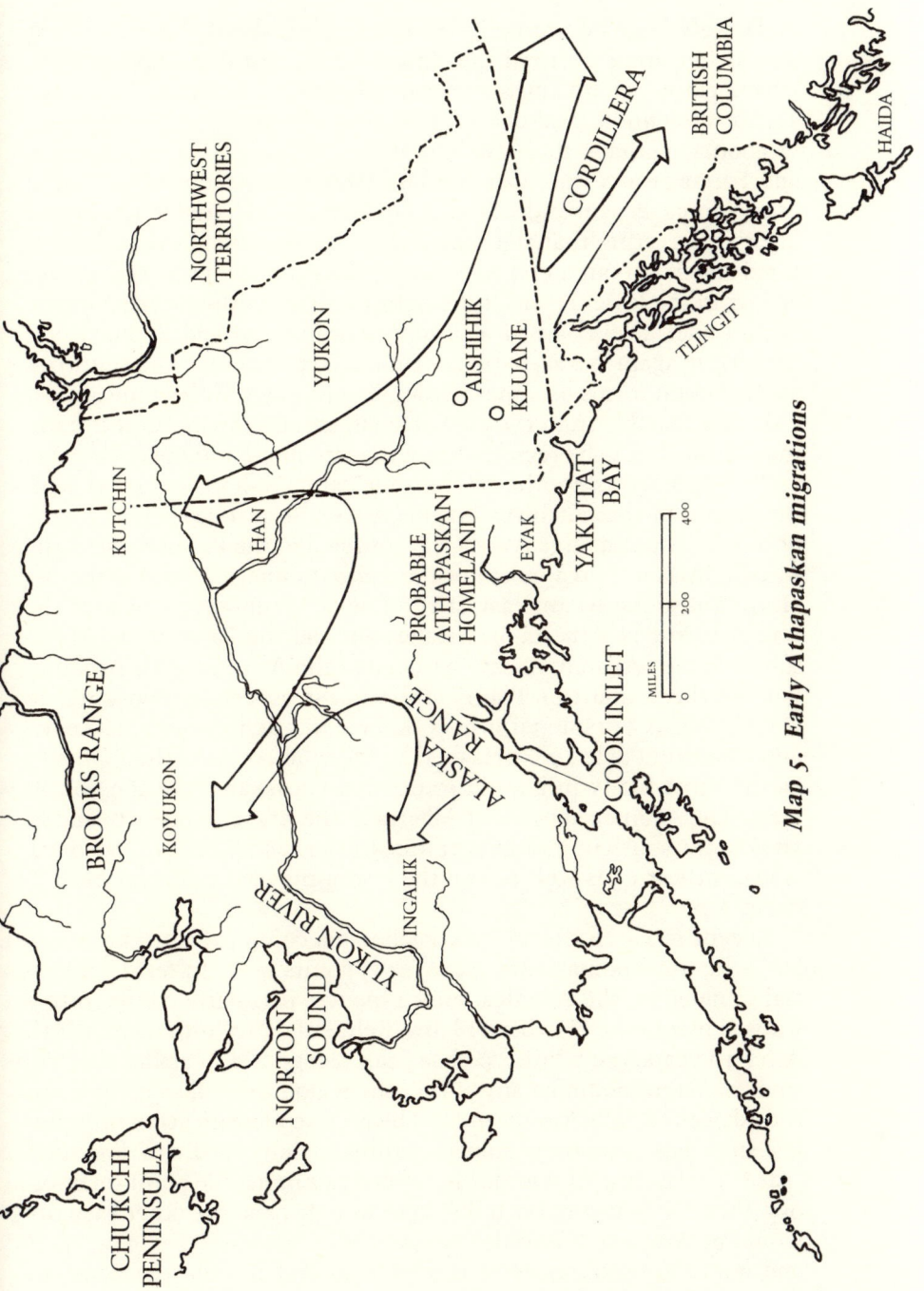

Map 5. Early Athapaskan migrations

"relatively large Besant points" (Wormington and Forbis 1965:132), and an apparent cultural continuity exists with the upper levels where points retain the same general shapes but become smaller. This is a technological change that suggests the appearance of new weaponry, perhaps the bow and arrow. According to Wormington and Forbis (1965:136), "At the Old Woman's Buffalo Jump, and at other jumps, Besant and related points have been found in the lowest layers, suggesting that the practice of driving buffalo over cliffs entered Alberta about 2,000 years ago." "Besant and related types" also appear in the lower levels of the Kenny site in southwestern Alberta, lying under a level dated A.D. 600 (Wormington and Forbis 1965:138). Here again is a stylistic continuity in points over the centuries as the Besant forms become smaller. Eventually they become almost indistinguishable from the type of small corner-notched points common throughout the region during the late prehistoric period.

The Avonlea is another archaeological complex associated with the region of the northwestern Plains. As Brian Reeves (1983:101) observes, "By and large Avonlea is confined to the Plains west of the Middle Missouri area, north of the Platte drainage, north of the Big Horn–Shoshone Basin, east of the Rocky Mountains, south of the Boreal Forest in Alberta-Saskatchewan, and the Parkland in Manitoba." Some researchers have associated the Avonlea with Athapaskan speakers, and this Plains affiliation is especially congenial to David Wilcox (1988) and others (Kehoe and Kehoe 1968; T. Kehoe and McCorquodale 1961; Haskell 1987), who consider the Plains to be the most likely migration route of Athapaskans into the Southwest. The Avonlea appears in Alberta in the first century A.D. and in sites to the south in Montana at A.D. 500 and 600 (Reeves 1983:102). Apparently it ends well before the beginning of the second millennium A.D.

Recent research has added considerable complexity to the Avonlea issue. As Thomas Foor (1988:261) points out, "In terms of spatial dimension, the Avonlea point type was originally confined to a limited part of the Northern Plains (Kehoe and McCorquodale 1961). After 20 years, the point type has been recognized in artifact collections made from almost any part of the region, as well as many from the adjacent Rocky Mountains." The precise identification of Avonlea sites has also been subject to discussion. As Lynn Fredlund (1988:181) notes, "If Avonlea is defined as a projectile point technology, then the Benson's Butte-Beehive complex and the other variants would be Avonlea. If Avonlea is assumed to have associated cultural and material traits, as defined by Reeves [1983], then the Benson's Butte-Beehive complex is not Avonlea since it only participated in the projectile point technology." In light of the tendency for the Avonlea complex to have come to seem more inclusive and culturally heterogeneous over the years, Leslie Davis (1983:5) observes that there is some skepticism about the validity of the Avonlea construct itself.

Avonlea points are small, usually notched and apparently associated with the bow and arrow.[3] Burials are primary, without evidence of reburial or other disturbance and without mounds, although they may contain grave goods. One Avonlea site in southeastern Alberta, however, does contain evidence of secondary burial, dated A.D. 560+/−90 (Milne 1988:65). Like the Besant and other peoples, the people associated with the Avonlea phase hunted bison in drives, using both jumps and impoundments. For the moment, though, it is uncertain which if any of the Avonlea sites might have been occupied by Athapaskan speakers. Reeves (1983:18) notes that "the picture today appears complex. In the mountains Avonlea technologically and lithically develops into . . . the archaeological representative of the prehistoric Kootenai people . . . In contrast, the Plains Avonlea develops into . . . the archaeological representative of the Prehistoric Piegan peoples."

David Meyer, however, suggests an Algonkian association for Avonlea. "It would seem that evidence for fairly free interaction between Avonlea and Laurel peoples in the Nipawim region [of Saskatchewan] and some interaction between Avonlea and Blackduck peoples in the Pas region has additional implications. It is generally considered that Blackduck pottery was made by Algonkians. The evidence from the Saskatchewan River, therefore, for interaction of Avonlea peoples with both Laurel and Blackduck peoples suggests that these Avonlea peoples were in contact with populations with whom they shared many cultural traits. In other words, it is likely that these Avonlea peoples were also Algonkian" (Meyer, Klimko, and Finnigan 1988:41).

George Ruebelmann (1988:200) points out analogies between rock effigy alignments at an Avonlea bison-hunting site in northern Montana and the practices of historic Plains bison hunters, particularly the Siouan-speaking Assiniboine. Ann Johnson (1988:141), meanwhile, suggests that ceramics found at Avonlea sites represent influences from outside the area, most likely the central midwestern United States.

It seems possible that the Avonlea was a technological style that influenced a variety of peoples over a wide geographic range. Although an Athapaskan presence in this region during the first millennium A.D. is a reasonable supposition, their identity among the scattered archaeological traces of hunters remains elusive. They may well have adopted some aspects of the Avonlea, whatever the origins of that complex might have been.

On the other hand, some of the regional manifestations of the Avonlea in Wyoming seem especially promising. At the Beehive site that Fredlund (1988) refers to, for example, located in the foothills of the Big Horn Mountains, there is a long record of occupancy underlying the level where Avonlea projectile points appear, dated A.D. 550 (Frison 1988:155). The stone tools are similar to other sites in the region. The site held the remains of one dwelling with charred juniper logs. George Frison (1988:160) notes that "the lodge was probably conical in shape and flat; sandstone slabs had been piled around the perimeter except for an opening to the east." We might note that Apache peoples throughout the Southwest built their dwellings with the doorways facing east.

Frison (1988:160) observes that the Benson's Butte Beehive stone tools are "remarkably similar" to those at the Irvine site in central Wyoming. Located on a steep slope, the site is dated A.D. 650+/−100 and includes bone tubes cut from jackrabbit tibia. Frison suggests that these were intended for decorative use, but we might also recall the use of bone drinking tubes among Athapaskan peoples during women's menstrual seclusion. Frison (1988:168) feels that these and other associated Avonlea sites in that region "appear to be intrusive into the Wyoming area and represent attempts at adaptation to the Archaic life style already dominantly present."

In northwestern Wyoming in the Jackson Hole region, other sites may shed more light on this phase of the Apachean past. According to Gary Wright (1984), several hundred sites in that area were associated with people who exploited multiple zones ranging from high elevations in the Tetons to valleys below 7,000 feet. Some of the sites in this area apparently functioned as base camps, showing repeated occupation with evidence of domestic functions. Others seem to have been sites for special activities associated with seasonal phases of the subsistence quest. The people responsible for these sites exploited a wide array of plant and animal foods in season, including bighorn sheep and elk at the higher elevations, using various zones within a radius of at least fifteen miles. Some of the base camps are in the high elevations, as well as in the valleys (G. Wright 1984:73). Knowing what we do about general Athapaskan patterns, this seems a familiar and perhaps recognizable profile.

Shoshonean peoples occupied this area in historic times, but the weight of evidence shows that they were not present before A.D.

1000 at the earliest and probably for several centuries afterward (G. Wright 1984:94). Discussing the people who might have inhabited the region before that, Wright (1984:104) rules out Siouan and Algonkian speakers, who are known to have arrived in the area more recently from the east. This would leave Athapaskan speakers as one of the few possibilities, and perhaps the most reasonable one.

If the general model of Athapaskan occupation of the mountain corridor is accurate, there ought to be other, more recent sites farther to the south that show some cultural resemblances. At the Ruby and Muddy Creek sites in the broken country of Wyoming, the Besant complex appears with dates between A.D. 150 and 280 (Frison 1971, 1978:221–223). At the Wardell site in Wyoming, a similar buffalo-hunting technique continues from A.D. 370 to 960, and on the basis of styles of ceramic ware found at the site, Frison (1978: 228–229) has suggested an Athapaskan association.

Still another Wyoming site known as Spring Creek Cave contained dried perishable materials as old as A.D. 225. One stone projectile point discovered at the site was set into a hardwood foreshaft with pitch. The foreshaft, in turn, was inserted into the hollowed end of a mainshaft, of which only a fragment remains. The mainshaft was wrapped tightly near the joint end, probably to bolster the socket of the enclosing shaft against splitting on impact (Frison 1965). A similar form was found at Wedding of the Waters Cave in Wyoming, except that the foreshaft itself was sharpened to a point, and no stone point was attached (Frison 1965).

These weapons are very similar to the Western Apache arrows from the nineteenth century, pictured in Grenville Goodwin and Keith Basso's (1971) book *Western Apache Raiding and Warfare*, although one of these has a metal point. Like the arrows in the Wyoming sites, the Apache arrows consist of compound shafts with a foreshaft of hardwood that has been inserted into a hollowed mainshaft. The mainshaft in turn has been wrapped near the joint end. According to Goodwin's Western Apache informant in the 1930s, the foreshafts "were set into the main shaft with pitch. They either put a stone point on the foreshaft or just left it plain and very sharp. Both kinds were used for deer and other game" (1971:227).

There is a further and rather intriguing hint that this might have been a very old and time-honored technique, established among Apache groups as the ideal way arrows should be made. Even when arrows were constructed with a one-piece solid shaft, which must have been much easier, they were made to appear as if the shaft were compound. "Right where the foreshaft would be set into a cane arrow," states the informant, "they would sinew around the wood shaft so it looked the same. The Chiricahua used to make lots of these arrows" (Goodwin and Basso 1971:227).

The archaeological record suggests that at least one new population, and possibly more, moved into the broken mountainous area of southern Alberta early in the first millennium A.D. and into the Wyoming region in succeeding centuries. The sequence implies a north-to-south movement. Based on some resemblances between artifacts and other items dating in the first few centuries A.D., there is reason to suspect that this population may represent an Athapaskan presence in the area.

Changing Conditions and Population Shifts

If Athapaskans had arrived in the Alberta-Montana-Wyoming region from the north early in the first millennium A.D., we can visualize a thinly dispersed population of Athapaskan speakers extending from Alaska down the Cordillera through southern Alberta into the Big Horn mountains of Wyoming. They would have operated in small mobile groups and tapped the resources of these varied ecological zones though subsistence strategies that were flexible, incorporating a range of food sources. This population, still relatively new in the region, expanded to fill a particular ecological niche and spilled out from the central Wyoming sites to occupy the areas they were able to exploit, learning, as Frison suggests, from earlier inhabitants of the region. The mountains were the avenue for their southward spread. The distribution of Northern Athapaskan peoples from Alaska to the southern end of the Subarctic Cordillera covers a far greater expanse than the remaining distance between the Canadian border and the Southwest. Even as the Athapaskan population shifted toward the south, though, changing conditions introduced another dynamic into their situation.

A cooling trend that had begun about 1,500 years earlier came to an end in the first centuries A.D. In succeeding centuries, the climate gradually moderated (Bryson and Wendland 1967; Harp 1978: 105; Workman 1978:63). As a consequence, the ranges of game species associated with subarctic conditions receded northward toward their modern distributions, and Athapaskan peoples who hunted these animals would have had to shift north in response. This process can account for the present southern boundary of Northern Athapaskan territory and the division between Northern Athapaskan and Apachean groups. As the leading edge of the population extended southward, the territory behind their expanding frontier would have been occupied by other peoples. They could have been Athapaskan speakers who remained where they were, increasing their population, or conceivably some other, unknown peoples. In the eastern barren grounds near Hudson Bay, the archaeological record provides one example of such a process. In levels associated with a cold phase, Dorset Eskimo artifacts overlay the traces of earlier occupants, to be replaced still later by other peoples (Harp 1978:105–106).

Hunting populations tend to disperse themselves thinly in any case, and in some regions of the Subarctic, the carrying capacity of the land is so low that despite small groups' occupation of vast expanses of territory, crowding with regard to the food supply is a potential problem. Because of this situation, if Athapaskans had retreated northward into a contracted territory, the process would have caused a telescoping of the population, with the associated stresses and strains that one could predict in such a situation. No doubt this would have involved some resistance on the part of the groups occupying the regions to the north. The linguistic split between Yupik and Inupiaq Eskimo on the distant coast of western Alaska, roughly 1,500 years ago, corresponds with the era during which the warming trend was making its effects felt to the south. As we have noted, Athapaskan groups pushing to the coast from the interior and intruding between sections of the Eskimo population might have caused the Yupik-Inupiaq Eskimo language split as a result of a chain reaction of pressure caused by the northward shrinkage of the caribou range far to the south.

In any case it is clear that not all of the Athapaskan population did withdraw to the north. Demographic problems caused by compressing the northern populations might have been one factor, but another probably was the result of subtle shifts in their subsistence. Caribou were always complemented by other food sources, and as they gradually became harder to find, the southernmost of these hunters might simply have come to focus more and more on other game. At some point these people ceased hunting caribou altogether in favor of deer, elk, mountain sheep, or even buffalo.

Probably some of these Athapaskan hunters had abandoned any major commitment to caribou long before. That focus had always been pragmatic in any case. If so, there was no particular incentive to move after caribou when their range contracted northward. In later centuries some of these people, at least, would become known as Apache.

The separation of Northern from Southern Athapaskans resulted from choices that led each of these populations to carry on a style of life they had developed over many generations. Glottochronology suggests that as early as A.D. 600 the Apachean dialects probably were distinct from most Northern Athapaskan languages (Hoijer 1956), although ties with some of the Canadian dialects persisted longer. If this estimate is correct or close to it, the split occurred several centuries after the warming trend had begun, during a period of animal and human population adjustments to changing conditions.

Intermittent contacts between some Northern Athapaskans and Apache may have occurred long afterward. As caribou became harder to find in the southern part of their former range and as the northern section of the Alberta-to-Wyoming Athapaskan population extended their food quest farther and farther into the Subarctic, these forays into the north would have increased the likelihood of their encountering other groups exploiting the same resources. Long-separated Athapaskan populations would again come into close contact in the northern regions.

A northward contraction of the population could have been especially pronounced at the end of the chain in Alaska, not only leading to an Athapaskan breakthrough at the coast of Norton Sound and a disruption of communication among the Eskimo population but affecting Athapaskan languages spoken in Alaska. Koyukon, Tanana, Ahtna, and Ingalik territories directly adjoin that of the Tanaina, but the deep linguistic divergences among them would be most likely to have occurred if speakers of these languages had once been more dispersed. A subsequent push northward would result in the juxtaposition of dissimilar languages.

During this period, in the middle of the first millennium A.D., the smaller projectile points usually associated with the bow and arrow begin to appear in the Alberta-to-Wyoming region. This technological innovation was an additional stimulus to population movements, allowing people to exploit certain resources more effectively than they had before.

Apache and Canadian Athapaskans

In the southern section of this Athapaskan-speaking population, the ancestors of the Chipewyan and Carrier were part of a single dialect group. Eventually linguistic differences grew as the Chipewyan expanded east of the mountains. If their movements resulted from population pressures on the local food supply, this pressure could have motivated people to expand and broaden their resource base. The introduction of the improved snowshoe and bow and arrow would have enhanced their possibility of doing so.

Much of the caribou population of North America consists of a few discrete herds. Their movements affect the movements of the human groups who hunt them, particularly on the barren grounds east of the Cordillera. Herds inhabiting that area spend the winter in the forests south of the tundra, moving north onto the open grounds in the summer when calving takes place (Gordon 1975). According to James Smith (1973:315), Chipewyan caribou hunters in the flat, barren lands east of the Cordillera "have traditionally followed the herds; some have told me that 'in the old days we lived like the caribou.' Others have likened their former existence to the wolves that also followed the herds." Elmer Harp (1978:106) has noted the historic linkage of caribou-hunting groups to the north-south movements of herds, and as he observes, "It is plausible to suggest that the Archaic Indian hunters might have operated to a like economic pattern."

But in some ways the historic strategies of the Chipewyan are a departure from the early Proto-Athapaskan pattern. If Athapaskans initially spread southward along the Cordillera, such groups as the Chipewyan, who occupied the open grounds to the east on the arctic drainage side of the mountains, moved into the barren ground more recently.

Many decades ago, D. S. Davidson (1937) advanced the hypothesis that only after the development of the refined snowshoe was human mobility on the tundra enhanced enough to make the exploitation of the eastern caribou herds feasible. He also suggested that the early introduction of the snowshoe into North America was associated with Athapaskan-speaking peoples. He proposed that, based on the geographic distribution and time sequences of subsequent modifications and refinements, these innovations also were Athapaskan developments that spread to other parts of North America. But for this issue, perhaps the most significant aspect of his classic study is the assertion that the light, efficient snowshoe opened some vast areas of the Northern Hemisphere to regular human habitation for the first time.

Linguistics provides additional support for the conclusion that the Chipewyan spread to the east was recent. The territory of the Chipewyan is easternmost of the historic Northern Athapaskan distribution. Westward toward the Cordillera lie the territories of the Sarsi, Beaver, and Sekani with the Carrier beyond that in the mountains verging toward the Pacific Coast. The degree of similarity between the Chipewyan and Carrier dialects is far greater than that between either of these and Beaver or Sekani, which are spoken in the territories lying between them.

Considering the distance that separates Carrier from Chipewyan and their apparent lack of any recent influence on one another, the linguistic similarity between these dialects must result from their having been the same not too long ago. With reference to Carrier, Dyen and Aberle (1974:250) conclude that "the deep divisions in the Carrier subdialects suggest long occupancy and a lengthy differentiation in the area. The alternative possibility, that Carrier is simply an amalgam of groups, is unlikely."

Although Carrier probably has long been established and stable in its present area, Chipewyan territory has fluctuated considerably even in historic times. In the early years of the fur trade, the Chipewyan expanded south and east at the expense of Inuit and Cree to control the trade routes from Prince of Wales's Fort on Hudson Bay at the mouth of the Churchill River (Yerbury 1976; Gillespie 1975, 1981; Rogers and Smith 1981).[4] There was considerable "push and shove" with the Cree, especially, with resultant territorial instability, until the horrors of the eighteenth-century epidemics became an even greater factor in the region.

The available evidence leaves little doubt that Chipewyan speakers spread eastward out of the Cordillera into the barren ground, eventually losing contact with their Carrier-speaking relatives in the mountains. Their pattern of open ground caribou hunting with snowshoes led to an even wider pattern of mobility and thinner population dispersion than had characterized their ancestors in the mountains.

The closest relationships of Apachean languages to northern dialects are with Chipewyan and Sarsi, but Chipewyan is far more closely related to Carrier than it is to Apache. Even now their differences do not exceed the level of dialect (Dyen and Aberle 1974:12). The Canadian Athapaskan dialect group, which shares cognates internally at the level of 77 percent or more and is thus considered by Dyen and Aberle (1974:14) to be a single language, certainly was even more uniform in this earlier period, suggesting that Carrier and Chipewyan were still the same when the Proto-Apache population separated from the northern groups.

Some caution is in order, however. It is misleading to visualize relationships among Athapaskan languages in the metaphor of a genetic tree or branching model (Krauss 1973b). Where speakers of a language are spread over a wide area but retain some degree of contact with one another, the regional dialects that form over time are likely to influence one another unevenly and in ways that confound attempts to determine past relationships in a clear-cut way (Krauss

1979:847–848). This can be even more complicated when speakers of these dialects move around a great deal and when people speaking related dialects rejoin after periods of separation. The Athapaskan languages and dialects have been subject to all of these phenomena.

Considering the wide dispersal of Athapaskan populations, it seems likely that there were regional variations in speech even at the time of the Apachean separation. Phonetic differences between eastern and western Apache dialects appear in Chipewyan sub-dialects as well. Because the Chipweyan eventually spread eastward, the Proto-Chipewyan, even at this earlier period, may have occupied the eastern slopes of the Cordillera that verge onto the flatlands. The eastern side of the Cordillera provides fewer fish but more abundant large game, including caribou (Dyen and Aberle 1974:276). The presence of these animals in large numbers would have been a pre-condition for some of the northern groups' eventually coming to specialize in hunting caribou on the barren grounds.

Contact between Proto-Apache and related segments of the Canadian Athapaskan population would not have suffered a sudden, distinct break. In both the Subarctic and the Southwest, historic Athapaskan groups were so mobile that treks of hundreds of miles on foot were not unusual (e.g., Hearne 1911; Goodwin 1969:69). With the capacity to range over so great a territory, these people might have encountered one another occasionally over many centuries. There is at least one report that Navajo in the late nineteenth century revisited northern Athapaskans, to whom they referred as other Navajo living far to the north (Morice 1914:155; Ellis 1974:113). Evon Vogt (1961:231) points out that Navajo speakers still can understand some Northern Athapaskan words.

The separation probably involved a gradual growing apart, as regional subsistence enterprises ultimately led to local populations pursuing different activities in areas more and more distant from one another. Proto-Apache remained in the Great Divide region of Wyoming for many generations, and the last tenuous contacts with their northern relatives took place only a few hundred years ago.

The Athapaskans who occupied the Wyoming area for centuries, the Shoshoneans who came after them, and the Siouans and Algonkians who followed were only the last of a long sequence of peoples entering the broken country of that region. The myriad reasons for these comings and goings probably will always remain beyond our comprehension, and the movements of Apachean peoples alone are far from clear.

Proto-Apache in the Southern Rockies

If Athapaskans arrived in southern Alberta in the first centuries A.D. and occupied the Wyoming region during the first millennium, more evidence of their presence between Wyoming and the Southwest would be tremendously helpful. A pair of archaeological sites in north-central Colorado do, in fact, appear to fill this gap. These sites are the remains of game drive systems. At one of them, known as the Murray site, James Benedict (1975:172) states that there is evidence of "a strong mountain orientation, and an economy based upon seasonal transhumance westward from the Front Range foothills." Located above the tree line, the site consists of stone structures lined up to guide animals to a point of ambush. Although the site apparently was abandoned, rebuilt, and reused in successive periods, the initial construction has been dated through a combination of radiocarbon and lichenometric techniques at 970+/−100 years B.P., or roughly A.D. 1000. Hunters at the Murray site took a variety of game species including elk, antelope, and mountain sheep (Benedict 1975:173, 161).

The projectile points associated with these activities include a small corner-notched form that Benedict refers to as the Hog Back type. Superficially, at least, they resemble the other small corner-notched points found in levels to the north in Wyoming that in some cases overlie Besant points. Benedict describes another site nearby called Scratching Deer that helps fill in the picture of this population's style of life. Again there are game drives on a tundra ridge above the tree line, with dates ranging from A.D. 435 to 1105, and small corner-notched points (Benedict 1975:276). These high-country game drives are associated with campsites in more sheltered valleys (Benedict 1975:276). They provide clear evidence of a versatile use of multiple zones of a mountainous area, including the treeless tundralike conditions at high altitudes. Benedict comments that the hunting strategies and techniques represented at the Murray site are more reminiscent of the Subarctic than of any of the surrounding regions in other directions. This insight, of course, fits nicely with the idea that Athapaskans were responsible for these structures.

Benedict also suggests that the earliest levels at these sites may be attributable to Shoshonean peoples who occupied the area in early historic times. But there appear to be strong arguments against this. Both Gary Wright (1978, 1984) and David Madsen (1975) have presented evidence that Numic-speaking Shoshonean peoples did not arrive in that general area until much later, as the result of an expansion from the southern Nevada region. Wright, in particular, discusses a series of sites in the Wyoming region in which recent levels attributed to Shoshonean peoples overlie traces of other, earlier inhabitants.

Wright also points out that except under conditions of extreme stress or deprivation, Shoshoneans have not been known to utilize the higher mountains. Their subsistence strategies have focused more intensively on the lower-altitude zones. This consideration alone might make a Shoshonean association with the high game drives of the Murray and Scratching Deer sites questionable, but apparently the earlier levels at these sites are too old in any case to have been Shoshonean. On the other hand, Ahtna and other Northern Athapaskan peoples normally built caribou drive structures at altitudes above the tree line, just as the people at these early Colorado sites did (cf. de Laguna and McClellan 1981:6–8). There is reason to think that Proto-Apache were present in the region at the time the Murray and Scratching Deer sites were first built and used and that subsequently, perhaps by the fifteenth century, Shoshonean peoples moved into the area. By then, or within a few decades of that time, the Apache had abandoned the northern Colorado area for the Southwest.

Still more recently, of course, Shoshonean peoples in the northern region were succeeded by Algonkian- and Siouan-speakers who entered from the east. But by then most of the Apache were established in the Southwest, and to casual observers, there would have been little evidence to suggest that they had ever been anywhere else. During the initial occupancy of the Murray and Scratching Deer sites, local conditions were colder than they are at present. This would have been much earlier in the general long-term warming trend that began early in the first millennium A.D. and continued into recent times and that set in motion the complex series of Athapaskan movements and population shifts in the North. In succeeding centuries this warming period with its associated dry spells culminated in the great drought of the thirteenth century. The region of the Great Divide Basin probably became less and less attractive to Apachean peoples during this period (Antevs 1955).

The area today is arid and, in general, rather barren and desertlike. The evidence from Benedict's Colorado sites not only suggests that the people lived there during a period of colder conditions but that, in utilizing the high tundra for their subsistence activities, they were pushing toward the extremes of available cold conditions in the region. Shoshoneans, on the other hand, expanded from the vicinity of Death Valley in southern Nevada into the Wyoming area. Shoshonean experience and food-getting strategies were attuned to hot, dry, lowland conditions. The climatic trends that would have made this region less and less suitable to the Apache might have made it more desirable from a Shoshonean perspective.

It is important to note that these northern Colorado sites are less than two hundred miles from the present New Mexico state line. The historic distribution of Northern Athapaskan peoples from Alaska through western Canada, by comparison, covered well over a thousand miles. In the nineteenth century, the Apache could easily cover more than forty miles a day on foot during journeys taking weeks at a time. This distance of a couple of hundred miles should not be considered a significant barrier between the Apache and the Southwest (Clum 1936:207; Goodwin and Basso 1971). In terms of geographic distance between Alaska and Arizona, they practically were already there.

Do we have any further indicators of the Apachean movement southward through the mountains? As it turns out, excavations in northwestern New Mexico reveal a dozen sites, linked on the basis of pottery to early Navajo, dating to the fifteenth century and possibly earlier. This is a region deep in the mountain corridor, hundreds of miles west of the Plains, and far older than any Athapaskan sites east of the mountains. Several of these are clustered in the La Plata River valley near the Colorado state line. These sites contain the remains of various structures, including a sweat lodge and dwellings similar to those of historic Navajo and other Apache. At this period the Navajo were far less differentiated from other Apachean divisions. Patrick Hogan (1989:54–55) observes that "these data suggest that ancestral Navajo groups occupied the upper San Juan drainage in the mid-sixteenth century and that these groups might have entered the area as early as A.D. 1450."

The Kiowa Apache Problem

At this point we can make use of evidence from other sources to add pieces to the puzzle. The background of the Kiowa Apache and their relationship with the other Apachean groups can shed more light on these events. Although traditionally the Kiowa Apache have been included with the rest of the Apachean divisions on the basis of language and other cultural similarities, the nature of their ties has been a matter of some debate (Gunnerson and Gunnerson 1971:3;

Hoijer 1971:5; Mooney 1898:241–248; Schlesier 1972; Brant 1949, 1953).

Throughout history the Kiowa Apache have stayed on the Plains, most recently associated with the Kiowa in a political/military alliance of sorts.[5] They lack some of the features that apparently resulted from the influence of Pueblo peoples or other groups in the Southwest that all of the other Apache divisions share, such as the use of masked dancers in ceremonies. There is no concrete evidence that the Kiowa Apache ever spent any time in the Southwest core area. All of the Apachean groups speak dialects of the same language, but Kiowa Apache is more divergent than any of the others and seems to be equally distant from all of them (Hoijer 1971). With regard to a range of phonetic features, Kiowa Apache clearly stands apart from the rest (Young 1983:394). All of this makes it appear that the contingent of people ancestral to the Kiowa Apache left the rest of the Apache population some time before they continued toward their ultimate destinations in the Southwest. In light of the reconstruction so far, it seems likely that they segmented off some time during the long period of the Alberta-to-northern Colorado occupation.

One nineteenth-century Kiowa Apache stated that many years ago they had "occupied a region known as the 'bad ground,' an exceedingly desolate and broken country between the headwaters of the Missouri and the Platte" (Keim 1897, quoted in Gunnerson and Gunnerson 1971:14). These river systems extend into the heart of the crucial Alberta-to-Wyoming region. Between them, they embrace many of the Wyoming archaeological sites that we have discussed. The earliest recorded location of the Kiowa Apache in the seventeenth century, before horses became such a significant part of their life-style, was in the vicinity of the Black Hills, only a few hundred miles east of their former homeland and still within reach of mountainous terrain (Gunnerson and Gunnerson 1971:14).[6]

The capacity of linguistic calculations to determine the time when the Kiowa Apache dialect separated from the others is debatable. Nonetheless, such calculations indicate that the Kiowa Apache diverged some time around the twelfth century A.D., which fits the picture quite well. These bits of evidence are far from conclusive. But the negative attitude conveyed in the Kiowa Apache reference to the "bad ground" may give some insight into the reasons for their departure. The earlier stages of the drying spell might have inclined the Kiowa Apache to seek more attractive areas even before the rest of the population departed.

The Proto-Apache Population

What can we determine from all the evidence? The distribution of Athapaskan populations during the second millennium A.D., at the northern end of the Cordillera from Alaska to southern Alberta and at the southern end of the Rocky Mountains in Colorado, New Mexico, and Arizona, is a historic fact. So is the past relationship among these populations. In the territory between, archaeological evidence for the preceding millennium indicates the presence of mountain-dwelling populations who exploited a variety of game at various altitudes from base camps, using such drive structures as many Athapaskan groups did in the Subarctic.

The evidence also indicates a number of population transitions in the Alberta-to-Wyoming region, with the appearance of small points associated with the bow and arrow in the first millennium A.D. At the Spring Creek Cave site in Wyoming, the arrows themselves apparently are identical with Apache arrows from the Southwest. The evidence also shows a similar population farther south in the mountains of Colorado early in the second millennium A.D., suggesting a movement toward the Southwest core area only a few hundred miles away. By the middle of that millennium, sites appear in the La Plata River valley of New Mexico between the San Juan and Chuska mountains.

Although Proto-Apache contact with the main Northern Athapaskan population dwindled toward the end of this period, sporadic encounters with a few of the Canadian Athapaskans, especially those who later became Chipewyan and Sarsi, might have occurred long afterward. Considering the mobility that characterized these peoples, who covered extensive areas in their quest for food, they might have maintained some mutual awareness. Perhaps each group even held a sense of other "people something like us" with regard to the other.

What were the people like? From the comparison of Northern, Southern, and Pacific Coast data, we have a basis for at least a general depiction of Proto-Apache culture. The number of people who constituted this population is difficult to determine. The earliest Spanish accounts of Apache groups in the Southwest, centuries later, use such phrases as "many and warlike." In the early 1600s, Father Alonso de Benavides refers to the "huge Apache nation."[7] Certainly these chroniclers were in no position to gather accurate census data. During the following centuries in the Southwest, the political impact of the Apache on other groups often caused them to loom large in the written records in more ways than one. There has been a marked, chronic tendency for their numbers to be exaggerated.

Even if accurate population records were available for the sixteenth- and seventeenth-century Southwest, though, they might well be misleading if they were projected back to previous centuries. We have noted that the Navajo, despite an extremely high infant mortality rate, have increased their numbers more than a dozenfold, from about 10,000 to over 150,000 in the relatively few generations since 1864. If population size can change so rapidly in little more than a century, there seems to be scant hope of establishing any firm estimates of the Proto-Apache population of three or four hundred years ago.

Language offers some insights, suggesting that the early population was dispersed at least enough for some phonetic variation to have existed among sections (Dyen and Aberle 1974:210). The t-k shift among the modern Apache dialects differentiates the western from the eastern groups, with the /t/ sound in Navajo, Western Apache, Chiricahua, and Mescalero replaced by a /k/ in Jicarilla, Lipan, and Kiowa Apache. The use of /t/ has been identified as a retention of the earlier Proto-Athapaskan form, with /k/ a later linguistic innovation (Dyen and Aberle 1974:210; Hoijer 1938; Brant 1949).

In historic times Kiowa Apache, Jicarilla, and Lipan have been the easternmost of the Apachean groups. The occurrence of the /k/ form in Kiowa Apache indicates that this linguistic innovation probably took place before they segmented from the others. The discovery that the t-k shift also occurs in Chipewyan, which is the easternmost of the Northern Athapaskan dialects, supports this (Haas 1968), implying that the Proto-Apache population itself encompassed elements from more than one section of the Athapaskan population.

All of this evidence indicates that linguistic differentiation took place deep in the past and far to the north and that the Proto-Apache population was scattered enough to maintain some internal variation over centuries. At the same time, though, the maintenance of language unity above the level of dialect implies that communication never was totally lost for any extended period. For this alikebut-different linguistic phenomenon to have maintained itself over so long a time is consistent with the model of a population scattered thinly over an immense area, operating on a day-to-day basis in small and mobile groups that had fluctuating, ad hoc compositions. This would have involved enough contact to retain language unity but not enough to wash out regional linguistic differences.

Benavides' account of the Apache population from 1630 depicts just such a situation. He states that "although, being one nation, it is all one language, since it is so extensive it does not fail to vary somewhat in some bands (*rancherías*), but not such that it cannot be very well understood" (quoted in Young 1983 : 394). At later periods, for obvious geographic reasons, Apache groups in the eastern section of the population showed a greater orientation toward the Plains than those groups to the west. For centuries the Apache occupied the eastern slopes of the Rockies, from which they could easily strike into the open country and return to the mountains whenever they wished, as they did during the historic period.

When the Spanish first encountered Plains Apache, whom they referred to initially as Querechos and later as Vaqueros, they described them as people who hunted buffalo on foot and transported the hides of these animals packed on the backs of dogs. These people had achieved the remarkable feat of exploiting buffalo so successfully on the open plains without horses that they could produce a sizable surplus for trade. On the other hand, they did not spend the entire year in the open country but returned seasonally to the mountains (D. Gunnerson 1974 : 126–127). In the early 1600s Benavides wrote that "they do not dwell in settlements, nor in houses, but in tents and huts, forasmuch as they move from mountain range to range, seeking game, which is their sustenance" (quoted in Schroeder 1974, I, 242). In the late 1700s, the Mescalero also were based in the mountains and moved onto the Plains to hunt buffalo seasonally (1974, I, 536).

The mountain orientation of most Apachean groups, including those who ultimately came to be considered Plains people, is well documented. Only the Kiowa Apache, and possibly those who became known as the Lipan, eventually committed themselves predominantly to the plains. Even so, the movements of the Lipan in particular were affected by conflicts with the Comanche from the eighteenth century onward. Before suffering a major defeat by the Comanche in 1723, they had been living near the Llaneria Grande (a big range of hills), north of San Antonio, Texas. By the 1770s the Comanche had driven them as far as the Texas coastal plain. Toward the end of that century, the Lipan were living in the mountains and the plains on both sides of the Rio Grande (Schroeder 1974, I, 499, 519, 521, 528). We might recall, too, that according to the earliest written references from the prehorse period, the Kiowa Apache were near the Black Hills. In addition to the variety of ecosystems encompassed in the Black Hills region itself, it is only a little over a hundred miles to the east of the Rocky Mountains.

By the nineteenth century, the conglomerate of Apache bands who became known as the Jicarilla had adopted a Plains/buffalo-hunting orientation, but Jicarilla statements attest to a strong nostalgia for the mountains and a feeling of unease in the open country (Opler 1936: 205). Albert Schroeder (1974: I, 436) concludes that "certainly there was no distinct plains people versus mountain people indicated in any of the Jicarilla history. All of these lived in the mountains and seasonally moved out into the plains, alone or with neighboring groups."

The ethnohistory of the Lipan Apache is more obscure, but on the basis of linguistic and other cultural evidence, there is little doubt that they and the Jicarilla share a close common heritage. This sequence of Apachean culture history, as much as any other, illustrates the dynamic and fluid nature of Apache social and political alignments. The historic Lipan and Jicarilla may both consist of aggregates of various Apachean groups noted throughout the seventeenth and eighteenth centuries in the Texas-Oklahoma Panhandle region. On the basis of archival evidence, Schroeder suggests that the nineteenth-century Jicarilla consisted of an amalgam of those Apache whom earlier documents referred to as Jicarilla, as well as others known as Cuartelejos, Carlanas, and Cipaynes, and that still other segments of some of these remained to the east to become known as Lipan.

The pattern seems to have involved two counterbalancing phenomena. A centrifugal tendency existed for local groups to become more and more differentiated as they scattered over a wide region, pursuing their own interests in a variety of niches, zones, and encounters with other groups. But there was also a centripetal tendency for these related peoples to coalesce occasionally, for much the same reasons. Perhaps the best we can do in this regard is to observe that apparently they did whatever seemed like a good idea at the time. Neither their social organization nor their cultural patterns inhibited the process to any significant degree.

The historic roster of Apachean groups in this area probably is misleading, since it conveys a sense of cleanly bounded "divisions" or social units of a sort familiar to Euro-Americans. What we appear to be viewing through the dusty lens of archival records is a broadly scattered population whose activities came to the attention of the Spanish in northeastern New Mexico, but which extended over an indefinite range in various directions. The regions to the north and northwest of the Sangre de Cristo Mountains and the Colorado Plateau were essentially unknown territory to the Spanish. Much of Arizona was unexplored by Euro-Americans until well into the nineteenth century.

Throughout these regions, mountains stretch to the north, west, south, and southeast into Texas, where they curve like a scimitar pointing to the area where the Lipan finally appear by name in historic records (Sjoberg 1953:76). After the introduction of horses, several of these groups began to spend more time on the Plains. Horses revolutionized life for many people after they acquired them (Secoy 1953). But despite, or perhaps because of, the ancient capacity of Apachean groups to exploit many types of zones, few of them became cut off from the mountains.

On the basis of all this evidence, we can visualize an early Apache population abandoning the region they had occupied for centuries and moving in small groups and bands through and along the mountain chain that would lead them into the Southwest. David Brugge (1983:489) asserts that "the central movement was along the mountain chains, spreading into the country on each side as techniques for exploiting new environments were mastered." He implies further that this binary division of the population over eastern and western mountain slopes could have been associated with the east-west distinctions perceived among the historic Apachean groups.

The complex structure of the Rocky Mountain chain, though, does not appear to lend itself to such a clear bifurcation of the population. The eastern face of the Rockies, verging on the vast grasslands of the High Plains, marks a clear boundary between ecological zones, but in the west there is no equivalent, sharp transition from one major zone to another. Instead, range after range of peaks undulate toward the west, verging on the Great Basin and the high Colorado Plateau before they gradually give way to dry, broken country and still more mountain ranges in California.

In any case, by the time the Apache occupied northern Colorado, the Southwest already was within striking distance. Goodwin notes that for groups in Arizona that "it was nothing for Apache to journey on foot southward into Mexico for two hundred miles or more to obtain horses." The avenue for these raids was the Sierra Madre Occidental mountain range (Goodwin 1969:93).

There are reports of "hogan-like structures" in the Colorado Rockies as far north as the White River headwaters, northeast of Denver (Huscher and Huscher 1942:80). Tree ring dates for what seem to be sites in the present Navajo region range from 1350 to 1514, although it is possible that these may have been built by Athapaskans at a much later date using old wood (Hall 1944). M. Jean Tweedie (1968:1133) places the northern boundary of "Old Navajoland" of early historic times at the La Plata Range in central Colorado. The recent discovery and dating of sites in New Mexico south of the San Juan Mountains is consistent with this sense of following the mountain ranges south. The Jicarilla, whose historic territory straddled the present Colorado-New Mexico border, laid claim to part of southern Colorado as far north as the Arkansas River, which is only a hundred miles or so south of Denver (Opler 1936b:202).

Researchers over the years have argued that the Apache entered the Southwest from the Plains to the east, bringing agriculture with them, but no Apache sites on the Plains predate the seventeenth century. The Plains migration model would also require some explanation why a mountain-oriented people would venture into an entirely different ecological zone, only to return to the mountains after traversing a great arc of many hundreds of miles.

The mountains were a source of nurturance, shelter, and increasingly at a later period, refuge for the Apache. It would not be surprising if small parties of hunters during earlier centuries had ventured briefly into the Southwest region on sporadic forays long before the people shifted in greater numbers to the south. Throughout history these peoples maintained the autonomy and wide options of independent small groups, and such a movement would have been more a collective result of myriad individual decisions, a trickling south of people over a long period rather than a single monolithic population shift. As conditions became harsher in the northern zone, the idea to move elsewhere may have appeared to be a good one to more and more family bands who already had a long tradition of exercising free options within an immense range.

From the first half of the sixteenth century, the Spanish were aware of a general east-west distinction within the general Apachean population, whom they referred to as Teyas and Querechos (D. Gunnerson 1971:20). The Teyas seem to have been more completely associated with mountain ranges, whereas the Querechos ventured far into the Plains to hunt buffalo, although the meanings of these designations are not entirely clear and perhaps not consistent in the records (Schroeder 1974, I, 97).

Aside from the east-west linguistic variance, though, there clearly was much cultural similarity among these clusters. We can be quite certain at this point that they exhibited a tendency toward matrilocal residence, a symbolic concern with femaleness expressed in avoidance restrictions and a ritual recognition of female puberty, a special set of attitudes and practices regarding death, and other ideological characteristics of Proto-Athapaskan culture. As segments of this population precipitated into a variety of geographical areas and niches throughout the Southwest, cultural diversification among the various divisions continued.

CHAPTER 7

On the Fringes of the Southwest

When the southward drift of the Proto-Apache led them to the threshold of the Southwest, they may never before have encountered sedentary village farming peoples. It is possible that some of the Proto-Apache had ventured far enough east over the Plains in the course of their food quest to encounter river valley agriculturalists before A.D. 1500. In earlier times, too, before the dry years of the thirteenth century, Southwestern farming peoples of the Anasazi tradition had spread north into Colorado, and it is conceivable that they might have had some encounters with Athapaskans in those northern areas as early as A.D. 1000. But if so, the interaction in the Southwest became more prolonged and intense.

By the mid-sixteenth century, the Apache population was scattered thinly from the Colorado Plateau eastward through the Sangre de Cristo Mountains of New Mexico, which verge onto the southern Plains. Communication between the extreme ends of this population tapered off, but this was merely a continuation of a long-standing phenomenon, as the t-k shift between the eastern and western sectors suggests. At the same time, the mobility of small groups within this population tended to allow a chain of continuous contact across the geographic spectrum, maintaining a general but gradually decreasing cultural homogeneity.

The game in this region overlapped what had been available farther north, but there were major shifts in proportion and some new sources of food. Elk abound on the Colorado Plateau, but for most of these peoples, deer replaced the moose and caribou of the northern Rockies and the Subarctic.

Deer and elk do not lend themselves as well as caribou and bison to the game drive techniques of the North. Among the Apache groups in mountainous regions where deer was a major food source, no evidence of the use of the drive technique survived. But farther to the east where the mountains give way to the Plains and herds of buffalo grazed over the flatlands, people continued to use drives until early historic times. Not long after that, horses revolutionized buffalo hunting.

Although the Southwest supported a greater quantity and variety of game than the Subarctic could provide, one of the most significant changes was in the relative availability of plant foods. Wild plants came to play a major role in the Apache food supply, and this emphasis coincided with a shift in the economic importance of women's contributions to subsistence. The traditional sexual division of labor meant that hunting was strongly associated with men. This continued to be the case in the Southwest, and while the acquisition of game remained important, the proportion of wild plant foods in the diet—generally gathered by women—grew to rival those derived from animals.

Another source of plant food in the Southwest had a great impact on Apache patterns in a different sense. The stable, sedentary farming villages of native peoples throughout much of the region often had stores of food, and through trading and raids, the Apache sought to include this in their subsistence quest. Their open receptivity to varied subsistence opportunities, which had enhanced their ability to survive in other situations in the past, now easily accommodated "enemy food," as the Navajo referred to corn, and other products of village farming.

In some cases they acquired this food through the exchange of products of the hunt for those of agriculture. In the late 1500s, the Spanish explorer Antonio de Espejo refers to people who might have been Apache, mentioning a "mountain people" near Acoma Pueblo who "came to the aid of the settlements and traded salt and game, particularly deer or rabbit and tanned hides for cotton *mantas.*" (Schroeder 1974, I, 188).[1] During the Pueblo Rebellion of the 1680s, some Pueblo refugees found shelter with Apache groups. Relations between Apache and Pueblo seem to have been somewhat unstable, though. By the late seventeenth century, the Apache acquired a great deal of their agricultural supplies through subsistence raiding.

The easy mobility and fluid nature of Apachean social organization amounted to a precondition that lent itself well to raiding. It facilitated the elements of surprise, rapid escape, and a general elusiveness that provided great advantages over the predictable, settled village life of intensively agricultural peoples. The orderly ritual calendar of Pueblo ceremonies attuned to the stately repetition of seasons is a striking contrast to Athapaskan concepts of a living universe peopled by capricious, unpredictable powers. To some extent these different views of the world reflect differences in the realities of these peoples.

Although there were times when a perceived common interest led to a fleeting coalescence of Apache local groups, this occurred only rarely even in later times. Considering the vital importance of free-ranging autonomy throughout the Athapaskan past, it would be surprising if it had. The actions of one aggregate of Apache did not necessarily have anything to do with those of any others.

The fundamental freedom of individual and small-group behavior that pervaded Apache social organization allowed them to pursue other options of interaction with farming peoples as well. Although one Apache group might raid a particular farming village, other Apache might maintain peaceful visiting relationships with the same community. There seems to have been some ambivalence on the part of the villagers in many cases, though. Pueblo peoples who welcomed friendly daytime visits by the Apache often were uneasy, nonetheless, about letting them spend the night within their walls and so required them to camp outside the village.

For the first few generations after they had arrived in the Southwest, though, there is not much evidence that the Apache raided sedentary peoples, and there is little indication of any general, coordinated overall raiding effort during the early period. Only after repeated Spanish attacks on Apache groups for slaves did raiding become an established pattern, often on Pueblo villages under Spanish control. Moreover, there are numerous instances of Apache groups forming alliances with certain Pueblo communities against the Spanish. Apache raids on pueblos are reported early in the 1600s, and by the latter part of that century, Spanish records indicate that because of these raids, a number of pueblos had been abandoned (Schroeder 1974, I, 268–269).

Eventually the Apache found themselves in chronic conflict with the Spanish. In the late 1500s, the Spanish were new to the area themselves and were advancing toward the north from relatively secure bases in Mexico. Renaissance Europeans in the process of expanding their empire, the Spanish represented a complex, hierarchical social order and an array of interest groups. The Apache who confronted them were mountain-dwelling hunters whose concepts of territory, political affiliation, and social relationships were vastly more egalitarian and individualistic. For the next several centuries, these mountain people not only would succeed in holding their own resource base but would contest the territory held by Europeans.

Eventually this struggle would end, but for the next several centuries, the process was to have profound effects on both peoples.

The raiding pattern also led groups of Apache into contact with peoples farther to the south. In a sense this was a manifestation of the general southward gravitation of the Apache that carried them down the mountain corridor in the first place. But the establishment of Spanish towns in Mexico provided a more specific attraction. The Apache's mobility allowed them to carry out raids on villages hundreds of miles away, retreating to their mountain base camps in regions that remained unknown to the Spanish. Their presence was felt far to the south of the territories that they actually inhabited.

The process of cultural differentiation among the Apache continued during their early years in the Southwest. As mobile as they were, local aggregates tended to operate more intensively in certain regions than in others, developing familiarity with local food sources and a degree of commitment to them. In doing so, they tended to become increasingly distinct from one another in dialect and to undergo cultural changes as a result of their historical experiences.

The Eastern Section

In some ways this diversification amounted to a continuation of more long-standing processes. In refining their ability to hunt buffalo successfully on the Plains, Apache groups in the eastern sector, these vaqueros, as the Spanish called them, shifted away from what earlier had been a basic, direct subsistence activity to hunting for trade, which gave them access to the agricultural products of the eastern Pueblo groups.

According to the early Spanish records, the buffalo-hunting Apache of the east used vast numbers of pack dogs to transport their products, not only to meet Pueblo demands but to take advantage of their growing Spanish clientele as well. Dolores Gunnerson (1974: 141) characterizes the enterprise as "commercial hunting." Our fragmentary glimpses of these people do not suggest a group that hunted only for their own food, and Spanish descriptions from the period probably depict a people who already had modified their ancient strategies in adapting to a new set of circumstances. No doubt these people had hunted buffalo and other large game for centuries, using drive techniques with origins in the north. They may have used dogs on a small scale long before their departure from their northern relatives. Gunnerson points out that the buffalo-hunting Apaches' use of dogs as pack animals rather than for pulling sleds or

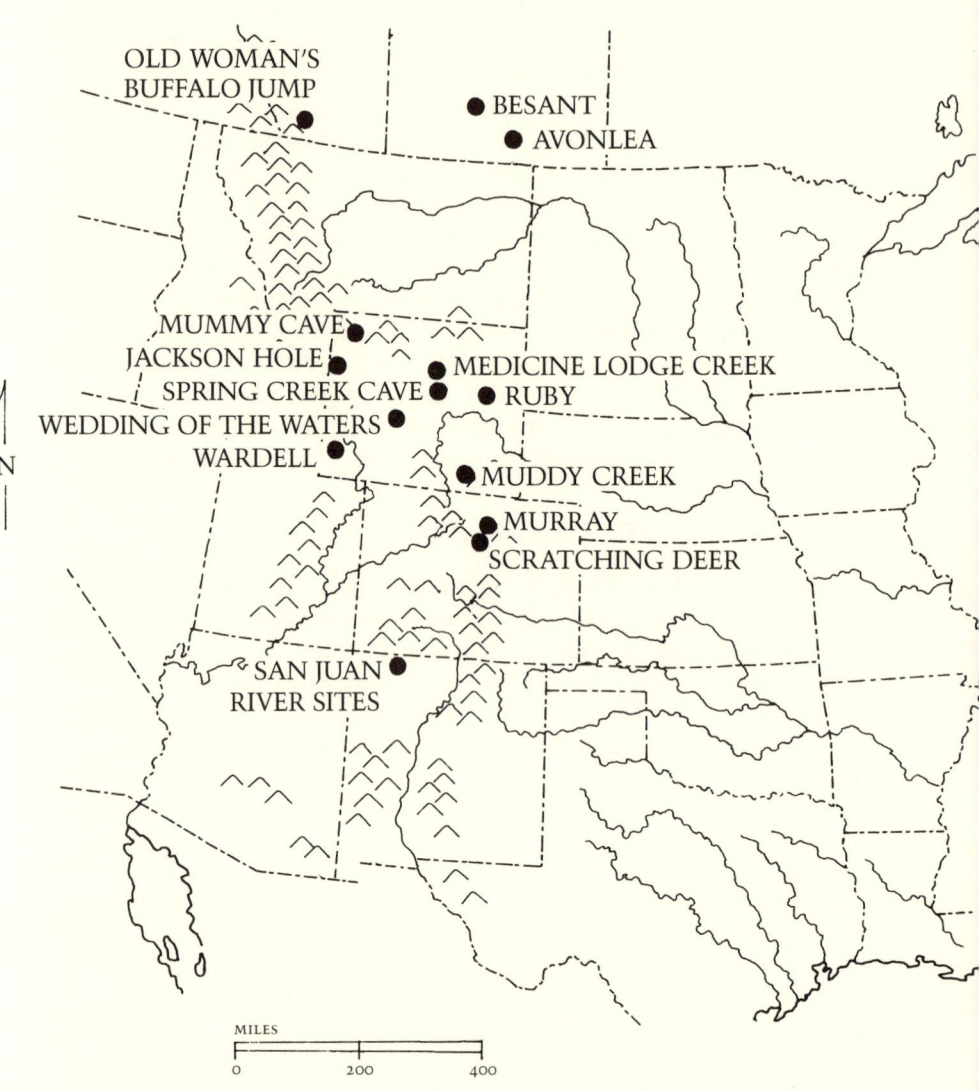

Map 6. Archaeological sites from Canada to New Mexico

travois made of poles attached to the animal's shoulders and dragged on the ground was also a Chipewyan pattern.

At the Spring Creek Cave archaeological site in Wyoming, where some of the artifacts bear a resemblance to later Apache materials, there were "several obliquely worn pole butts with wear patterns suggesting use of dog travois frames" (Wedel 1978:206). Although the Plains Apache did not use the travois in historic times, the poles for their hide tents were tied to the dogs' sides and allowed to drag behind them on the ground. Gunnerson (1974:17, 128, 145) suggests that Athapaskans introduced these dog-packing techniques to the Plains region. Dogs can be a mixed blessing for subsistence hunters.[2] It might be important to have enough dogs to meet the needs of household transport and perhaps to assist in hunting, but to have too many dogs can create problems, not the least of which is the dogs' need for food, which places them in potential competition with humans for sustenance. For this reason alone, we might expect small hunting groups to have had a few dogs, but not the hundreds the Spanish encountered when they finally observed the people who had been supplying all the buffalo robes. But by that time systemic changes had occurred in Apache subsistence patterns. As the size of the buffalo kill increased in response to the demands of trade, the need for more dogs to transport these goods also grew. Greater kills provided a surplus of meat and by-products that made it possible to maintain a large number of working canines.

As we noted earlier, many writers have argued that Apachean peoples arrived in the Southwest after having migrated through the Plains rather than the Rocky Mountain system and that they interacted with Plains agriculturalists before encountering Pueblo peoples. Some of the eastern Apache population had ventured far out onto the Plains by at least the early seventeenth century. Researchers have claimed that a scattering of archaeological sites as far away as western Nebraska show evidence of an Apache presence. The cultural remains at these sites, referred to as the Dismal River complex, indicate that the inhabitants practiced agriculture.

Evidence for an Apache association with the Dismal River complex, though, is a matter of debate.[3] Much evidence consists of a distinctive type of pottery similar to Jicarilla Apache ceramics, made from micaceous clay. Others have pointed out that many aspects of the sites, particularly the method of burial, are not consistent with Athapaskan patterns (Opler 1971). The significance of the Dismal River sites for Apache population movements is a pivotal point in a long-standing discussion. If the sites demonstrate an early population of agricultural Apache on the Plains, many argue, they would add support to the idea of an Apache migration route through that area.[4] But even if the Dismal River complex does turn out to be associated with the Apache, all of the known sites are dated at a period when the Apache are known to have been in the Southwest (Wilcox 1981:223).[5]

Whatever the affinities of the Dismal River complex may prove to be, the sites are too recent to shed direct light on Apache migration routes into the Southwest. The earliest dates associated with these sites are no older than the seventeenth century, and the presence of iron implements underscores this relatively late occupation.[6]

David Wilcox (1981) has argued that the Black Hills region of South Dakota may have been the starting point for a general Apachean migration into the Southwest through the Plains, based on the early historic Kiowa Apache presence there. But linguistic and other cultural evidence makes it appear more likely that the Kiowa Apache split from the rest of the Proto-Apache population in the north. In that case the Kiowa Apache association with the Black Hills does not indicate anything about the movements of other Apache.

Throughout their migrations the rest of the Apache could have exploited the seasonal food resources available in the flatland and perhaps even ventured hundreds of miles east of the mountains. But the linguistic similarities of all the historic Southwestern Apache groups indicates that they maintained communication among themselves until historic times, and there is no evidence that the western portion of the population ever went into the Plains at all. The eastern groups continued their affinity with mountainous regions, keeping them in touch with their relatives farther west. The Kiowa Apache, on the other hand, did separate more completely from the rest and move east at an earlier time, as the linguistic differences indicate.

The eastern Apache groups experienced more intensive contact with Europeans than the western aggregates did during the early years in the Southwest, and consequently we have more historical references to them. To some extent, though, this confuses rather than clarifies the picture. The ambiguity in the historic records is tantalizing. Having reconstructed the long process of Athapaskan prehistory to this point, we now have the first eyewitness glimpses of the Apache as they appeared to the Spanish. If only the picture were clearer!

Aside from the general terms such as Querechos, Teyas, or Vaqueros by which the Spanish referred to Apache or possible Apache groups, the documents also record names of specific aggregates. Typically these are Spanish names—Palomas, Sierras Blancas, Carlanas, and so on, or, like the term Querechos, names that were bestowed on them by other native peoples. Indeed, the very terms *Apache* and *Navajo* have such origins. This might reflect the fluid nature of Apachean groupings. Among the Apache themselves, these aggregates probably were not named corporate entities except to the extent that they consisted of people associated with a particular locality or region.

The Spanish were accustomed to dealing with named sociopolitical entities that maintained distinct political boundaries and stability through time. In their experience with New World populations, they had encountered complex urban societies and intensive agriculturalists in Mexico. Even in the Southwest, they found permanent farming communities that tended to be highly structured and self-contained independent societies in themselves. But the Apache population maintained far greater social flexibility, as they had long before in the Subarctic. The Spanish rarely experienced intimate contact with these Apache groups during the early phases of encounter. More often they glimpsed the Apache in brief hostile exchanges and identified them on the basis of scanty evidence and erratic criteria.

The interplay between Apache subsistence raiding and the Spanish policies aimed at preventing and retaliating for these raids created volatile relationships. But although the interactions were often violent, they were not uniformly hostile. In some instances, too, relationships became strained among the Spanish themselves. When livestock from Apache raids in Sonora to the south frequently appeared in the Spanish markets of New Mexico, Sonorans understandably objected.

Apachean receptivity to innovation led to a variety of adaptations among the various local Apache populations throughout the Southwest, and their small-group autonomy accommodated a wide spectrum of interaction ranging from guerrilla raids to peaceful trading. In the early 1700s, according to Spanish records, the Jicarilla had established a close relationship with Taos Pueblo in New Mexico and had settled in permanent villages. The documents portray them living in masonry dwellings as "peaceful farmers" with irrigated fields (J. Gunnerson 1969). At the same time, they maintained contact with their relatives on the Plains who hunted buffalo and traded the robes made from buffalo hides at Taos and other communities.

During their close association with Puebloan peoples, the Jicarilla modified many of their ancient Athapaskan cultural features. Recognition of female puberty in the Southwest came to involve public ceremonies among all of the Apache groups, and among the Jicarilla it included a ceremonial relay race and an episode during which the young woman ritually ground corn on a metate (Opler 1944:75). Like the other Apache peoples of the Southwest, in contrast with the Kiowa Apache who remained on the Plains, the influence of Pueblo cultures also led the Jicarilla to the ceremonial use of masked dancers who represented benevolent deities.

At a later historic period, when the Jicarilla had given up sedentary farming and had turned their subsistence focus to hunting buffalo on horseback, they saw themselves as a society consisting of two groups: the Ollero and Llanero, or Sand People and Plains People. Some researchers have suggested that this dual division reflects a reunion of some of the earlier Plains Apache population with the group that had briefly turned to farming, although this also has been debated (Opler 1936b).[7]

The eastern Apache retained a pattern of matrilocal residence that required a married couple to live with the wife's family, but by the nineteenth century they had developed bilateral social organization, which gave equal recognition to relatives on both the father's and mother's side rather than emphasizing descent through women. They also had a general prohibition on the marriage of cousins (Dyen and Aberle 1974:234). This idea had the effect of maximizing the scope of marriage ties, extending them beyond the range of known relatives among a population that exploited vast regions of the Plains.

The Lipan Apache seem to have been in close association with the Jicarilla, and both may represent the coalescence of some of the earlier Plains and transitional zone Apache who were noted by chroniclers in the region of northeastern New Mexico, the Texas-Oklahoma Panhandle, and the southwestern Nebraska regions. By the 1700s the Comanche advancing from the north pushed them into west Texas, where again they established themselves in the vicinity of mountainous terrain. We can see reflections of their mobility in scattered references to the confrontations they had with the French and their Pawnee allies in eastern Texas, and there is some evidence that they had further sporadic contact with the Kiowa Apache to the north (Dyen and Aberle 1974:15).

Other groups alluded to in Spanish records farther south in Mexico may also have been Apache. Segments of the general Apachean population could have found their way that far south, but we know very little of these groups, and the weight of evidence does not support their identification as Apache (Forbes 1959).[8] On the other hand, many Apache groups based in New Mexico did spend a large portion of the year far south of the Chihuahua border.

The Western Section

As these complex interactions were occurring in the eastern zone of Apache territory, the western section of the population was relatively unaffected by early Spanish contact. There are very few descriptive accounts of these people until much later. Even in this earliest phase of their Southwest occupation, though, we can see some Apache diversification and a range of historical encounters with other groups. In the broken country far to the west of the Plains, some of these people eventually came to be known as the Coyotero, Arivaipa, Pinal, Sierra Blanca, or collectively, the Western Apache.

In the early 1600s, the extensive region occupied by the Apache, ranging from the southern Plains westward into the complex mountain system verging toward the Basin, was relatively unknown to the Spanish chroniclers, and because of Apachean occupation, they had little access to it. There is no doubt that after the Apache's first century in the Southwest core region, the process of differentiation among local groups was well under way. Regional populations already had begun to precipitate into various niches. But continued interaction among them made the process far more complex than a simple branching off.

In 1630 Father Alonzo de Benavides (1965:39–57, quoted in Dyen and Aberle 1974:213) referred to Apaches de Xila, Apaches de Navajo, Apaches del Perillo, and Vaqueros and noted that these people spoke a single language with some variation in dialect. In subsequent accounts the Apache's geographic distribution gradually increased, with the notable exception of the eastern groups' retraction and loss of territory in the face of Comanche pressure (Secoy 1957). The overall trend in Apachean movements was to the south. Benavides' account provides an early glimpse of a continuous process. Differentiation continued, and Apache territory increased until the late nineteenth century. No doubt the population grew as well, although to some extent this may have involved a rebounding from earlier losses that resulted from their initial exposure to European diseases.

Apparently the central and western segments of the Apache population gave rise to the historic Navajo, Western Apache, Chiricahua, and Mescalero, but the process by which this occurred is not altogether clear. The Chiricahua and Mescalero dialects are very similar, partly a result of the reservation period, when in 1913, a group of 187 Chiricahua were granted permission to move from Oklahoma to the Mescalero reservation (Schroeder 1974, I, 536).

In the earlier period, the Mescalero, referred to as Faraones, conducted their raiding activities to the south, north, and east from a region on the east side of the Rio Grande. At one point they refused to live on the west of the Rio Grande with an Apache group known as Mimbres, who were part of a more general regional Apache population that the Spanish referred to collectively in many earlier documents as Gila Apache. The Faraones did not consider themselves closely related to these people, nor were they very well disposed toward them (Schroeder 1974, I, 166).

It was in the Gila population, including the Mimbres, that the Chiricahua apparently originated. One observer in the mid-1800s stated that the Gila Apache, different from the Mescalero, were among themselves "identically the same people in language and habits, they range over the same country, are intermarried" (Michael Steck, quoted in Schroeder 1974, I, 172).

Despite their linguistic similarities to Navajo and Western Apache (Dyen and Aberle 1974:216–217), the Chiricahua and Mescalero dialects share significant resemblances with Jicarilla and Lipan as well. The Mescalero spent some time on the southern Plains and may even have been the first native American group to acquire horses. Eventually they withdrew farther into the mountains of New Mexico because of Comanche pressure, but for a time they experienced close and intensive contact with the Jicarilla.

From this perspective the issue of whether or not the sections of the Apache population ancestral to the Chiricahua and Mescalero might have been more closely affiliated with the eastern or western groups may not be particularly meaningful. They had a variety of associations and interactions with each end of the population spectrum.

During the 1600s, from the time of their first appearance in the historic records, the Chiricahua Apache were established in the southeastern Arizona region. Apparently they were named after the mountain range that was thought to be their base of operations, as was the case with many of the other Apache divisions. They raided assiduously and relentlessly to the south into Mexico. Their closest interactions were with groups on the west side of the Rio Grande in central New Mexico, who were known collectively as the Apache of the Gila drainage, including the regional populations called Mimbrès, Coppermine, and Mogollon.

The Mescalero remained to the east of the Rio Grande, raiding south into Chihuahua. Antonio Cordero (quoted in Schroeder 1974, I, 536) writes of the Mescalero in 1776, "This group dwells, generally speaking, in the mountain ranges near the Pecos River, extending northwards on both banks as far as Comancheria. It uses this locality particularly in the proper seasons for the buffalo hunt, on which occasions it joins with the plains group which is its neighbor." The neighboring Plains group probably were Lipan Apache.

Although all of these groups were extremely mobile, apparently most, if not all, planted small plots of corn here and there within their territories. For the most part, they operated out of the mountain ranges scattered throughout New Mexico and Arizona. In 1777 Teodoro de Croix (quoted in Schroeder 1974, IV, 73) described the area between El Paso and Sante Fe as largely uninhabited, being "surrounded on all sides by hills on which the Apaches live and from which they come down to commit hostilities without risk of suffering retaliation."

The earliest reports of Apache late in the sixteenth century focus on the northeastern corner of New Mexico. But the locales of reported Apache in Spanish documents might primarily reflect the places where the Spanish happened to be, rather than the range of the Apache. Aside from a reference to possible Apache near Acoma Pueblo in the 1580s, the earlier accounts generally refer to the regions east of the Rio Grande and indicate a general southward movement of Apache activities over a number of decades.

Although the areas west of the Rio Grande were much less known to the Spanish, by the 1600s the records contain references to Gila Apache and later, more specific references to Mimbres, Coppermine, and Mogollon Apache. Gila Apache territory on the west side of the Rio Grande near the Arizona border ranged from just south of Zuni almost to Mexico.

Through the nineteenth century, the Chiricahua acted as hosts to Apache raiders from other divisions among the Gila groups, occupying a strategic mountain pass that was used regularly as a gateway south into Sonora (Schroeder 1974, IV, 183). No doubt their relationship with other Apache groups helped to maintain, and perhaps even to establish, cultural similarities among them. The Chiricahua may have gravitated into their southerly location to gain an advantageous position for raids into Mexico. Whatever the case, though, their geographic base eventually gave them an identity apart from the other Apache of New Mexico and Arizona. Yet despite this separate identity, in 1859 government agent Michael Steck (quoted in Schroeder 1974, IV, 184) wrote that although the Chiricahua were a distinct group, they were "intimately connected with those of the Mogollon Mountains by intermarriage and habits and if a reservation should be established they should at once be compelled to locate with them on the Gila." In the succeeding reservation period, they were indeed grouped with the Gila divisions, and as a result, the diversity that had begun to develop among these regional populations tended to blur (cf. Schroeder 1974, IV, 138).

Once again in this period in the Southwest, the merging and rejoining of local Apachean populations continued much as it had in the past, albeit for different reasons. Circumstances led to the rejoining of groups whose diverse activities had led them to grow apart, and other ethnic divisions that had not existed before began to develop.

By the mid-1600s, other groups west of the Gila Apache of New Mexico, in what is now east-central Arizona, became more prominent in the literature. They were referred to as Pinal, Arivaipa, and Coyotero, and later came to be known collectively as the Western Apache. Their earlier relationships with the other Apache groups is not clear, but throughout the literature there is evidence of significant differences between these people and the Gila Apache. A strip of uninhabited territory separated them from the Mogollon section of the Gila Apache to the east (Schroeder 1974, IV, 138). Occasionally they joined efforts with the Gila population for enterprises that they conceived to be in their common interest, but in a government report of 1858, a brother of the prominent Gila Apache leader Mangas Coloradas was quoted as saying that his people "had no connection with the Coyoteros."[9]

Apparently the Western Apache had a common origin with the Navajo in the westernmost section of the Proto-Apache population. On the basis of shared linguistic innovations, the Navajo and Western Apache dialects form a distinct unit apart from the other five dialects of Apache. Nonetheless, the depth of the division between Navajo and Western Apache is much greater than those among the other five. The Western Apache (San Carlos) dialect shares cognate words at the level of 94 percent with Navajo, 95 percent with Chiricahua, and 94 percent with Mescalero. Among themselves, Chiricahua, Mescalero, Jicarilla, and Lipan share cognates at the average of 95 percent (Dyen and Aberle 1974: 13). With regard to shared innovations in kinship terms, "early inter-influence was probably followed by a fair degree of isolation, to judge by the number of unshared innovations in San Carlos." (Dyen and Aberle 1974:225). Although Navajo and Western Apache seem to share a common base within the Apache population, that base is fairly old compared to past relationships among the other groups. In some ways the Navajo and Western Apache are more different from one another than the Chiricahua, Mescalero, Jicarilla, or Lipan are among themselves.

Western Apache traditions indicate that they once lived in northern Arizona near the Navajo and Hopi, but that encounter probably would have been too recent and brief to account for the linguistic evidence. Apparently the Navajo entered northern Arizona for the first time from the east in the 1860s as a result of military pressure (cf. Schroeder 1974, I, 478–482; Kelley 1980). They were unfamiliar with the region at that time, and in the course of their migration into the area they had a series of hostile confrontations with Western Apache who were already there. There is no suggestion in the records that the Navajo had any previous, remembered acquaintance with these people.

Much of what we know about the Navajo, in fact, indicates that they might have been among the last of the Apachean groups to enter the Southwest and that they arrived substantially later than the others. Quite the opposite view is held by a number of researchers (Brugge 1981; Schaafsma 1981), but the geographic position of the Navajo as northernmost of the Apache, with the exception of the Kiowa Apache, is consistent with this. At times other Apache groups on the Plains side of the Rockies may have occupied regions to the north of them, but these seem to have been later incursions onto the Plains from a base in the Southwest. The Spanish in the 1600s perceived the Navajo as a group distinct from other Apache (Schroeder 1974, IV, 190, 194). They also seem to be the only Apache who maintained a belief that other people like them lived far to the north (Ellis 1974:47–52).

On the basis of the frequencies of twenty-four blood group genes, Emoke Szathmary (1977:117) concludes that although there is little difference among Apache in general, the Navajo are more similar to Northern Athapaskan populations than are the other Apache. Moreover, with regard to the Northern Athapaskan population, they also score closer to the Slave, Sarsi, and Chilcotin at the southern range of the distribution than to the Kutchin or Tutchone farther to the north.

This suggests something about Apachean migration patterns into the Southwest. Although some of these population movements probably took place along the eastern slopes of the Rockies, there is no reason to see the migration as having been limited to that side of the mountains, since this historic Apachean population was spread widely from east to west. The western region around the Colorado Plateau was largely unknown to Europeans well into the eighteenth century. The western groups of Apache not only share a number of distinctive linguistic and cultural features among themselves but also patterns suggesting some contact with Uto-Aztecan groups who inhabit the western side of the Rockies verging toward the Great Basin.

Some of these features could be the result of later influences, but others, such as the dome-shaped willow-covered house form, appear in very early accounts. Some researchers argue that early Navajo pottery resembles a type found in certain Plains sites dated in the 1600s, but it also is typical of a type of utility ware made throughout a broad range from the Plains westward through the Great Basin. The Navajo pattern, in fact, is almost indistinguishable from Paiute ware (Ellis 1974:47–52).

Considering the linguistic, historical, and ethnographic evidence, it seems most plausible that the Navajo and Western Apache shared a common past in the region north of their present territory and that the Western Apache preceded the Navajo into the Southwest. By the time they encountered each other again in northern Arizona, they had become strangers. They could still communicate through dialects of the same language, but their interactions were tentative and often volatile.

Western Apache legend attributes their departure from the Navajo in northern Arizona to the activities of a quarrelsome woman, whose banishment along with her relatives gave rise to the Navajo (Goodwin 1969:71–72). No doubt there is another side to this story. But in any case, after a series of Navajo incursions into Western Apache territory south of the Mogollon Rim in the 1860s, both populations apparently withdrew to leave a buffer zone between them that each tended to avoid for fear of encountering the other.

Whatever the exact reason for their departure, in a wider context it represents another manifestation of the diversity among segments of the Apachean population. Whether metaphorical or not, the tale of the quarrelsome woman expresses the tone of the relationship between these groups, which seems always to have been uneasy and often hostile, in the absence of formal social structures capable of mediating disputes between such autonomous, free-ranging aggregates. Despite their recognition of shared cultural features, a certain amount of distrust and a fair degree of active conflict characterized interactions between the Western Apache and the Navajo throughout the historic period.

An old-style dwelling, San Carlos

Much evidence indicates that the Apache entry into their present territories progressed southward through New Mexico along the east side of the Rio Grande, with some of the population, drawn by the establishment of new Spanish settlements in Mexico, later crossing to the west side in southern New Mexico to become known as the Gila Apache (Schroeder 1974, IV, 512). This model seems plausible as far as it applies to the groups of New Mexico, but it appears more likely that the Western Apache entered their region from the northeast, from the direction of the Hopi. The early sites in the La Plata River Valley and the San Juan drainage of New Mexico tend to support this idea. The territory between Pueblo communities and Spanish settlements was largely devoid of population, and small groups of Apache would have found it easy to pass through these almost empty lands whose inhabitants were clustered in small, scattered agricultural communities.

It would be difficult to account for the Western Apache's differences from Gila groups if they had been a recent offshoot of the Gila segment of the population. On the other hand, if the Western Apache had diverged from the rest of the Apache population farther north and finally had ended up adjacent to their former kin by way of a different route, their distinctness is more readily accountable. The uninhabited strip of territory between these groups underscores their differences. A similar uninhabited zone also separated the Western Apache from the Navajo.

By the time the Navajo and the Western Apache encountered each other in northern Arizona, each had had generations of experience in the Southwest. The Navajo had a fair amount of contact with the Jicarilla during at least certain phases of their history, and at various times they engaged in hostile and friendly relationships with Utes from the northwest. The Jicarilla, Navajo, and other Apachean groups bore the impact of a Ute-Comanche alliance in the 1700s.

The Navajo also experienced far more intimate and sustained contact with Pueblo peoples than the Western Apache did, and they incorporated entire contingents of Pueblo peoples into their population. In the process the Navajo adopted many Puebloan cultural features (Ellis 1974: 106–116). Like other Apache they engaged extensively in subsistence raiding, and perhaps more than the other groups, they developed long-standing visiting and trading relationships with Pueblo communities. The most intensive Puebloan influences on them probably came as a result of the Pueblo Revolt against the Spanish in the late 1600s. During those years an influx of Pueblo people found refuge among the Navajo, and numerous intermarriages occurred. As a result, many aspects of Navajo ideology, ceremonial, and material culture show the influence of Pueblo cultural systems. The entire Navajo creation myth, in fact, appears to correspond almost exactly to the Jemez Pueblo version (Ellis 1974: 116).

The adoption of agriculture was one of the most important changes affecting the Navajo at an early period. They developed the present form of their system of matrilineal clans in association with this change in subsistence, although the fundamental principle of matrilineal descent was a part of the general Apachean cultural repertoire. Navajo territory does not have a particularly rich natural food supply compared with many other regions of the Southwest. Hence, agriculture, and later sheep herding, became increasingly important to them, first as a source of food to be acquired through trading and raids on agricultural peoples, and later as a means of producing food directly for their own use. By the mid-nineteenth century, Navajo food production had become such an essential part of their subsistence quest that a military campaign to destroy their fields and orchards effectively undermined their political autonomy.

The Navajo surrender to the United States government and their removal to Fort Sumner in New Mexico is probably the most bitterly remembered and tragic event in their past. Many of them died, either on the way or during their confinement. After they finally were allowed to return to northern Arizona, however, their population increased to the extent that they now have become one of the most populous native American groups in North America.

It may have been during the early years in Arizona when the Navajo and Western Apache were still in fairly close contact that the Western Apache also began to practice agriculture more intensively. This shift in the Western Apache food quest could also have been a response to Pueblo influence, either directly or through interaction with the Navajo. The Western Apache clan system shows a number of specific resemblances to the Navajo system, including some clans with the same names (Goodwin 1969:109–110).[10] The Western Apache associate agriculture with the benevolent *gaan* (mountain spirits resembling Hopi *katcinas*) who, according to one tradition, showed a young woman how to grow crops at a time when the people were starving during the period when they lived near the Navajo. But the *gaan* are associated with hunting as well, and they may have more ancient continuities with supernatural powers associated with the food quest in the North. Their association with mountains underscores this older cultural base, and in a sense they may represent a personification of an ancient abstract concern of Apachean peoples (Goodwin 1969:71–72).[11]

It is conceivable that the Pueblo communities had a special motivation to encourage agriculture among the Apache. Since the Apache had incorporated agricultural foods into their subsistence pattern, it might have been preferable from a Pueblo point of view to have the Apache grow their own crops rather than acquire them through subsistence raiding. Whatever the circumstances of the acquisition of agriculture might have been, though, Western Apache contacts with the Pueblo communities were far more intermittent and less intense than Navajo interactions with these sedentary farming peoples. Consequently, Puebloan influences on Western Apache culture have been far weaker.

Below the Mogollon Rim, the Western Apache directed their attention less toward the Navajo than to the village peoples in southern Arizona and Mexico. From their camps in the mountains of the Gila and Salt river drainages, they struck southward through mountain trails to raid the towns and ranches of Sonora. The Western Apache reliance on crops never became their sole or even their primary means of subsistence. The natural food supply in Western Apache territory was richer and more varied than it was in Navajo territory to the north, and they probably could have given up their gardens at any time and survived on wild foods (Goodwin, cited in Opler 1972).

But perhaps the most important factor was that eventually the Western Apache, like the Chiricahua, Mimbres, Mogollon, Coppermine, Mescalero, Jicarilla, Lipan, and Navajo, all developed a raiding complex that focused on sources of livestock in Mexico as a major component of their food quest. The following pages will examine the life-style associated with this era in Western Apache culture history more closely.

CHAPTER 8

The Western Apache

By the time the Western Apache had established themselves south of the Mogollon Rim, a sense of relationship among widely separated sections of the Apache population probably was fading. As the others adapted to their particular situations, the Western Apache took advantage of opportunities that the natural food sources in eastern Arizona afforded them. They focused the thrust of their subsistence raiding toward the villages of the south and established farm plots associated with groups of kin who were related by descent through women.

In the early nineteenth century, they held most of eastern Arizona as far south as the city of Tucson. The Pinal section of the Western Apache operated from the mountains near the junction of the Gila and San Pedro rivers. After the Sobaipuri Pima withdrew in the face of Apache raids, the Arivaipa Apache occupied the area to the south. The Coyotero Apache held lands to the northeast in the mountains from the Gila River to the Sierra Blanca range south of the Mogollon Rim.

Throughout this territory a variety of ecological zones offered subsistence at various times of the year, just as in the other regions their ancestors had occupied. The food quest ranged from the relatively low areas of the northern Sonoran Desert in southern Arizona to the higher altitudes with grassland and forest toward the north. The Western Apache had access to a wider variety of wild plant foods than any other group in western North America (Jorgenson 1980:127). In this region they maintained ancient strategies derived from the Subarctic. They camped in small clusters and moved from place to place, attuned to the subsistence opportunities of the moment. They gathered in larger aggregates when possible and scattered easily when it was necessary. Their farm plots added to this repertoire, providing temporary bases to which groups of people would return at certain times of the year, to depart subsequently for other locales. In some ways the encampments near farm plots were analogous to the base camps of the Subarctic near salmon rivers or caribou drive sites.

They added the strategy of subsistence raiding to their pattern without modifying it, at first, in any radical way. Small parties could depart on raiding excursions hundreds of miles to the south into Mexico and after a few weeks return to their seasonal camps with livestock.

Cultural Modifications

In the course of the Western Apache's adaptation to the Southwest, old patterns were modified and refined even as they persisted. The ideological concern with femaleness took a more positive form, possibly, as mentioned earlier, as a result of women's direct contribution to subsistence. But contact with other groups in the Southwest also influenced the practices associated with this aspect of belief. Puberty recognition shifted away from an emphasis on seclusion, with its associated behavioral restrictions and their implied sense of danger, toward more celebrative, public ceremonies. They may have held public female puberty ceremonies before they entered the Southwest, since these occurred in all of the Apache groups. A similar pattern occurs among the Carrier and the Athapaskan peoples of the Pacific Coast (Jorgensen 1980:282). Even so, the prominent role played by the masked *gaan* impersonators and the incorporation of corn grinding and other features gave the ceremony a distinctly Southwestern flavor.

The ceremonial structure under which the initiate danced with her female companion continued among the Western Apache as a remote echo of the seclusion hut. But increasingly, the emphasis on health, strength, beauty, and long life for the young woman, as well as the beneficial influence she could bestow on those around her while she was in that special condition, came to predominate. The female power that imbued her condensed ideologically as an anthropomorphic, benevolent female deity.

Nonetheless, direct continuities from the past are clear. The ancient scratching stick and drinking tube continued to be used in the puberty ceremony, with the stipulation that the young woman drink only warm water and keep her eyes cast down. The bull roarer retained its place in the culture through the long migration south. The potential threat associated with certain aspects of femaleness, particularly regarding the direct exposure of men to childbirth or menstruation, retained its place in Apache thought, but this more dangerous aspect was relatively downplayed.

The abstract power of femaleness became far more benevolent and less threatening than it had been in the Subarctic. Perhaps it is significant in this regard that, according to some Western Apache traditions, it was a young woman to whom the *gaan* gave agriculture, saving the people during a time of starvation. Moreover, Western Apache women had substantial influence and status. The matrilocal residence pattern, which entailed that a married woman continue to live with her parents, sisters, and unmarried brothers, may have reinforced women's position to some extent, providing them with considerable domestic support. Other aspects of culture, ranging from the concept that the wife owned the couple's dwelling to the importance of her contribution to subsistence, must also have strengthened women's position in Western Apache society. The generally high degree of male absenteeism that the northern subsistence pattern had demanded continued in the Southwest, although the resources differed.

Some aspects of Western Apache ideology seem to have changed very little in the journey to the Southwest. Ghosts continued to be a source of dread. They whistled in the dark or appeared to people in dreams or in the form of owls, and they could cause sickness through fear. People continued to take ancient measures to guard against them. They removed the bodies through holes made in the walls of their dwellings and buried their dead with all personal belongings. Relatives did not mention the name of the deceased, and they destroyed or abandoned the dwellings. In the 1930s one Western Apache told Grenville Goodwin (1969:521), "When someone is dead, you can't call his name. You must not do it where the kin of the dead people are. If you did and they heard you, they might get mad and say: 'Do you see where he is standing? He is not here. What do you want to call him for?'"

As Athapaskan peoples did in the Subarctic, they used the sweat bath for enjoyment and good health, although preparatory sweating acquired a religious aspect in the girls' puberty ceremony. The Western Apache acquired numerous other features after their departure from the North as well. The mythological character Coyote, who also appears in the mythology of the Pacific Coast Athapaskans, has a widespread distribution throughout much of western North America. But Coyote is not a feature of the Subarctic region, which is outside the animal's range. Joseph Jorgensen (1980:183) notes that "the Coyote was an important mythological character among all Shoshonean Uto-Aztecan speakers" and occurs among northern Plains groups to the east. The Apache may have acquired Coyote during the transition from the North during the Apachean migration from either side of the Rockies.

The Western Apache also adopted the Great Basin-style dome-shaped dwelling, made of a frame of bent poles and covered with brush or hides with a smoke hole left in the top. Ranging from four to ten feet in height at the center, it usually was built on the surface of the ground without an excavated floor and with the entrance facing east or northeast. This type of dwelling differs in many details from those of the Navajo, who used both a squat, conical structure of forked poles joined at the top and later, a hogan with horizontal log walls.[1]

Like the rest of the Apachean populations, the Western Apache acquired the general Southwestern aversion to fish or any other water-dwelling creatures as food. There is little evidence of such a pattern among Northern or Pacific Coast Athapaskans, for whom fish often constituted a vital resource. In some of these northern groups, though, fish are more an expedient than a preferred food.[2] Many Pueblo peoples also consider fish unacceptable as food.

The Food Quest

Beyond the multitude of relatively minor cultural additions and modifications, the Subarctic derivation and continuity of Western Apache culture from their northern heritage is recognizable. Remote as central Arizona may be from the mountains of the Subarctic, many of the same essential strategies that had proved successful in the North continued to be effective in the Southwest. A nonspecialized pattern of exploiting the multiple zones of mountainous areas through small, mobile, autonomous social aggregates allowed the Apache to hold a vast and hotly contested territory for centuries. In its most salient aspects, eastern Arizona was a suitable medium for the Apachean pattern in the sense that their ancient strategies from the North could apply there without radical changes.

It seems clear that the factors that led the people into Arizona in the first place had a great deal to do with their continuation of older subsistence practices in equivalent ecological settings, rather than abruptly shifting into a different milieu. From the viewpoint of Apache subsistence, in many important respects, Arizona was more like the Subarctic and the Rockies than it was different.

Goodwin's (1969 : 157–158) description of the nineteenth-century food quest, some three centuries or so after the Apache arrival in the

Southwest, sheds some light on the patterns of previous generations. Hunting continued throughout the year and focused on a variety of game, particularly deer.[3] The Western Apache hunted elk and various birds and small mammals, although they avoided peccaries and fish. Apparently they had abandoned the game drive system because of a lack of large herd animals.

Late fall and winter were the most important times for hunting. Mescal sprouted on the southern mountain slopes in early April, and groups traveled to these areas to harvest and prepare it in a manner long used by Mexican peoples. With the spring rains in May, families gravitated toward their garden plots in river valleys, where they usually stayed until their corn plants had gotten off to a good start in early July. In the following weeks, small groups would tend to drift away from the gardens, some of them making their way into the low desert regions to harvest saguaro cactus fruit. In midsummer ripe acorns attracted scattered groups to the stands of Emmory's oak in the higher elevations, where families picked the nuts by the thousands as they camped together to socialize and enjoy the harvest.

Acorns probably constituted the basic staple for the Western Apache. At this time of year, small expeditions would also venture back to check the gardens for green corn, but it was only in September that they fully harvested the plantings. During August, in the meantime, some people gathered mesquite beans in the lower desert regions, returning to their gardens eventually to harvest whatever had been produced. Still later in the fall, they gathered piñon nuts and juniper berries. Raiding, which was also an important part of the Western Apache subsistence pattern, took place during the fall and winter.

Although there is no way of telling precisely when the Western Apache added farming to their yearly round, even in the nineteenth century it had not come to dominate their subsistence. For the most part, it was a quantitative addition to their food quest rather than a qualitative change. Goodwin is explicit about this, stressing that to some extent agriculture was a "luxury" to the Western Apache. Interspersed throughout their territory were families and local groups who did not grow crops, interacting regularly with those who did. "Agriculture was not an integral part of their culture, and they could easily get along without it if they had to, as in all parts of the W.A. territory there were sufficient varieties of wild plants growing, and game on which they could sustain themselves alone."[4]

There is little reason to doubt the ultimate Pueblo origins of Western Apache agriculture.[5] When the Apache occupied the northeastern region of Arizona, they acquired it as an appendage to what remained predominantly a hunting and gathering base. It also seems likely that during their early farming period, the association of kin groups with desirable farm plots, as well as the influence of other groups in the Southwest, influenced the form in which the Western Apache system of matrilineal clans developed.[6]

The Clan System and Social Organization

Whether the presence of strong matrilineal clans among the western Pueblos affected the historic form of the Western Apache system, the basic ingredients for this system had long been a part of Apachean social organization. Matrilocal residence was an aspect of the ancient culture base, and the principle of defining interpersonal relationships through women was a fundamental aspect of Athapaskan cultures. It is not surprising that, when conditions allowed or stimulated the development of a more complex system of descent groups, they were built on the theme of matrilineal ties. At the same time, though, the association of clans with farm plots did not lead to any rigid territorial system that might have interfered with the mobility of these aggregates or, by implication, with their capacity to subsist.

The Western Apache clan system of the nineteenth century and probably earlier was uniquely suited to the needs of a people whose priorities still emphasized a high degree of option and movement among small independent local groups. The clans did nothing to curtail that mobility, but at the same time they provided a far-flung abstract network of individual ties with strong interpersonal attachments. These amounted to obligations and expectations that bound people together over wide territories without hampering their autonomy.

The most salient concrete unit in the Western Apache social structure was the matrilocal joint family (*gota*). Typically this consisted of a senior couple with perhaps one or two unmarried children, composing a central household linked to those of their married daughters with their husbands and children. The size of a *gota* could vary considerably, but such a group might include thirty or more people. This was the basic unit of Apache society, a cluster of people who were essentially self-sufficient and capable of operating independently on a day-to-day basis. In these *gota* the Western Apache raised their children, planned raids, and gathered, prepared, and ate their food. The husbands married into the *gota*, but the women and children were matrilineal "blood" relatives, members by birth. The numerous Spanish accounts of Apache *rancherías* attacked in the seventeenth and eighteenth centuries throughout the Southwest note Apache casualties ranging from a dozen to forty or so, suggesting that such a residence pattern probably was typical of the other Apache populations during those times as well.

As children grew up in such a setting, the people they knew best and interacted with every day were their mothers' sisters and their families. The other children of the *gota*, a child's closest playmates, were parallel cousins—all matrilineal kin. Every person had many other relatives throughout the region as well, but in Western Apache society the experiences of one's early years were structured to nurture strong feelings of personal bonds to the close matrilineal relatives. As a social unit, the *gota* had a rather short "structural duration" (Gluckman 1968). A particular *gota's* existence depended on the life cycle of its constituent members. Usually it would end when the senior couple died, whereupon the married daughters with their families might form new *gota* of their own. Because of these factors, a particular *gota* might last for less than the lifetime of an individual, even though the *gota* as a form of social organization was endlessly replicated. This temporal instability tended to enforce the frequent readjustment of the population, maintaining the flexibility so vital to the subsistence pattern (Perry 1972).

Although the individual *gota* could operate by itself, gregariousness was a prime Western Apache virtue. Whenever the situation allowed it, *gota* would tend to cluster. *Gota* headed by sisters would sometimes join to form larger aggregates, in which case all of the people except for the men who had married into the *gota* would be matrilineal kin. On the other hand, marriage of a man to a woman of his father's clan (or from a woman's perspective, to a man of her mother's brother's wife's clan) was the preferred form. Anthropologists refer to this as classificatory patrilateral cross-cousin marriage.

This marriage pattern results in linkages between pairs of clans. In a matrilineal system, a man belongs to his mother's clan. If he marries a woman of his father's clan, this marriage reiterates the linkage between the two clans expressed in his parents' marriage. Because of this, it would not be unusual for several of the in-marrying husbands to be members of a single clan. But these patterns were not rigid. *Gota* could form larger aggregates for a number of reasons, and for at least as many reasons, they could separate. These linkages among *gota* were even less stable than the *gota* themselves.

The belief system, particularly those aspects having to do with death, impelled this dynamic, shifting process still further. The feeling of dread associated with the scene of death, the destruction of the dwelling, and the abandonment of the site all tended to ensure that groups would not become "locked into" any particular locality but would continue to cover wide territories. By the same token, strictures against mentioning the name of the deceased effectively prevented any deep genealogically based structures that might have led to more rigid social units.

Western Apache clans were abstract social categories whose members were recruited by the fact of birth, but they required no record keeping of past relatives. A person belonged to a particular clan simply because his or her mother did. In other localities there often were people who belonged to the same category, for the same reason of birth. But unless people were very close relatives, it was unlikely that they would keep track of their specific kin ties. Instead, there was a tacit recognition that they and their people shared a common identity, demonstrated in their clan name. Members of the same clan referred to one another by the same terms used for siblings. They were expected, ideally, to behave toward one another in a manner appropriate to the relationship that the use of brother and sister terms implied.

The Western Apache also considered clans to be related to one another in several degrees of closeness (Goodwin 1969 : 68). The obligations and expectations incumbent upon members of the same clan extended to members of related clans as well, but to a weaker degree. Prohibition of marriage was probably the most clearly defined aspect of this relationship and extended to members of all related clans. The preferred marriage of men to women of their fathers' clan linked those clans to one another through affinal ties. This system may never have been followed rigidly, but even in recent times the Western Apache felt that members of certain clans usually married one another.

In the nineteenth century, Western Apache kinship terms that grouped the father's brother's children and mother's sister's children with one's own brothers and sisters expressed these clan ties. Anthropologists usually refer to cousins of this sort, children of siblings of the same sex (the mother and her sister, for example), as parallel cousins. In the Western Apache case, this terminological category reflected the fact that most, and perhaps all, of these people would be members of one's own clan. Not only were parallel cousins called by the same kin terms as siblings, but these sibling terms applied to people of the same generation throughout the rest of the clan as well (Opler 1937). On the other hand, children of a person's mother's brothers and father's sisters, whom anthropologists classify as cross-cousins, were referred to by terms different from those that applied to parallel cousins and siblings. This is a classic Iroquois type of cousin terminology.

Given the clanwide extension of kin terms, the preferred marriage of a man to a woman of his father's clan meant that he would marry a woman who stood as his father's sister's daughter. Conversely, a woman in that situation would marry a man who stood as her mother's brother's son. These were not literally first cousins; the kin terms reflected categories of clan membership. It is interesting to recall that the same pattern, producing a repetition of marriage ties between pairs of clans, also characterized the Ahtna of Alaska and other Northern Athapaskan groups (de Laguna and McClellan 1981:653).

The maintenance of option and flexibility in Western Apache social organization precluded a total adherence to this pattern, but the kin terms are structured as if this were the usual practice. One of the most striking things about the way in which the organization of personal ties was transmitted into far-flung clan networks, though, is the degree to which a complex system of abstract social categories came to pervade and link the population over thousands of square miles without hampering the mobility of small family units in the least.

In the late nineteenth century, the Western Apache had well over sixty clans, each with its traditional place of origin. Accounts of clan origins were not sacred tales or myths. By the early twentieth century, the origins of a few clans had been forgotten, but in most cases accounts of clan origins seem to have been straightforward recollections of the farm plots with which they had been associated, perhaps blurred a bit through time. For the most part, these traditions relate specific clan histories in terms of geographic associations, without a precise sense of chronological duration.

Except for a few clans that originated with outsiders who had been adopted into the Western Apache network, the places of origin of all clans are in the northern part of historic Western Apache territory or somewhat farther to the north of their range, either strung out along the Little Colorado River Valley or its tributaries or below the Mogollon Rim. The north-to-south pattern is clear in Goodwin's (1969, inside covers) map of clan migrations.

The Western Apache viewed the clan system as something that they had always had. The local Southwestern origins of many of the clans might seem to contradict this, but the generation of scores of recent clans in the nineteenth century does not preclude the prior existence of a more ancient structure from the North. Many of the Athapaskans of the Subarctic Cordillera had matrilineal clan and moiety systems. From the perspective of its underlying principles, at least, the perception that the Western Apache clan system had ancient roots seems valid (Goodwin 1969: 103–104).

The Raiding Complex

Apache raiding patterns became a significant factor in the history of the Southwest, and in later periods the character of raiding came to resemble warfare. It is difficult to tell when raiding began as a normal, regular activity for Apache groups, but in many ways it must have been an outgrowth of the pragmatic and varied subsistence pattern that the people had brought with them from the far north—a pattern that entailed the use of a wide range of available resources.

The historical record does not reveal any major divisions of the Apache population which were not involved in raiding at one time or another in their history, from the Lipan who battled French and Pawnee in Eastern Texas to the Western Apache who raided as far west as the Gulf of California in Mexico. Whether this implies an early origin for the raiding pattern among the Proto-Apache population or the rapid spread of an idea at a later time is difficult to ascertain. It is clear that raiding was fundamentally compatible with the sociocultural organization of all of the Apachean groups. On the other hand, it is clear that the intensity of raiding, if not the pattern itself, was stimulated by hostile actions on the part of other groups in the Southwest, particularly the Spanish engaged in slave raids. Trade, rather than thefts, characterized Apache interactions with sedentary peoples until the 1630s.

When the people came into the Southwest via the Rocky Mountain system and encountered sedentary, town-dwelling agricultural peoples, they quickly saw these villages with their stored food as an additional source of subsistence, whether through trade, raiding or both on an ad hoc basis. The distinction between game free for the taking and livestock grazing on the open range, which often displaced game, may not have been particularly convincing to the Apache, especially when it involved a sense of ownership quite different from Apache concepts of legitimate rights. The early phase of Apache raiding, violent as it often was, was primarily a facet of the food quest. As a subsistence method, raiding involved no implicit motivation to destroy or drive out the people who were responsible for the production of these resources (Spicer 1962: 239). In later generations, when peoples of European origins moved into the Southwest in greater numbers, the pattern was continued and was extended to them as well. The element of hostility on the part of Apache varied with time, place, and circumstance.

There is reason to suspect that up to the sixteenth century, Uto-Aztecan speakers occupied the central and southern Arizona region. Movements and disruptions among the Pima and Opata of northern Sonora and southwestern Arizona during that time may have led to a migration of the Opata from the Arizona mountains into the valley regions of northern Mexico (Spicer 1962:87, 233). If so, this would have coincided with an Apachean population establishing themselves in northern Arizona. They might already have developed a pattern of striking south from the region of the Mogollon Rim, eventually helping to cause the earlier inhabitants of the area to abandon it.

From the perspective of the Spanish who attempted to secure their northwest frontier in Sonora, the areas to the north of the familiar Opata villages were inhabited by elusive, dangerous bands of nomads who struck by surprise and disappeared into unknown regions without allowing reprisal. The situation at first did not permit the Spanish to differentiate the raiders from one another. Some of them, such as the Suma and Jocome, may have been speakers of Uto-Aztecan or Hokan languages. They have long since disappeared without their identities ever having been firmly established in history (Spicer 1962:233).[7] It is not until after 1600 that the term *Apache* becomes well established in Spanish records. By the early years of the next century, the people known by this name appear to have held exclusive domain over the eastern part of Arizona (Spicer 1962:229).

During these years, which probably encompassed the first few generations of Apache in the Southwest (when the people incorporated raiding and farming into their already varied subsistence activities), they extended their sovereignty throughout thousands of square miles of territory. Their informal leadership and the independence of small joint family clusters which had been an ancient part of their heritage persisted throughout this era. Each small group had its respected senior figures whose authority rested mostly on personal abilities and the respect they inspired, but the records are consistent in underscoring the independence of individuals. On occasion, the draw of an exceptional man might attract a greater number of families to associate with his group, but such large aggregates were ephemeral. The population remained essentially fluid and loosely structured.

As the Western Apache precipitated into various local regions, people in particular localities developed a degree of cultural distinctness that gave rise to divisions which later became known as Arivaipa, Coyotero, and Pinal. Subtle differences in speech and cultural style developed among the various bands, and geographic distance and social or topographic barriers between groups cultivated this sense of identity. But these differences were much less marked than the changes that already had set the Western Apache apart from the Navajo to the north and the Chiricahua and Gila Apache to the south and east.

Unlike Apache groups farther east, such as the Jicarilla and Lipan, from whom the Western Apache now had been separated for a number of generations and might no longer even have known about, the Western Apache had very little close contact with non-Apache peoples. In addition to the mutually hostile regard that followed their separation from the Navajo, contact with the Apache of the upper Gila drainage, including those who later became known as the Chiricahua, apparently was sporadic. From the late seventeenth century on, it probably consisted mostly of passing through Chiricahua lands on raids into Mexico, even though in the nineteenth century they still regarded themselves as similar peoples.

The Western Apache saw the Pima, Papago, Opata, Spanish, and other groups to the south as producers of potential resources. Only in some circumstances, which eventually became more frequent, did they also define them more absolutely as enemies. Unlike the Navajo, whose continued, if ambivalent, contacts with the western Pueblo Villages and Spanish led them to incorporate many features from these groups into their culture, the Western Apache remained much more culturally isolated. This conforms to the assessment of Dyen and Aberle (1974:224–225), who suggest on the basis of the linguistic evidence of unshared innovations that the Western Apache's earlier contact with the Navajo "was probably followed by a fair degree of isolation."

By the mid-1600s Apache raiding parties often set out on foot across the Gila River southward down through jagged peaks and mountain valleys to strike two hundred miles or more from the home camps in the north, where their families awaited their return. Parties ranging in size from two or three men to a dozen or more slipped easily between the line of presidios the Spanish had built across Sonora Province. The Western Apache struck by surprise deep in Mexico, making off with livestock and anything else of value to them and retreated into the vastness of their own territory before military reaction was possible. Although they exploited the settlements of Sonora for centuries, their main concern was property

(Spicer 1962:239). To the frustration of the Spanish, they avoided battle whenever possible and used ambush and other guerrilla tactics when pursuit became too hot. To the east the Mescalero and the Apache of the Gila drainage pursued the same pattern in Chihuahua.[8]

Edward Spicer (1962:239) writes that "in the second half of the eighteenth century, it was evident that the Apaches had perfected a way of life which called for no increase in their territory and no desire to defeat the Spaniards in what the latter called battles. The Apaches aimed merely at supplying their shifting camps in the mountains of southeastern Arizona and southwestern New Mexico by raids whenever they wished."

At times contingents of Spanish troops ventured north of the Gila looking for Apache raiders and killed the few people they encountered. But these Spanish expeditions had little effect on raiding except to add an element of bitter vengeance for relatives who had been slain, providing extra motivation for subsequent raiding parties.

In the earlier years, the Spanish tended to underestimate the distances traveled by the raiders. In at least one instance, they attacked and killed Sobaipuri Pima in southern Arizona who had had nothing to do with Apache raids except that they had been victims of the same pattern (Spicer 1962:234, 338).

Over the decades the Western Apache came to depend more and more on raids for livestock, including horses, which they used mostly as food. Their domination of the vast area from the Navajo territory to the Sonora frontier in Mexico kept them far more isolated from Spanish influence than many of the other Southwestern groups, and as a consequence, there are few reliable descriptions of them in the literature of the period. What occurred during these years, though, was more a shift in the balance of old patterns than a revolutionary change. They added a "war dance" as a preparatory ritual before embarking on sorties to the south, and to the ancient female puberty ritual they added celebrative victory ceremonies in which women played a major part following successful raids.

At this time and for generations afterward, the Western Apache carried out raiding and warfare in an individualistic way with recruitment on a voluntary basis, or at most, involving a sense of collaboration among relatives. The pattern did not give rise to authoritarian leadership. Only after a party embarking on a raid had entered foreign territory south of the Gila River did the raid leader exercise complete authority. His functions were to coordinate the enterprise and to fortify and encourage the other raiders. He was referred to by a term meaning "he destroys dew" because he walked ahead toward the enemy, and the example of his own courage was as important an aspect of his leadership as his exhortations to his companions. But his position as leader existed only in the context of raiding. When the enterprise was over, he was "just a common man" (Goodwin and Basso 1971:254, 255).

Throughout these centuries there were numerous attempts to establish peaceful relationships. Late in the eighteenth century, the "Galvez reforms" imposed significant changes in Spanish policies that for a short time, at least, seemed effective. Recognizing that any decisive military solution was unlikely, the Spanish attempted to attract Apache groups to their posts peacefully by offering rations. The Spanish reasoned that as long as ample food was supplied, there would be less incentive for the Apache to bear the risks and effort of raiding.

As a few Apache groups came in to partake of this windfall, the Spanish attempted to create a chronic dependency on their largess. The people were encouraged to drink heavily, and the Spanish tried to exacerbate any frictions that occurred when these formerly wide-ranging bands were drawn together to interact with each other at close quarters in an unusual setting. The Spanish hoped to encourage feuds in order to further nullify the Apache as a military threat.

In succeeding years this policy had its effects, particularly, as might be expected, among groups whose territories were southernmost and who therefore had the easiest access to the Spanish settlements. A few seem to have lost their independence as well as the respect of both the Spanish and other Apache groups. Some, who became known as Apaches Mansos ("tame" Apache), lived in southern Arizona into the nineteenth century and came to be considered enemy people by the Western Apache and Chiricahua (Goodwin 1969:86; Spicer 1962:240).

The full potential of this program for undermining the ancient autonomy of the Apache never was realized, since after the Mexican war of independence from Spain, funds for the rationing program dwindled. As the various Apache aggregates began to turn away from the rationing centers and to move north into their old territories, raids increased. The people of Sonora formed volunteer armies. Small, isolated villages of farmers, who struggled to produce enough to survive, had little hope of defending themselves effectively, and even the organized expeditions were poorly equipped and ill trained. Many had no firearms and had to use bows and arrows.

The governors of Sonora and Chihuahua offered bounties in pesos equivalent to fifty to one hundred dollars for each Apache scalp, a practice that resulted in the deaths of large numbers of people, often children and women who were surprised at their encampments. The carnage grew to the extent that the number of scalps turned in exceeded by far the funds available to pay the bounty (Spicer 1962: 240–241).

Yet throughout this period, the situation was far more complex than a simple enmity between two groups. By many accounts, the Apache spent considerable time in Mexican towns, and some Apache even entered into *compadrazco* relationships with Mexicans, becoming godparents to their children. They not only traded but played cards and drank together, which often proved to be a volatile situation, however, and at times Mexican authorities unsuccessfully tried to prohibit such exchanges.

To understand this situation, it is necessary to realize that Apache perceptions of the Mexican population reflected the way the Apache perceived themselves—as small groups of independent, politically autonomous people. In Apache thought, peaceful relationships with one Mexican village might be honored without breach, but this had no bearing on their actions toward other villages. The Mexican authorities, on the other hand, accustomed to defining populations in terms of state systems, seem to have had difficulty understanding or dealing with the atomistic nature of Apache social organization. They often tended to visualize interactions in terms of larger social categories which had no meaning to the Apache. This sometimes led to claims of betrayal and to mistaken accusations of one Apache for the actions of another.

Things were complicated still more by bad feelings that arose between different Mexican provinces over the Apache. At times, for example, the people of Sonora suspected that the Apache who camped peacefully near Chihuahua presidios raided Sonoran villages and fled back into Chihuahua, where they were safe from pursuit. In Chihuahua the Comanche also raided in large groups and engaged in hostilities with the eastern Apache as well as Mexicans, although the Western Apache rarely, if ever, encountered them. Bandits from the Mexican population also disguised themselves as Apache to steal livestock from other Mexicans. Finally, by the early nineteenth century, Anglo-Americans became more common in the area. Some of the most notorious were attracted by the bounty. One "Santiago" Kirker, hired at one point by the Mexican government as a mercenary against the Apache, was dismissed subsequently because the authorities found his methods dishonorable and reprehensible.

Many Apache were captured and sold as slaves throughout the eighteenth and nineteenth centuries, and some of the Apache sold captives for the slave market as well. The effect of the slave trade on native American populations in the Southwest was such that one observer in the nineteenth century maintained that almost every household in New Mexico had Navajo children as domestic servants (Ellis 1974).[9]

By the early nineteenth century, most Apache had come to regard the people of northern Sonora not only as a source of raiding booty but as enemies in a more absolute sense. More and more of the Apache had had relatives killed by Mexican troops or bounty hunters, and more and more, the acquisition of property as an incentive to raid was coupled with the quest for revenge. According to George Bancroft (quoted in Schroeder 1974, IV, 365), as a result of Apache attacks between 1820 and 1835, "no less than 5000 lives had been lost . . . at least 100 ranches, haciendas, mining camps, and other settlements had been destroyed; . . . from 3,000 to 4,000 settlers had been obliged to quit the northern frontier [of Mexico]; . . . in the extreme north absolutely nothing was left but the demoralized garrisons of worthless soldiers." Captives and slaves were taken by both sides, and in some cases the Apache brought back Mexican captives to be killed by women who had lost relatives (Goodwin and Basso 1971:284). But the Apache also adopted captives, who became integrated into their social system. In some cases these captives later declined the chance to return to their former people and chose instead to remain with the Apache.

It was in the time of intensive conflict in the 1840s, during what could be considered true warfare with the people of northwestern Mexico, that the Western Apache began to encounter significant numbers of English-speaking Americans in their territory. In earlier times a few fur trappers had appeared along the Gila River, and individual traders had made contact with the Western Apache in their territory (Goodwin 1969:95).[10] Despite their growing animosity toward Mexico, the Western Apache considered the Anglo-Americans to be a different people—a view that seems consistent with the Athapaskan perspective that tended to assume the autonomy of people associated with different localities or who displayed other distinguishing characteristics. In subsequent years many Apache groups applied this interpretation to Anglo-Americans themselves, considering trappers, for example, to be a different category of people from army troops or ranchers.

In 1850 a small party of Americans came through Western Apache territory and informed the people that they had defeated Mexico in a war (Spicer 1962:245).[11] For the most part, the Apache reacted to the Americans as allies who had opposed a common enemy. Despite isolated incidents, the earliest phase of Anglo-American contact was fairly peaceful, if tentative.[12]

In a number of cases, Apache groups allowed outsiders to settle within their territory in exchange for payment. The Apache almost certainly viewed this as a courtesy extended to allies rather than as the simple impersonal sale of land. The Apache saw the reciprocal exchange of gifts and hospitality as a social interaction. Anglo-Americans tended to interpret such encounters as transfers of exclusive rights to property. This sort of misunderstanding, with both parties operating by different rules that they erroneously assumed to be mutually understood, had an inherent volatility. The tenuous relationship of amity did not last long.

One source of tension between the Apache and the United States at the outset was disagreement about relations with Mexico. Neither the Mexicans nor the previous Spanish government ever had succeeded in occupying Apache territory. When Americans told the Apache that Mexico had given their lands to the United States as a part of the war settlement, the position seemed absurd. The Americans told them that since the war had ended, their raids across the border into Mexico must cease.

Such arguments had little apparent effect on Apache raiding activities in the next few decades. Nonetheless, not much violence was directed at Anglo-Americans until an incident involving Chiricahua leaders and an army lieutenant in 1861. Having invited a number of Chiricahua to a meeting to negotiate the release of a Mexican captive, the lieutenant tried to take them hostage. The renowned leader Cochise escaped, but the others, who included one of his close relatives, were hanged.

Earlier, in 1857, Cochise had agreed with the government to allow Overland Mail carriers to cross Chiricahua territory unmolested. But Apache forbearance ended with this incident, and attacks on settlements and travelers erupted throughout eastern Arizona. As federal troops that year withdrew to the east for the Civil War, Arizona once again became Apache territory.

The troops returned, though, and the succeeding years were times of extreme pressure on the Western Apache. For the most part, their guerrilla tactics served them well in campaigns against conventional troops whose strategies were adapted to a European battlefield pattern. They could avoid confrontations until they chose to strike and disappear among the mountain crags they knew so well, as they had when they harassed the Spanish for generations. But more and more the army used Pima, Papago, and other Apache as scouts to track them. Troops were able to penetrate to the heart of Apache territory and find their farm plots. Eventually Apache *gota* were kept moving so relentlessly that they were hard-pressed to find enough food.

The chronicles of this period in the Southwest are voluminous, and details of actions and encounters are easily available (e.g., Thrapp 1968). But several features appear to stand out from this era of the "Apache Wars." The small-group autonomy inherent in Apachean social organization was also an aspect of their combative pattern. The independence of Apache aggregates meant that agreements with one cluster of families had no bearing on others. Referring to the Gila Apache in 1778, Croix (quoted in Schroeder 1974, IV, 87) complained of "the difficulty of coming to an agreement with a nation so dispersed in which every Indian was a free republican." There are cases of extremely prominent and respected men, such as Diablo of the Eastern White Mountain band, making agreements that a sizable part of the Apache population accepted (see Goodwin and Basso 1971:101). But even in such instances their acquiescence was voluntary.

In 1850 U.S. government agent Michael Steck (quoted in Schroeder 1974, IV, 172) said of the Apache that "they have no civil regulations that give their chiefs power to act for and controll [sic] their people. At their councils the old men or chiefs talk for the tribes, but as soon as they separate every one acts as an independent agent, and refuses to be controlled and the chief has not the influence with others to compell him to obey as they seem to fear each other." Referring to the prominent Gila Apache leader Mangas Coloradas, John Cremony (quoted in Schroeder 1974, IV, 149) noted that "he could assume no authority not delegated to him by his people. He never presumed to speak for them as one having authority but invariably said he would use his influence to perform certain promises and engagements."

In keeping with this concept of small-group autonomy, there was no sense whatever of any "Apache society" as a collective, corporate entity. An individual's greatest obligations of loyalty and affiliation were defined by ties of blood, marriage, and clan membership, and only beyond that to the division or "band" to which he or she belonged (Goodwin 1969:10). Despite the people's recognition of cultural similarities to other Apache groups, any implication of their consequent unity appears to have been almost nonexistent. Certain warring practices such as scalping generally were not used on Chiricahua because they "were considered *nde* (Apache people)" (Goodwin 1969:83), but scalping was rarely practiced by the Apache in any case. And fighting among the Western Apache themselves was not unheard of, by any means. This condition of autonomy allowed some Apache bands to participate in capturing others during the early reservation period. In an odd way, this phenomenon may have contributed to the frequency of homicidal treachery employed by Anglo-American "citizens' groups" against the Apache in the waning years of their sovereignty in the Southwest. In the last part of the nineteenth century, there were almost always times in which some groups were not involved in fighting while others were, and in some cases much peaceful interaction occurred between the Apache and the Anglo-Americans. All of this set the stage for the treacherous incidents, so numerous in the records of the period, in which unarmed Apache were massacred, often in peaceful meetings with Anglo-Americans.

There was an infamous poisoning of twenty-four people who had been invited to a peace negotiation near Miami, Arizona, during the 1860s, although apparently they were mostly Yavapai rather than Apache. In 1863 the Arizona territorial government openly advocated genocide for the Apache population. Atrocities reached an extreme with the Camp Grant massacre of 1871, when citizens of Tucson stole upon a nearby camp of sleeping Apache of the Arivaipa group who had established peaceful relationships with the surrounding population. The attackers clubbed women and children to death and kidnapped some forty children to be sold as slaves in Mexico.[13] This incident was exceptional only in degree, however, and was consistent with the prevailing attitudes of the populace. When the perpetrators were brought to trial at the insistence of President Ulysses S. Grant, the jury acquitted them after a few minutes' deliberation.

By 1872 the federal government set aside several reservations for the Apache, and during the next two decades, the people were confronted with circumstances dramatically different from those they had encountered in the past. For the first time, their movements were restricted. Eventually their ability to get food and survive, which had carried them through so many different settings and localities in the past, was curtailed.

The Eclipse of Sovereignty

At this point in the Western Apache cultural continuum, we can see that, underlying the evident changes, the continuation and modification of older patterns gave direction to the processes of adaptation in the Southwest. The nonspecialized food quest adapted to mountainous zones, with its roots in southern Alaska or possibly even beyond the Bering Strait in Siberia, not only had been a facet of

Proto-Apache movements south along the Rockies but constituted a precondition for the Apache's receptivity to the varied and unpredictable food sources they found in the Southwest.

When the people encountered village farmers with surpluses of stored food, they easily incorporated this resource into their subsistence pattern through the dual means of trade and raiding. At the same time, the pattern of mobility and the independence of small groups lent themselves well to this strategy. They could strike sedentary farming villages at will without hampering other aspects of the hunting and gathering cycle.

But subsistence raiding set off a dynamic sequence of changes in the Southwest that fed back to Apache culture itself. As raiding proved to be successful, it extended farther south to encompass more villages still deeper in Mexico. As settlers encroached on Apache territory and displaced game with livestock, the livestock came to be an important and valued part of the Western Apache diet and a commodity to trade. At the same time, townspeople of the Southwest engaged in trade networks with the Apache, even as they attempted to guard their own herds from raids. During their first few centuries in the Southwest, Apache reliance on raids grew to be more and more significant.

The role of cultivated foods in the Western Apache diet also grew as a result of their adoption of agriculture. Both farming and raiding stemmed from their early contact with sedentary peoples. Apache raiding might even have been an incentive for Puebloan peoples to encourage and perhaps instruct them in growing their own crops. Cultivated foods appeared early among the Apache and continued to be a significant, but still supplementary, aspect of the food quest. Neither farming nor raiding initially supplanted the older pattern of mobile, "mixed bag" subsistence involving the exploitation of extensive mountainous regions. Both activities were added to a subsistence pattern whose dominant characteristic had always been multifaceted.

Ultimately these changes generated problems for the Apache. After the end of Spanish jurisdiction and the establishment of an independent Mexican government, the reactions of other groups to Apache raids came to involve an escalation of violence and intensified volatility in intergroup relations. While early Apache raids had been primarily acquisitive with little intention of destroying or driving away the villagers who provided a constant source of food, Spanish and Mexican governments directed more and more campaigns against the Apache population itself. This reached its most extreme manifestation in the actions of mercenaries and bounty hunters in the nineteenth century. As attacks on the Western Apache increased and more deaths occurred, bitterness over the loss of relatives and the desire for revenge also grew as an important element of raids.

In the period following Mexican independence, and even more so after the United States acquired claim to Apache territory, escalated hostilities came to interfere with the Apache's food quest and both increased the dangers of raiding itself and affected the Apache's seasonal rounds. No longer were the stages of the agricultural cycle or the availability of food in a given locality the sole considerations in determining Apache movements. Outsiders who had established towns in Arizona formed parties of "Indian hunters" who, despite their general lack of success, committed periodic atrocities against peaceful Apache camps and constituted an additional harassment. In some cases, particularly after native American scouts were used by the U.S. Army to locate Apache fields, groups were kept moving too relentlessly to harvest their crops or effectively to harvest wild foods in the proper season.

Eventually these various forces would curtail the effectiveness of the Western Apache food quest by disturbing their ability to respond to subsistence opportunities through the free movement of small clusters of people over extensive areas. It was this, as much as any other factor, that led to their ultimate loss of sovereignty.

To a great extent, the remainder of Apachean culture history has been a matter of attempting to adapt to a series of fluctuating situations that have constrained the full capacity to make decisions over their own affairs. For thousands of years, the people had dealt with a spectrum of environmental settings from the Arctic to the Sonoran Desert. But the loss of political sovereignty, coupled with the efforts of outside forces to alter these ancient patterns, vastly complicated the process of adaptation. Yet cultural continuity, resting on the maintenance of options and autonomy within a network of far-flung kinship bonds, was not entirely broken. The following chapter will consider the responses of the Western Apache to this new context.

CHAPTER 9

The Reservation Years

Federal reservations for the Apache were established in the early 1870s in areas remote from any likely Anglo-American settlement. General George Crook, given charge of pacification in Arizona, announced in 1871 that he would hunt down and kill any Apache who failed to report to the reservations by a specified date (Spicer 1962:250). The government designated Camp Apache (later Fort Apache) and Camp Grant to the south for the Western Apache. In 1872 San Carlos Reservation was established, and Camp Grant was abandoned.

Many of the Western Apache came to these reservations in the early 1870s. The original San Carlos Reservation encompassed a sizable tract of land within the general Western Apache territory where the people had the status of prisoners of war and were kept as much as possible within sight of the troops (Ogle 1970). The army took daily roll calls and designated leaders of "tag bands." They required each member of these administrative bands to wear metal "dog tags" to facilitate supervision of the population. The government required permits to leave the reservation or to travel to other parts of it in search of food. With their subsistence quest curtailed, the people had no choice but to depend on rations for survival.

The government also brought people from many of the Apache groups, including the Chiricahua, to San Carlos. People who were used to moving at will over thousands of square miles camped together now in close quarters. Old feuds and antagonisms flared under crowded, stressful circumstances. Sanitary conditions deteriorated, and diseases spread among the concentrated population. Despite the government stipulations, many fled the reservation. Perhaps the most famous instances were the departures of groups of Chiricahua and Gila Apache led by Victorio, Geronimo, Juh, and others.[1] As sporadic feuding and homicides continued to occur during these early years, the administration organized an Apache police force to help keep order. When killings occurred, the perpetrators often became "renegades," apparently because one who had killed believed that inevitably the victim's relatives would take vengeance. Giving up any hope of resuming former relationships, such people in despair of their lives sometimes began killing everyone they met (Goodwin and Basso 1971:314, n. 114).

Many young men enlisted as scouts during the last quarter of the nineteenth century and helped the army track renegades and Apache bands who refused to return to the reservations (Adams 1971: 118). Government scouting became one of the earliest experiences of wage earning in which any sizable number of Apache participated. In the late 1870s, the military withdrew to the periphery of the reservation, largely through the demands of reservation agent John Clum. It was Clum who organized the Apache police, selected to represent the various local groups. Clum also arranged for additional wage work, which mainly consisted of building roads and irrigation ditches for scrip that could be used as local currency at the agency store (Spicer 1962: 252–253; Clum 1936). During these years a number of Apache families resumed farming. Clum resigned in 1878, a time when it appeared that economically, at least, the Apache's situation was promising. The concentration of bands relaxed a bit, and the government allowed the White Mountain and Cibecue people of the northern sector of the Coyotero population to leave San Carlos and return north to their familiar territory around Fort Apache.

But there were more problems and disruptions during the next decades. In one case a group of people from Cibecue attacked San Carlos and killed the chief of police, although the uprising that they had hoped to provoke did not occur (Goodwin 1969:23). A decade or so later, some people were killed along the San Carlos River, and the leader of the group to which the perpetrators belonged ambushed some scouts, anticipating retaliation. After a few days, though, this group surrendered in Globe and were returned to San Carlos (Goodwin 1969:32; Goodwin and Basso 1971: 316, n. 16). Then in 1881 people were killed at Cibecue in the violence that ensued after troops attempted to arrest the leader of a newly founded religious movement (Goodwin and Kaut 1954). For the most part, though, such incidents in the San Carlos and Fort Apache reservations did not amount to anything approaching the intensity of conflict of earlier years.

The several campaigns of Geronimo, Chihuahua, Loco, and other Chiricahua leaders, culminating in the surrender of Geronimo to

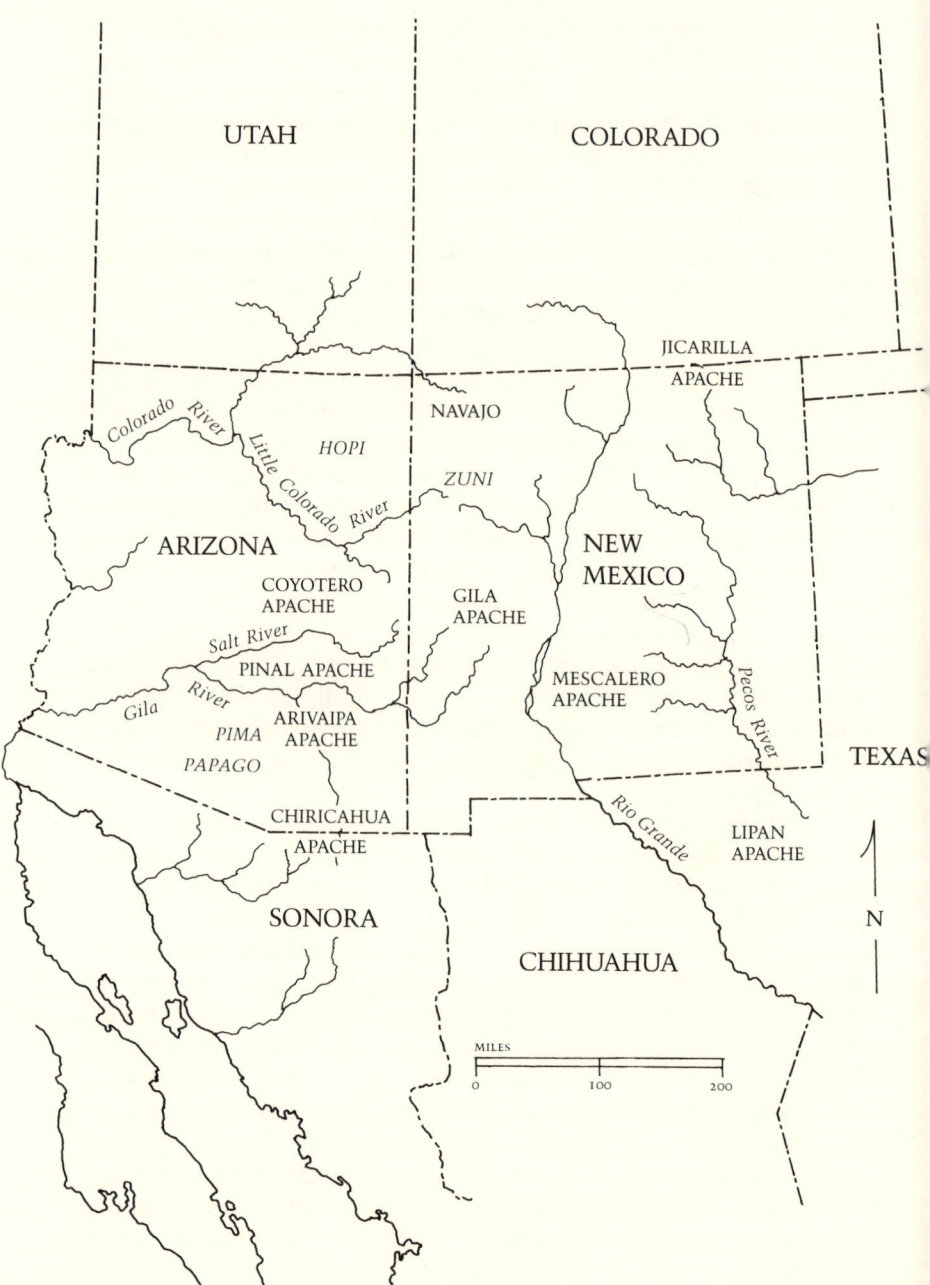

Map 7. Apache and neighboring groups in the Southwest, nineteenth centu

General Nelson Miles in the Sierra Madres of Mexico, drew far more attention. In the wake of these actions, the U.S. government transported all of the Chiricahua to Florida, including the many who had not left San Carlos. Government strategists apparently believed that in Florida the Chiricahua would become too weakened and disoriented to pose any further threat to the established order and certainly would be unable to continue their forays into Mexico. The ensuing history of the Chiricahua is a tragedy in its own right, with their children taken from their families and placed in a boarding school where many of them died within a few years. Only decades later, after several relocations ending in Oklahoma, were the Chiricahua given the choice of returning to the Southwest. Toward the end of the nineteenth century, though, after the Chiricahua were taken off to the east, only Western Apache and a few Yavapai resided in San Carlos.

Remarkably, a handful of Apache were able to elude capture in the Sierras of Mexico well into the 1930s. They maintained their freedom in mountain strongholds, avoiding capture. The Western Apache of San Carlos knew about them, which suggests that some communication occurred, but they considered them "wild" and dangerous, possibly because of their desperation. In the mid-1930s one of their little girls was captured in Mexico and tethered to a tree. She died before she could be rescued. Grenville Goodwin wrote in a letter to Morris Opler (1973:56) in January 1934 that "my own friends, the W. Apache, are scared to death of them and have no contact . . . These people are only rarely seen by Mexicans and whites, and then only by accident. They live back in the Sierra Madre." Goodwin estimated that these Apache numbered only about thirty people, and he was concerned about their survival. After this time no further mention of them is found. Most likely they were unable, at last, to avoid the forces that hunted them.

This implacable refusal to relinquish their sovereignty well into the twentieth century was a strategy that most of the Apache population, who were unable to elude the U.S. Army, did not or could not follow. Life continued on the reservation context under the surveillance of the U.S. government, and a series of executive orders removed large portions of valuable reservation lands and placed them in the public domain. As the final decade of the nineteenth century ended, wage work in San Carlos had increased to the extent that the Western Apache were considered one of the major sources of labor in the Southwest. Many Apache people spent most of their adult lives in agricultural work or in highway construction. When silver and

Two Apache men, 1888 (National Anthropological Archives, Smithsonian Institution)

copper mines opened in the area in territory that had once been part of the reservation, many of them found jobs in these operations.

In 1970 an elderly Apache woman reminisced, "When I was a little girl we used to move from San Carlos to the mountains. My father gathered wood and brought it into Globe in a wagon to sell." At the same time, some people developed successful farms near the San Carlos River. Around the turn of the century, many Apache worked on the construction of the railroad through the San Carlos Reservation (Adams 1971: 119), and by 1901, rations were discontinued at San Carlos on the grounds that they no longer were necessary.

The large San Carlos Reservation that had seemed remote from Anglo-American settlement a few decades earlier now fell to an increasing degree under pressure from competing interests. In 1888 the Arivaipa group, who had settled within the boundaries of the reservation near the mouth of the San Pedro River, were forced to move north because of threats from Anglo-Americans who wanted the land (Goodwin 1969: 29). Mining interests exploited the copper discovered on lands that had been excised from the eastern and western ends of the reservation. The agent at San Carlos and the commissioner of the Bureau of Indian Affairs both invested heavily in the new mining operations and profited from the Apache's loss of resources.

Mormon farmers encroached on the Fort Apache Reservation. Southeast of San Carlos, other Mormon settlers diverted so much water from the Gila River for their own farms that the Apache irrigation ditches downstream almost ran dry. During this period the federal government also leased most of the potential grazing land on the reservation to Anglo-American cattle ranchers, which resulted in a prolonged legal battle decades later when the Apache attempted to regain use of it for their own cattle.

The late nineteenth century had brought many assorted school teachers, missionaries, and other civilian personnel to the Western Apache. Small children were carted to school bound in chains to prevent their escaping back into the secure refuge of their families, and as late as the 1930s Apache children were kept in barbed wire compounds and beaten if they spoke Apache, or if they spoke to another child of the opposite sex. A standard punishment at that time was to force a child to carry a ball and chain (Spicer 1962: 257).

Boarding schools a great distance from the reservation held a still greater threat for children and the parents who feared for them. In the early part of this century, the forebodings of a Navajo mother might have been echoed by many Apache parents: "I hated to send

People waiting to be issued rations at San Carlos, 1880s
(National Anthropological Archives, Smithsonian Institution)

this boy to school. I knew I was saying goodbye. He would come back a stranger" (Institute for Government Research 1928: 574). An Apache man in the 1920s said, "I know the results of the reservation school but when we send our children to non-reservation schools we do not see these children for a long time, and sometimes they die" (Institute for Government Research 1928: 574). Sometimes children died in the schools, and sometimes in desperate lonely treks to get back to the nurturance and support of their families and relatives on the reservation.

The government's "educational" strategy was to remove the children from a traditional setting, shielding them from the influence of Apache elders in order to "open" their minds and help them to learn "new ways." The experience of formal schooling, with its implicit and often explicit attacks on the identity, the sense of worth, and even the bodies of Apache children, left many with a feeling of bitterness and resentment that continued beyond their generation.

The people tried to adapt themselves to these circumstances. A report published in 1928 by the Institute for Government Research and titled *The Problem of Indian Administration*, widely known as the Meriam Report (1928: 614), quotes an essay written by one Apache schoolchild: "When the Indians return from school they want books. In a tepee there is so much smoke and noise and women. It is impossible to think good thoughts and to work with books in a tepee under those circumstances." During these years probably almost all Apache children had some school experience. Despite the cruelties perpetrated and the traumas experienced in many of these institutions, at least some children made a great effort to attend school. In 1970 a man in his seventies said, "When I was young I did my best to get educated. I used to hitchhike to Globe every day. For lunch I had nothing but a bowl of beans, for ten cents in those days. I did my best to play football."[2]

This man's experience illuminates a poignant contrast between the motivations of many Apache regarding education and the officials who administered it. The government and others saw formal education as a means of weaning Apache children from their ethnic heritage, often with a brutally heavy hand. But many Apache sought schooling as a means of acquiring the instrumental skills they would need to subsist in their immediate circumstances. It was an adaptive strategy that they felt would help them to survive as Apache and would enable them to address the problems they confronted in their contemporary situation.

According to the Meriam Report, "In Globe schools Indian segregation from whites is fairly complete." Yet despite this laconic, rather ominous statement about social relations in this part of Arizona in the 1920s, the report adds that through the efforts of one compassionate teacher (who unfortunately remains unnamed), Apache children in the Globe school were cheerful, outgoing, and eager in their schoolwork, having overcome their "customary shyness" (Institute for Government Research 1928:695). Such episodes in the history of the contact period seem far from typical, however.

Although many Apache had become accustomed to wage work in these years and had experienced the inexorable need for cash that is part of the twentieth-century context, this does not necessarily indicate that cultural assimilation of the Western Apache into Anglo-American society was impending. Little reason exists to think that the Apache at this time or any other have been inclined to relinquish their sense of cultural identity and to submerge themselves in the wider society. Working for wages was another of the many subsistence strategies that the people employed in the past. But as such, wage labor in principle did little to challenge or strain the core of traditional patterns.

Apache workers retained close ties to their relatives. Jobs that would have involved isolation from their interpersonal network of kin bonds for any length of time were not attractive to most people and, in fact, usually were unacceptable to them. Some communities of Apache grew up near mining operations where, to some degree,

The wife and child of an Apache laborer, early twentieth century (National Anthropological Archives, Smithsonian Institution)

they could accommodate the demands of wage work and close ties with relatives at the same time.[3] But the established pattern among Apaches was to engage in intermittent, short-term projects that could provide a temporary surplus of means and allow the worker periodic, regular returns to a congenial social milieu (see Krutz 1971).

This way of life with its alternating dispersion and gregarious clustering was inherent in the ancient patterns of hunting and the more recent subsistence raiding. It fit comfortably with intermittent stints of scouting for the government during the 1870s and 1880s, when scouts were paid after each expedition and reenlisted for the next one only if they felt like it. The pattern also accommodated many of the early construction projects in the immediate vicinity of San Carlos. It does not, though, conform to the traditional Euro-American ideal of dogged, endless toil as a virtue in itself. Apache wage labor was a means of attaining continued existence in new and shifting circumstances.

There is little doubt that the use of Apache workers in Arizona around the turn of the century was fundamentally exploitative. In 1902 a Globe mine workers' union lodged a formal public protest against the use of Apache labor, based largely on the low pay for which the Apache were willing to work. They worked for much less than union miners demanded (Adams 1971:119), and no doubt much of the demand for Apache labor in these years was associated with employers' awareness of that fact. A passage from the *Literary Digest* of 1920 refers to the alleged capacity of the Apache to work in conditions that would be intolerable to others (Adams 1971:121)— an obvious and disturbing parallel to such rationalizations for the use of slave labor in the southeastern United States.

The Meriam Report provides an example of the Apache labor experience that contrasts starkly with other, more optimistic reports. In this instance some Apache workers had traveled to San Carlos to sign up for a job that, according to the local agent, would pay $2.50 per day. After the workers, many of whom had their families with them, had been loaded into a truck and driven to the job site, they discovered that the gross pay was to be only $2.00 per day. From that $2.00, half was deducted for board and five cents was taken out for a "hospital" fee, leaving ninety-five cents for a day's work. Nor did transportation to the work site turn out to be a round trip. At the end of the job, those workers whose families had accompanied them had not made enough to pay for a ride back to San Carlos, and they were left to return with their children on foot (Institute for Government Research 1928: 687).

Despite these conditions, in the first few decades of the twentieth century, the Apache became more and more involved in wage labor, and job opportunities burgeoned to the extent that the U.S. government hired an employment officer to facilitate the hiring process (Spicer 1962:257). This boom time for jobs continued through the 1920s until the Great Depression. Many Apache farms were doing well in the meantime, despite the problems of water rights. In the 1920s the Bureau of Indian Affairs instituted a cattle-raising program and encouraged families to raise beef for the market, as well as for their own use. Part of the plan was that Apache families might disperse throughout the reservation with their cattle herds in the fashion of the Navajo with their sheep. This did not happen to any great extent, but eventually cattle raising did become one of the largest sources of income in San Carlos.

During the same decade, the government decided to build Coolidge Dam across the San Carlos River. The dam amounted to the last major construction project on the reservation and the last source of large-scale employment for the Apache. Along with the cattle program, the dam marks the beginning of the most recent phase of Apachean culture history, in which a sense of cultural identity and social boundary was intensified in many ways.

The proposers of Coolidge Dam conceived it as a means of impounding water to enhance agriculture in southern Arizona. The lake that the dam created on the San Carlos Reservation eventually would flood many of the best and most prosperous Apache farms. Among those destined to lose their farms were many Arivaipa, who in 1888 had been driven from their earlier settlement by Anglo-Americans and who still earlier, in 1871, had been victims of the Camp Grant massacre. Some of the major beneficiaries of this water would be commercial farmers to the south as far as Tucson.

Senator Carl Hayden of Arizona presented the dam project to Congress as a means of helping the impoverished Pima to the south. The *Arizona Republican*, the principle newspaper in Phoenix, emphasized this rationale, presenting the Pima as Indians who had helped the Arizona pioneers defeat the "marauding Apaches." The paper also noted, however, that the bulk of the water would help create an "agricultural empire" in Arizona by supplying commercial farms. Few, if any, of these ventures in agribusiness were owned by either Apache or Pima (*Arizona Republican* 30 Dec. 1923, sec. 15, p. 5).

Apache relationships with the Pima and Papago had generally been hostile since the earliest raiding days of the seventeenth century, and the tone of that relationship has not entirely disappeared. Some of this animosity in the early days resulted from an explicit "divide and conquer" policy of the Spanish. Goodwin quotes an Apache man in the 1930s who claimed that Apache people could never encounter the Pima without getting into a fight, and he notes that this seemed to be true (Goodwin 1969: 87–88). Apache bitterness over losing the farms that they had worked for decades to establish, then, was only accentuated by their perceptions of the ultimate purpose of the dam.

When the finished structure was dedicated, the government officials who had organized the ceremony arranged to have a marching band of Apache children play their instruments as a train carrying President Calvin Coolidge steamed to a halt on the reservation near the old Lutheran school. The president stood at the back of the last car and waved to the people. Decades later, an Apache man who had been among the marching band as a child noted that the president never left the car. The train quickly lurched into motion again and disappeared down the tracks into the distance.

It is worth noting that over forty years later, Congressman Morris Udall in a letter to Congressman Wayne Aspinall pointed out that the Pima farms were impoverished because of a lack of irrigation. He noted that they had never received the water from the dam that the planners had projected.[4] Commercial farms in Arizona did, however, benefit substantially.

When the Depression struck, the loss of Apache farms was accompanied by a loss of wage work. William Y. Adams (1971:119) estimates that because of the loss of their jobs during the 1930s, "virtually every member of the Apache Tribe returned to the reservation." The cattle industry was beginning to become a significant enterprise, but with the inundation of the prime lands under San Carlos Lake, farming all but came to an end on the reservation.

The U.S. government attempted to persuade the Apache to establish new farms in another area, but only a few desultory efforts to grow crops resulted. Disillusionment and anger had soured the people's receptivity to farming and made such an enterprise seem futile. As late as 1970, an elderly woman stated that "lots of people used to have farms at Old San Carlos. I had a big farm. The old people used to like to grow corn. Then they took our farms to build the dam, and people never have farms anymore. They just don't care now." Far from Coolidge Dam on the Fort Apache Reservation to the north, farming still is important. But in San Carlos, the cattle industry is the primary economic activity.

In some ways this combination of events in the early twentieth century caused a drawing-in of the San Carlos Apache community. Exclusion of the Apache from the labor market involved widespread and flagrant ethnic discrimination, and the experience of Coolidge Dam could only have compounded the resentment and anger. At the same time, the cattle industry provided some hope of economic survival within the reservation setting that involved minimal contact with outsiders (Krutz 1971).

Through the experience of a generation or more, the people had learned that, divested of their sovereignty and the opportunity to control their own lives, they would draw the short end of the bargain time and again. The cruelties of the early schools, the confiscation of reservation lands by mining interests with government complicity, the exploitation of Apache labor at below-standard wages, the flooding of the farms, and other experiences all had become a part of the ideology of the people, traditional wisdom that was passed on to new generations. But as in the past, the source of strength, comfort, and a satisfactory life was perceived to lie within the network of kin and the Apache community, rather than on the outside.

Throughout the twentieth century, Apache people have continued to leave the reservation for various reasons. Many fought in World War II, Korea, and Vietnam. But attitudes toward the outside became decidedly and perhaps permanently negative. To some extent, though, this negative tone is only one side of the coin. The Western Apache in the reservation period have confronted chronic poverty and attempts by outsiders to alter aspects of their traditional ways, including attacks on their language, their belief system, and even their residence patterns. They have experienced ethnic discrimination and raw racism in the towns that outsiders have built up all around them. They have had authorities take away their children and beat them for speaking the language of their parents, and they have systematically been denied the opportunity to run their own affairs and control their own resources. Throughout all of this, their cultural continuity has persisted.

Reflections and Reprise: San Carlos in the Later Twentieth Century

San Carlos Reservation in 1990 is a community of about ten thousand people, most of whom live in a few small population clusters. A handful of others live scattered over the hundreds of square miles of reservation land, many of them involved in the cattle industry. During the late summer, many people move up to the higher areas, where women gather the acorns that cover the ground by the hundreds of thousands, filling their fringed burden baskets and bringing them down to the lowlands in pickup trucks. People banter with one

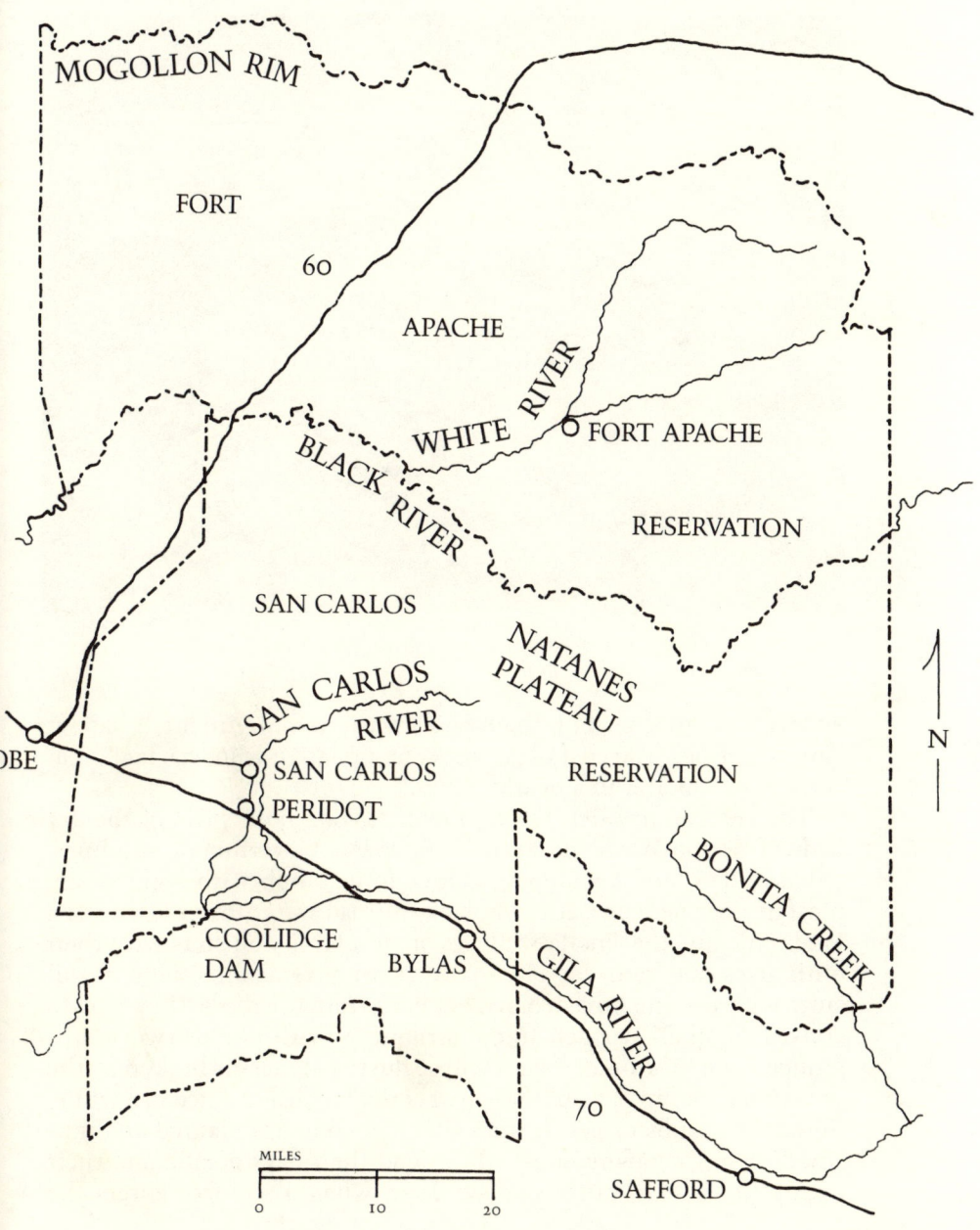

Map 8. The San Carlos and Fort Apache reservations

The San Carlos community

another in Apache, but their conversations now might be about cattle auctions, the cost of gasoline, or a relative who was laid off at the copper smelter in a nearby town.

The community lies among low mesas on both sides of the dry beds of Gilson Wash and Seven-Mile Wash. Government buildings, tribal offices, and a shopping center form a hub with solid stone-masonry permanence. An old black railroad water tower looms as a landmark, and the small dwellings of joint family clusters with their outhouses and ramadas are scattered in several directions on all sides with diminishing density. Set back from the roads, they tend to consist of small wooden frame structures with one or two rooms grouped widely around spaces whose dusty bareness is broken by the occasional clump of tumbleweed or scrub brush and, once in a while, flowering shrubs or peach trees that someone has planted and nurtured. A few scrawny dogs, who spend their days dozing and their nights in combat, raise a noisy alarm when a stranger enters the area.

Apache children go to school. Many of them watch television. Like adults, they dress in the same styles as those worn by other Arizonans, although most adult women still own at least one of the

Apache Children, San Carlos

older type of long, full cotton "camp dresses" based on nineteenth-century Mexican styles. A few older women wear them most of the time. Since the 1930s men have had their hair cut short and typically wear jeans, western-style shirts, and cowboy hats.

San Carlos today is a community with problems. Like many of the western reservations, it is plagued by severe poverty, with a per capita income so far below the national average that there is almost no basis for comparison. Infant mortality is staggering, often from the dehydration caused by infant diarrhea. Tuberculosis, long a disease of poverty, has diminished from extremely high levels a decade or so ago, but other health problems afflict the community. The tragedy of teenage suicide is terribly frequent—many times the national average. So, too, is homicide and other acts of violence. Chronic alcoholism afflicts many of the people—itself a product of crushing poverty and frustration, and a cause, in turn, of many other problems. Twenty-year-olds have died of cirrhosis of the liver, and fetal alcohol syndrome has become a growing concern.

How could this have happened? Why are the Western Apache beset by problems now that threaten their very existence, after having survived through so many centuries in a variety of circumstances that physically, at least, must have been far more challenging?

In the past the process of surviving led them from a hunting exis-tence in the mountains of the Subarctic to a period of political domi-nance of the Southwest that lasted several centuries. The situation of the modern San Carlos community is far too complex to be dealt with fully here, but even to begin to comprehend it we must have some sense of how it came to be. This necessarily involves a sense of change at two levels.

One level has to do with the historic events in the Southwest that culminated in the Western Apache's political eclipse and the estab-lishment of the reservation system. The other has more to do with the range of long-term processes that underlay, shaped, and led to the culture of the Apache population in the first place and that help to account for how they came to be who they were when they en-tered that historic theater. This study, for the most part, has focused on that long-term aspect of Apache history. It has been an attempt to understand the cultural processes that have characterized their past and that provide the cultural momentum that continues to affect their present and their future.

In trying to account for their present situation, a crucial factor, perhaps, is that throughout the changes they underwent, they were able to adapt and make choices as an autonomous population. They drew on their own repertoire of traditions and to some extent were constrained by it. But these traditions, more than defining their range of choices, maximized the options of individuals and small groups in their pursuit of subsistence. This strategic openness, a cul-tural "style," developed in the mountain ranges of the Western Sub-arctic where sparse and erratic resources stimulated an ecological sensitivity and a quick responsiveness to opportunity.

The mobile capacities that developed in that setting and a recep-tivity to a variety of resources opened a vast ecological zone to them. Following the mountain chains to the south, they pursued the same subsistence patterns throughout an environmental zone that over the course of thousands of miles was consistent, in the sense that it provided a variety of ecological niches at different altitudes. Even-tually the mountain corridor led them into the Southwest, where their exploitation of new food sources, including raids on sedentary peoples, persisted until their sovereignty was wrested from them by still another population new to the area.

At every step the changes that occurred were consequences of the past. They built on what had gone before, perpetuating it, adding to it, and in some cases reacting to problems caused by it. Their mi-gration south was more a matter of expanding throughout the same ecological setting than of moving from one zone to another. The Rocky Mountains, with their drastic differences in altitude, provide Subarctic conditions within a few miles of warmer lowlands, even in Colorado.

The Apache's eventual political demise and loss of autonomy resulted to a great extent from the U.S. Army's success in curtailing the free pursuit of their subsistence patterns. Hampered in their raiding forays and unable to garden or to carry out the seasonal gathering and hunting cycle while scouts pursued them, they finally found themselves in such straits that acquiescence to a life under government administration became the only reasonable choice.

Since that time the political control over their own affairs by a state system, with all of the powerful interest groups that implies, has resulted in their loss of copper-bearing lands, farmlands, irrigation water, and other potential resources. It has relegated them to reacting to conditions, often without full information, rather than creating them, and to working for low wages or receiving meager government assistance in order to survive.

The people of San Carlos now have no apparent connection with the Western Subarctic except in the continuities of their culture. Scores of generations have passed, experiencing profound changes from the Proto-Athapaskan culture base that the Western Apache share with other Athapaskan speakers, but much of that culture continues in the living Apache community. Some aspects of San Carlos culture still echo their common heritage with the Eyak of southern Alaska and probably have been retained from the period before the Eyak-Athapaskan split.

In San Carlos, people still avoid the names of the deceased, although for the past few generations, funerals and wakes have become common practice. Contact with a ghost can cause illness, even among young people. Owls inspire dread. Dogs, ubiquitous in San Carlos, are not seen in the same light as the pets that dominate typical middle-class American homes. Older patterns of interpersonal behavior still are appropriate. Staring into another's eyes is rude.

Matrilocal residence predominates in the joint family clusters scattered about the community—a pattern that persisted in spite of the government's attempts to isolate nuclear families in a "modern" pattern by establishing single-family houses in rows along streets. Arranged marriages may be rare now, but adult brothers and sisters still treat each other with diffidence and decorum, and men try to avoid their mothers-in-law to show their respect. The significance of matrilineal descent remains strong and continues to be expressed in the structure of the clan system. A person who refers to "my close

Sunrise Ceremony, San Carlos, early 1960s

relatives" usually means matrilineal kin. That phrase in San Carlos is laden with connotations of mutual aid, reciprocity, and support. There is no seclusion for young women at puberty—that pattern probably was abandoned before the Apache entered the Southwest— but the celebrative female puberty ceremony continues to be a major event of great significance and emotional impact for the people of San Carlos. Once in danger of disappearing, these ceremonies are now a central focus of the community and occur from early spring throughout the summer and fall.

The extent to which these constitute hollow carryovers from the past or continuing, meaningful aspects of contemporary Apache culture could be debated at length. They represent the kinds of choices people in San Carlos make in conducting their lives. They reflect the intellectual framework by which people interpret their experience. The people of San Carlos are fully aware of the cultural alternatives that surround them, and many have selectively chosen some of them. In 1970 there were many avid professional football fans among the Western Apache. People in San Carlos are not oblivious to the appeal of cars and pickup trucks and the rest of the material cornucopia on display in U.S. society. Nor are they unaware of their own economic, social, and political circumstances or the extent to which these are associated with their relationship to the wider society.

In such a situation, it is questionable whether many of the ancient patterns constitute a disadvantage. They differ from those of the U.S. mainstream and thus continue to set the people apart. But what sets the Apache apart in a more devastating sense is the political structure that keeps them in relative poverty and precludes political and economic sovereignty. Matrilocal joint families still nurture kinship ties, and wizened old people still can spend congenial hours bestowing their affection and the benefits of their years on small grandchildren and great-grandchildren. People carry into adulthood a sense of bonds and obligations to the close matrilineal kin with whom they share their earliest memories. These patterns are valuable—perhaps more than whatever they might gain by surrendering them.

The situation for the people of contemporary San Carlos is complex, and the concept of underdevelopment does not appear to be an appropriate framework for helping to clarify it. Underdevelopment implies that the Western Apache have not yet developed the ability to "stand on their own feet." But in that regard, the people had done very well until an expanding state extended hegemony over their territorial base. At that juncture, decisions over the control of their resources—the subsistence pattern, writ large—were no longer theirs. If the Western Apache were ever to regain control their situation could change.

It is not the old ways that cause poverty. Poverty is a result of a loss of power and enforced dependency. Certainly the people of San Carlos, like all people, must adjust to new circumstances when they are faced with them, but for many centuries it has been part of the Apachean tradition to adjust and adapt. That process has involved building on strengths drawn from the past to cope with new situations. Restoration of control over their own affairs could enhance this possibility for the Western Apache.

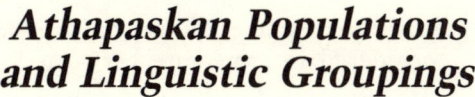

Athapaskan Populations and Linguistic Groupings

Divisions Used by Dyen and Aberle (1974: 11–14)
Athapaskan languages. These are based on lexicostatistics, with a provisional language limit set at 77 percent of shared cognates from the Swadesh 100-word list.

Northern Athapaskan Languages
    Tanaina
    Ingalik
    Tanana-Koyukon
    Atna
    Canadian Athapaskan (includes the following dialects)
      a. Kutchin-Han-Nabesna (Lower Tanana)
      b. Hare-Dogrib-Slave-Chipewyan-Beaver-Carrier
      c. Sarsi
Pacific Coast Languages
    Mattole
    Hupic (includes all other dialects)
Southern Athapaskan Languages
    Apachean (includes the dialects Navajo, Jicarilla, Lipan, Chiricahua, Mescalero, San Carlos, and Kiowa Apache)

Divisions Used by Krauss and Golla (1981)
Northern Athapaskan languages. Major dialect chains, characterized by a high degree of mutual intelligibility, are noted through parenthetic cross-references.

    Ahtna
    Babine
    Bearlake (closely linked to Hare, Mountain, and Slavey)
    Beaver (closely linked to Sekani)
    Carrier
    Chilcotin
    Chipewyan
    Dogrib

Han
Hare (closely linked to Bearlake, Mountain, and Slavey)
Holikachuk (considered intermediate between Ingalik and Ko-
    yukon)
Ingalik
Kaska (closely linked to Tahltan and Tagish)
Kolchan (closely linked to Lower Tanana [Nabesna], Tanacross,
    and Upper Tanana)
Koyukon
Kutchin
Lower Tanana (Nabesna) (closely linked to Kolchan, Tanacross,
    and Upper Tanana)
Mountain (closely linked to Bearlake, Hare, and Slavey)
Sarcee
Sekani (closely linked to Beaver)
Slavey (closely linked to Bearlake, Hare, and Mountain)
Tagish (closely linked to Kaska and Tahltan)
Tahltan (closely linked to Kaska and Tagish)
Tanacross (closely linked to Kolchan, Lower Tanana, and Upper
    Tanana)
Tanaina
Tsetsaut
Tutchone
Upper Tanana (closely linked to Kolchan, Lower Tanana, and
    Tanacross)

Divisions Used by Krauss (1979)
Athapaskan languages and dialects. Based on "sociological criteria
as well as linguistic" (Krauss 1979:848).
    Twenty-one Northern Athapaskan groupings
        Ahtna
        Tanaina
        Ingalik
        Holikachuk
        Koyukon
        Upper Kuskokwim
        Tanana
        Tanacross
        Upper Tanana
        Han
        Kutchin
        Tutchone (possibly divisible into two languages)
        Tahltan (probably mutually intelligible with Kaska and Tagish)
        Dogrib (mutually intelligible with Hare, Bearlake, Slavey, and

Mountain, with which it forms a "Mackenzie drainage" language group)

Slave (see Dogrib)
Mountain (see Dogrib)
Bearlake (see Dogrib)
Hare (see Dogrib)
Chipewyan
Beaver
Sekani
Sarcee
Carrier
Babine-Hagwilgate (traditionally included with Carrier, but seen by Krauss as a distinct language)
Chilcotin

Two extinct and poorly recorded "intermediate islets"
Nicola
Kwalhioqua-Tlatskanai

Four Pacific Coast languages
All Oregon Athapaskan dialects except for Umpqua
Umpqua
All California Athapaskan dialects except for Hupa-Chilula-Whilkut
Hupa-Chilula-Whilkut

Apachean
Seen as "a single close-knit substock"

Divisions Used by Osgood (1936b)
Northern Athapaskan divisions based on perceived ethnographic distinctness.

Atna
Bear Lake
Beaver
Carrier
Chilcotin
Chipewyan
Dog Rib
Han
Hare
Kaska
Koyukon
Kutchin
Ingalik
Mountain
Nabesna

Sarsi
Sekani
Slave
Tahltan
Tanaina
Tanana
Tsetsaut
Tutchone
Yellowknife

Divisions Used Here, with Comments

Consensus groupings

These are seen as distinct ethnic units in all of the listings cited above.

Northern Athapaskan
Ahtna
Beaver
Carrier
Tanaina
Chilcotin
Chipewyan
Dogrib
Han
Ingalik
Kutchin
Sarsi
Sekani (included by Dyen and Aberle [1974:15] within Canadian Athapaskan)
Tutchone
Tsetsaut

Decision groupings

Decisions to treat groups individually or collectively are based on (1) consideration of their linguistic similarity, with regard to its implications for the degree of cultural distinctness; (2) the extent to which they have been treated as distinct populations in the ethnographic literature; and (3) the degree to which ethnographic data on them are available.

Northern Athapaskan
Beaver, Sekani
These will be treated separately but cross-referenced because of their extremely close relationship. Asch notes that "as Jenness (1937:8) pointed out, 'it is impossible to draw a sharp line between Sekani and Beaver Indians, and the Indians of Hudson Hope, who are usually classed as

[western] Beaver, might be included with almost equal justice among the Sekani'" (Asch 1981:351).

Chilcotin

Chilcotin is not given major attention in Dyen and Aberle's (1974:236) listing (see above), presumably because of a dearth of linguistic documentation. They appear to see it as a separate dialect of Canadian Athapaskan, as do Krauss and Golla (1981). The Chilcotin are consistently treated as a distinct ethnic population in the literature, however, and will be so treated here.

Kaska

Krauss and Golla (1981) group Kaska with Tahltan and Tagish as a group of closely related dialects. Tahltan and Kaska are distinguished by Osgood (1938), who does not recognize Tagish. The three are discussed as separate cases by Dyen and Aberle (1974). They will be grouped together here under the listing "Kaska" because of their close linguistic relationships and contiguous populations.

Koyukon

This language is linked with Tanana by Dyen and Aberle (1974) on the basis of lexicostatistics, but the Koyukon generally are considered distinct in the ethnographic literature. They are sufficiently well described to be treated as a separate case.

Slave, Hare, Mountain, and Bearlake

These are seen as a series of closely related dialects by Krauss and Golla (1981). All of these are seen as dialects of Canadian Athapaskan by Dyen and Aberle (1974). All four, however, have been treated as distinct ethnic populations in the literature. Krauss and Golla (1981:79) state that "the groups known as Slavey, Mountain, Bearlake, and Hare speak closely related dialects of a single language." Gillespie (1981:311) notes that "From scattered and limited historical materials it can be gleaned that there were a couple of groups of both Dogrib and Hare that were associated with the Great Bear Lake region. At least one group of each people, as well as some Slavey and Mountain Indians, were continuously trading at Fort Norman and gradually merging with the others through intermarriage." Although the data are sparse on the Bearlake group, they will be treated separately here. All four groups will be listed separately, but cross-referenced.

Tanana

Tanana is treated by Krauss and Golla (1981) as a dialect chain which includes Upper Tanana, Lower Tanana (Nabesna), Tanacross, and Kolchan. There is insufficient ethnographic evidence to treat each dialect group separately, and their linguistic relationship justifies grouping them as a single ethnographic population for the purposes of comparison.

Pacific Coast

Dyen and Aberle (1974) set Mattole apart as a separate language on the basis of lexicostatistics, grouping the rest under Hupic. Shipley (1978) defines four Pacific Coast Athapaskan languages: Tolowa (including all of the Oregon Athapaskan dialects); Hupa-Chilula-Whilkut; Mattole (including Bear River); and Wailaki-Nongatl-Lassik-Sinkyone-Kato. Krauss (1979; see above) also suggests four Pacific Coast Athapaskan languages, but his groupings are Umpqua, the remaining Oregon languages, Hupa-Chilula-Whilkut, and the remaining California Athapaskan dialects. The ethnographic evidence seems compatible with the treatment of Mattole as a distinct case. Few data are available on Umpqua traditional culture. In general, Shipley's four groupings appear to provide the most useful divisions for present purposes and will be used here. It is clear in any case that differentiation among these dialects (and languages?) is shallow. They constitute local populations whose traditional cultures have been described with varying degrees of thoroughness, and they display a high degree of similarity in many respects.

Southern Athapaskan

Chiricahua, Jicarilla, Kiowa Apache, Lipan, Mescalero, Navajo, and Western Apache will be treated individually despite the similarities of their dialects, since they have usually been treated as distinct populations in the ethnographic literature, and generally have operated as such in historic times.

Exclusions

Holikachuk

Little ethnographic information is available. The ethnic distinctness of the population speaking this dialect from surrounding Athapaskan populations has only recently been established (cf. Krauss and Golla 1981).

Kolchan, Lower Tanana, Tanacross, Upper Tanana

These are treated ethnographically as a single case under Tanana (see discussion of Tanana above).

Tahltan, Tagish

These are subsumed within Kaska (see the discussion of Kaska above).

Tsetsaut

Excluded because of sparse ethnographic information.

Babine

Krauss and Golla (1981) consider Babine to be a distinct language rather than a dialect of Carrier as it had formerly been treated. Nonetheless, this population has conventionally been included ethnographically with Carrier and will be so treated here.

Yellowknife

This population apparently disappeared in the nineteenth century and seems to have merged with the Chipewyan (cf. Gillespie 1981).

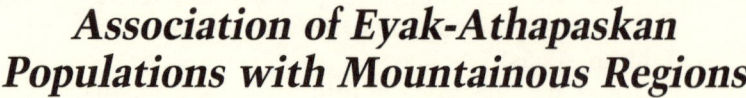

Association of Eyak-Athapaskan Populations with Mountainous Regions

Eyak
> "The Eyak occupied the mainland east of Prince William Sound, including the Copper River Delta" near Mount St. Elias (Birket-Smith and de Laguna 1938:341).

Athapaskan
Northern
Ahtna
> "The Alaska range, from the Mentasta Mountains on the east to the gateway of present McKinley Park on the northwest, formed the Ahtna northern boundary" (de Laguna and McClellan 1981:641).

Beaver
> "The Beaver Indians occupy the region of the Peace River from the eastern base of the Rocky Mountains in British Columbia along the Peace River to the falls about forty miles below Vermillion" (Goddard 1917:208).

Carrier
> "They live in the mountainous northern interior of British Columbia between the Rocky Mountains and the Coastal Range" (Tobey 1981:413).

Chilcotin
> "Chilcotin territory encompasses Cariboo Parklands, Subalpine Forest, and Northern Alplands biotic areas" (Lane 1981:402).

Chipewyan
> "The territory occupied by the Chipewyan in proto-historic and earliest contact times was the northern transitional zone of the boreal forest and the Barren Grounds beyond" (J. Smith 1981:271).

Dogrib
> "But the greater portion of the Dobrib range is in the low

hills and rock outcrop of the Canadian shield, where the forest cover becomes progressively sparse and stunted toward the east" (Helm 1981 : 291).

Han

"The part of the Yukon River occupied by the Han is a heavily forested region just upstream from the area known as the Flats" (Crow and Obley 1981 : 506).

Hare

"These widespread geographic features—the Barren Grounds, the tree-line, Great Bear Lake, and the Mackenzie River—mark the informal borders of the territory that is currently travelled over and utilized by the people. Their domain constitutes the northeastern part of what was once the aboriginal range of the Hare Indians" (Savishinsky 1974 : 4).

Ingalik

"The Yukon and Kuskokwim river basins are two extensive lowland areas formed by the valleys of the two great rivers." "There are highland areas of tundra and barren country covered with small shrubs, lichens, sedges, grasses, weeds, and mosses" (Snow 1981 : 602–603).

Kaska

"Lying between the Rocky Mountains on the east and the Coast Range to the west the country is bounded north and south by water sheds of considerable height" (Honigmann 1964 : 11).

Koyukon

"The Koyukon territory is a vast region that cross-cuts several ecozones." "The two Yukon divisions share the lowland flats with their myriad bogs, sloughs, and small lakes, as well as the adjacent forested rolling and mountainous upland areas. . . . as one goes farther north it becomes more arid with numerous uplands and mountains, and a greater proportion of open taiga" (A. Clark 1981 : 584).

Kutchin

With regard to the Yukon and Mackenzie flats, "The culture of these areas is that of people who live along small streams, turning periodically to the highlands for hunting, then returning to the comfortable protection of their small isolated valleys." However, "the Upper Porcupine River Kutchin and those of the Peel River are primarily mountain people" (Osgood 1936 : 16).

Mountain

"Between the high peaks, often above the timberline, are alpine tundra and river valleys covered mainly with white and black spruce, and birch, tamarack, and willow are found in certain areas" (Gillespie 1981:326).

Sarsi

"At the beginning of the nineteenth century they ranged from the Saskatchewan and the Missouri and from the Rocky Mountains far out on the Plains; but their true habitat was the prairies south of Beaver hills and the adjacent foothills" (Curtis 1964, XVIII, 91).

Sekani

"The country of the Sekani includes rolling foothills, mountains, and high plateau areas, dotted with lakes and cut by numerous rivers and streams" (Denniston 1981:433).

Slave

"In general the area consists of gently rolling plateau country which extends east to Great Slave Lake and the foothills of the mountains" (Honigmann 1946:17).

Tanana

"The terrain to the south beyond the river floodplain consists of a series of rolling hills, and beyond them comes the rugged Alaska Range, with peaks ranging from 10,000 to over 20,000 feet" (McKennan 1981:563).

Tanaina

"The country of the Tanaina surrounding Cook Inlet impresses every visitor with its grandeur. Approaching from the Kodiak group of islands, one sights great mountains rising from the western shore of the sea to more than ten thousand feet of altitude, with the upper parts ever freshly whitened with snow" (Osgood 1937:17).

Tutchone

"The Tutchone homeland is the Yukon Plateau between the towering Saint Elias Mountains on the west (which merge into the coastal range on the south) and the Pelly and Selwyn mountains on the east" (McClellan 1981b:493).

Pacific Coast

Tolowa

A coastal location, but a territory that included "an area of steep mountains ranging from 1,000 to 2,000 feet in elevations of the Siskiyou Mountains to the east. Oak-covered flats of varying sizes occurred between these mountains and furnished an abundant supply of acorns of at least three edible species" (Gould 1978:128).

Hupa, Chilula, Whilkut

"Except for the level valley floor, one to two miles wide, the country is mountainous and difficult of access" (Wallace 1978:164).

Mattole, Nongatl, Sinkyone, Lassik, Wailaki

These groups "occupied the extreme northern part of the Coast Range geomorphic province. This is a system of longitudinal mountain ranges usually from 2,000 to 4,000 feet elevation, with occasional peaks reaching altitudes of 6,000 feet or so" (Elsasser 1978:192).

Southern

Chiricahua Apache

"Within the territory recognized by a band as its own there were favorite places—places easy to defend and difficult to storm; spots where the winter's food supply could be safely cached; comfortable and secluded refuges, often surrounded by mountains and inaccessible country, to which retreat was always possible in time of trouble" (Opler 1955:129).

Jicarilla Apache

"But no sooner were they out of reach of the mountain refuges which marked their boundaries than a great uneasiness seized them. No time was lost in finding the buffalo, securing the meat and hastening back to their own territory. Psychologically they were anything but a Plains people" (Opler 1936b:205).

Kiowa Apache

"Many years ago they occupied the region known as the 'bad ground,' an exceedingly desolate and broken country between the head waters of the Missouri and the Platte" (Keim 1877, quoted in Gunnerson and Gunnerson 1971:14). "When McAllister worked among the Kiowa Apaches in 1933–34, their 'Medicine Lake' was said to be located in the Black Hills region of South Dakota" (Gunnerson and Gunnerson 1971:14).

Lipan Apache

"The Lipan Indians, at the time of earliest contact with Europeans, probably lived with other Apaches in eastern Colorado or northeastern New Mexico. By the beginning of the eighteenth century, a number of these tribes—many of them as yet undifferentiated in the historical records—were forced south and east into the Llano Estacado or High Plains region of Texas as a result of pressure by the recently arrived Comanche" (Sjoberg 1953:76–77).

Mescalero Apache

"The area associated with them is characterized by a series of mountain ranges with peaks that soar to 12,000 feet, separated by valleys and flats" (Opler 1983b: 419).

Navajo

"Set a stretch of sagebrush interspersed with groves of small evergreen (pinyon and juniper trees) against a background of highly colored mesas, canyons, buttes, volcanic necks, igneous mountain masses clothed in deep pine green, roofed over with a brilliant blue sky, and you will have a generalized picture of the Navajo landscape" (Kluckhohn and Leighton 1947: 13).

Western Apache

"Characterized by great diversity, it is a region of jagged mountains and twisting canyons, of well-watered valleys and arid desert" (K. Basso 1971: 13).

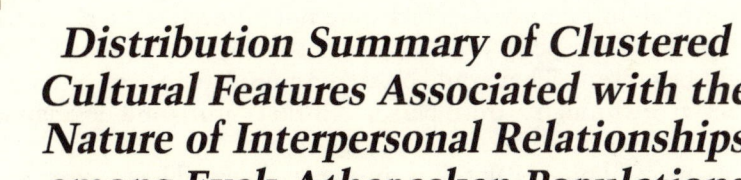

Distribution Summary of Clustered Cultural Features Associated with the Nature of Interpersonal Relationships among Eyak-Athapaskan Populations

Aspects of the cluster:

a. Emphasis on relationship through women as a theme for defining interpersonal ties, taking the form of matrilineal descent in many cases, but with individualistic, interpersonal bonds generally more significant than corporate group membership.

b. Preferred matrilocal residence, whether permanent or temporary, as in bride service.

c. Avoidance/respect relationships among siblings of the opposite sex.

d. Mother-in-law avoidance.

e. Ideological treatment of femaleness as a transpersonalized, transcendent power with ambivalent connotations. Associated practices to deal with the situation include measures to control dangers associated with menstruation, such as the use of scratching sticks, drinking tubes, menstrual seclusion (whether symbolic or actual), fresh meat and cold water dietary restrictions on the menstruant, restrictions on her gaze, a strong symbolic dissociation from male activities which involve some degree of uncertainty or anxiety such as gambling and hunting, and more emphasis on female puberty than male, with a strong focus on menarche.

f. Restrictions on males regarding association with childbirth.

g. Arranged marriage.

Eyak

a. Matrilineal descent, with moiety exogamy (Birket-Smith and de Laguna 1938:131).

b. Traditional postmarital residence is uncertain. Bride service took place before marriage after the turn of the century. Informants in the 1930s give contradictory views on traditional residence, including assertion of matrilocality (Birket-Smith and de Laguna 1938:132).

c. "Grown-up brothers and sisters were not allowed to be alone together, even to speak to each other, though the brother's wife might be present. They could only communicate to each other indirectly, or through a third person" (Birket-Smith and de Laguna 1938:137; see also de Laguna 1937:70).

d. "A man could not speak to his mother-in-law and had to step out of the trail if he saw her coming" (Birket-Smith and de Laguna 1938:133).

e. Puberty seclusion for females for several months' duration in a special hut away from dwellings. The young woman used special dishes of her own, drank water through a bone tube, and used a bone scratcher. She was not allowed to see, touch, or eat fresh meat or fish; violation would offend the animals (Birket-Smith and de Laguna 1938:70). Women were prohibited from touching hunting weapons (de Laguna 1937:73). An adolescent girl who looked at the sky could cause bad weather (de Laguna 1937:74).

f. Men were supposed to leave the house during childbirth (de Laguna 1937:70).

g. Arranged marriages (Birket-Smith and de Laguna 1938:132).

Northern Athapaskan

Ahtna

a. Matrilineal clans with exogamous matrilineal moieties (non-localized) (de Laguna and McClellan 1981).

b. Bride service (de Laguna and McClellan 1981:658).

c. Avoidance ("shyness," "shaming") between siblings of the opposite sex (de Laguna and McClellan 1981:656).

d. Mother-in-law avoidance; there were no terms of address for "father-in-law," "mother-in-law," "son-in-law," or "daughter-in-law" (de Laguna and McClellan 1981:656).

e. Parallel puberty observances for males and females, in both cases involving seclusion and the use of the drinking tube. Both sexes wore a large hood of moose skin, with "fringes falling over the face to shield living things and the sky from the wearer's baleful glances and was hung with rattling hoofs to warn others" (de Laguna and McClellan 1981:658). The initiates were not allowed to speak, eat, or drink for the first three days of their seclusion (de Laguna and McClellan 1981:658). They used a drinking tube of swan bone and were not allowed to eat food that was less than three days old (de Laguna and McClellan 1981:658).

f. A special birth shelter was used at some distance from the dwellings (de Laguna and McClellan 1981:657).

g. Arranged marriages (de Laguna and McClellan 1981:658).

Bearlake
a. No evidence of matrilineal descent.
b. Matrilocal residence (Osgood 1932:78).
c. No evidence of cross-sex sibling avoidance.
d. No evidence of mother-in-law avoidance.
e. Insufficient evidence of ideological treatment of femaleness.
f. Birth restrictions included one case of "a Great Bear Lake woman following birth as forced to break a new trail through the snow, lest ill success in hunting or some other calamity would beset an Indian who incautiously should tread in her footsteps" (Osgood 1932:75).
g. Arranged marriage (Osgood 1932:77).
Beaver (see also Sekani)
a. Bilateral recognition of kinship, but Iroquois cousin terminology suggesting a former unilineal emphasis (Ridington 1981:353).
b. Matrilocal, with bride service (Goddard 1917:221).
c. No mention of opposite sex sibling avoidance.
d. Father-in-law avoidance (Goddard 1917:221).
e. Boys wishing to become good runners used a bone drinking tube to prevent contact with water. This was done only on a hunt. There were prohibitions on eating leg meat or bone marrow, eggs of any kind (Goddard 1917:226).
f. Insufficient evidence of birth practices.
g. Arranged marriage, with exceptions (Goddard 1917:221).
Carrier
a. Matrilineal in historic times, but earlier social organization is uncertain (Tobey 1981:418; Jenness 1937). Cross-cousin marriage preferred in some Carrier groups, but practices and terminology were variable (Tobey 1981:424).
b. Bride service, with subsequent patrilocal residence common (Tobey 1981:428).
c. Insufficient evidence of cross-sex sibling avoidance.
d. No evidence of mother-in-law avoidance.
e. Seclusion for females for one or two years at puberty. Restrictions on eating fresh meat; only dried fish, berries, roots, and bark were allowed (Tobey 1981:427). A drinking tube of goose or swan bone was used, as well as a scratcher (Tobey 1981:428). It was believed that her hair would fall out if she combed it (Jenness 1937:524). She stayed in a hut out of sight and was forbidden to touch a hunter's snowshoes, tools, or weapons in the belief that it would spoil his success. It was also believed that "if a man so much as saw her face he might die" (Jenness

1937 : 523). If the group moved, she would follow far behind on the trail (Jenness 1937 : 524).

f. The husband built a special birth hut. He was the only male allowed to enter (Tobey 1981 : 427).

g. Marriage depended on the choice of the woman and her parents (Tobey 1981 : 428).

Chilcotin

a. Descent was probably bilateral, and kinship ties are characterized as "highly individualistic" (Lane 1981 : 407).

b. Bride service was expected (Lane 1981 : 407).

c. No mention of opposite-sex sibling avoidance.

d. No mention of mother-in-law avoidance.

e. Puberty seclusion for females, with the use of the drinking tube and scratching stick. (Males underwent special training and a vision quest at puberty, but there was no ritual observance for them parallel to that for females.) (Lane 1981 : 407).

f. "Birth occurred out of doors and away from camp." The husband might assist at delivery (Lane 1981 : 404).

g. Arranged marriages (Lane 1981 : 407).

Chipewyan

a. Bilateral descent, but with cross-cousin marriage suggesting former unilineal descent (J. Smith 1981 : 277).

b. Bride service (J. Smith 1981 : 279).

c. "From the early age of eight or nine years, they are prohibited by custom from joining in the most innocent amusements with children of the opposite sex" (Hearne 1911 : 302).

d. "The familiar mother-in-law taboo was known only as a Cree custom" (Curtis 1964, XVIII, 41). However, Curtis later refers to mother-in-law avoidance among the Chipewyan (Curtis 1964, XVIII, 108n).

e. At puberty, young women "generally go a little distance from the other tents for four or five days, and at their return wear a kind of veil or curtain, made of beads, for some time after, as a mark of modesty" (Hearne 1911 : 304). There was no ritual observance of male puberty.

f. Birth took place in a small tent, with women as attendants. "No male, except children in arms, ever offers to approach her" (Hearne 1911 : 131). "A Northern Indian woman after childbirth is reckoned unclean for a month or five weeks; during which time she always remains in a small tent placed at a little distance from the others, with only a female acquaintance or two; and during which time the father never sees the child" (Hearne 1911 : 131).

g. Arranged marriage (J. Smith 1981:277).

Dogrib

a. Bilateral kinship, but bride service (Helm 1981).

b. Bride service generally lasted at least until the birth of the first child (Helm 1981:301).

c. "Traditional Dogrib norms required reserved behavior between a man and his sister" (Helm 1981:301).

d. Insufficient evidence of mother-in-law avoidance.

e. Menstrual restrictions for females; no ritual for males (Helm 1981:301). At puberty, boys should no longer play with girls or they might become weak (Helm 1981:301). "For the rest of her reproductive life, each menstrual or postpartum period required that she stay apart from men's gear, that she walk aside from the trail, and that, generally, she remain apart from the family so that her condition would not adversely affect her husband's hunting or her children's health" (Helm 1981:301).

f. Insufficient evidence of birth practices.

g. Insufficient evidence of arranged marriage.

Han

a. Three exogamous matrilineal clans (two in one moiety) (Crow and Obley 1981:508; Osgood 1971:40).

b. Bride service was expected.

c. Insufficient evidence of cross-sex sibling avoidance.

d. Insufficient evidence of mother-in-law avoidance.

e. Puberty observance for females included seclusion for a year and a prohibition on eating fresh meat. Male puberty received minimal observance (Crow and Obley 1981:508). "When outside the shelter, the girl wore a special hood that prevented her from looking anywhere except at the ground in front of her, and she was not allowed to walk in an established trail" (Osgood 1971:49).

f. Childbirth took place away from men (Crow and Obley 1981:508).

g. "Marriages were generally arranged by parents during their children's infancy, although consideration was given later for the wishes of those involved" (Crow and Obley 1981:508–509).

Hare (see also Slave, Mountain)

a. Bilateral reckoning of kinship ties, but bifurcate merging kinship terms in the first ascending generation and Iroquois cousin terms, which usually are associated with unilineal descent. Evidence of an earlier practice of sister exchange (Savishinsky and Hara 1981:319).

b. "A man was expected to fulfill a period of bride service for his wife's family, and postmarital residence was therefore initially uxorilocal" (Savishinsky and Hara 1981:319).

c. Insufficient evidence of cross-sex sibling avoidance.

d. Insufficient evidence of mother-in-law avoidance.

e. Menstrual seclusion. "There were a large number of food and touching taboos" (Savishinsky and Hara 1981:320). "Menstruating women were forbidden to step over fish nets and hunting implements and prohibited from skinning or eating the parts of certain animals to insure the success of men in subsistence activities and the well-being of their families and children" (Savishinsky and Hara 1981:320). There was no ritual for male puberty (Savishinsky and Hara 1981:320).

f. Insufficient evidence of birth practices.

g. Arranged marriage (Savishinsky and Hara 1974:47).

Ingalik

a. Bilateral (Snow 1981:610).

b. Bride service (Snow 1981:609).

c. Avoidance between siblings of the opposite sex (Snow 1981:610).

d. Insufficient evidence of mother-in-law avoidance.

e. Seclusion of females at puberty for a year in a corner of the dwelling. No puberty seclusion for males. During his daughter's seclusion, a father observed ritual restrictions similar to those associated with childbirth. There was no seclusion for male puberty (Snow 1981:610). A young woman in seclusion was dangerous to men if she looked them directly in the eye. Her gaze could cause them to lose hunting, fishing, or political power (Snow 1981:610).

f. Restrictions on men during childbirth.

g. Insufficient evidence of arranged marriage.

Kaska (includes Tagish and Tahltan)

a. The Tahltan had matrilineal clans (MacLachlan 1981:463, 464). The Tagish had matrilineal clans and exogamous moieties with Tlingit names, although "far back in their history the Tagish may have had matrilineal descent and exogamous clans with Athapaskan names" (McClellan 1981a:485). Matrilocal extended family, with bifurcate merging and Iroquois kinship terminology (Honigmann 1981b:446).

b. See above. Bride service was expected.

c. Respect/avoidance between siblings of the opposite sex (Honigmann 1981b:446).

d. Reserved relationship between husband and mother-in-law.

e. Boys underwent training at puberty. Female menstrual seclusion was practiced, and women were restricted from touching hunting gear. A menstruant in seclusion wore a hood over her head to obscure her view, especially of the sky (Honigmann 1964:125). Contact with menstrual blood was believed to cause sore legs in men (Honigmann 1964:124). Tagish puberty seclusion for females involved the use of a large hood over a willow frame to restrict the woman's vision. "Male puberty was equally important, but observance was not so dramatic" (McClellan 1981a:488).

f. Birth fluids were considered dangerous to men and especially unlucky for hunters (McClellan 1981a:487). Men were expected to stay away from the scene of childbirth (Honigmann 1964:447).

g. Arranged marriages.

Koyukon

a. Matrilineal clan system with three exogamous clans and Iroquois cousin terms (A. Clark 1981:589).

b. "Initial matrilocal residence," which tended to weaken after the turn of the present century (A. Clark 1981:589).

c. No mention of cross-sex sibling avoidance.

d. No mention of mother-in-law avoidance.

e. Menstrual seclusion at puberty for almost a year with a hood worn over the head to restrict vision, a prohibition on eating fresh meat, special mittens to prevent the young woman from touching her own skin, and a special cup and bowl for her to use. She was expected to keep her eyes downcast (A. Clark 1981:591). A young woman in seclusion wore a special decorated hat or a moosehide hood, drank small amounts of water through a tube, and was prohibited from eating fresh meat or berries (Cruikshank 1975:4). "The menses . . . has its own spirit that contains the essence of femininity, and it can bring bad luck with animals, feminize men and alienate animals from them, or even cause sickness and death" (Nelson 1983: 25). In the central Yukon, women had a special term for a girl who has become a woman, but none for a boy after puberty (Cruikshank 1975:13).

f. "Birth almost always occurred outside the family dwelling" (A. Clark 1981:590).

g. Arranged marriages (A. Clark 1981:590, 591).

Kutchin

a. Matrilineal clans until 1840, although with regard to the concept of corporate group membership as a criterion in defining interpersonal relationships. "All aspects of Kutchin social life exemplified two further and overriding principles, namely, flexibility and opportunism" (Slobodin 1981:517). Hawaiian cousin terminology. "Family curses—physical blemishes or behavioral peculiarities were held to be inherited matrilineally" (Slobodin 1962:526).

b. Regarding matrilocal residence, "it was customary for a newly married daughter to occupy the other half of the lodge until her own family increased to a size that required a separate lodge" (McKennan 1965:51). Matrilocal residence "until at least the birth of the first child" (Slobodin 1962:42).

c. Respect between siblings of the opposite sex (Slobodin 1962:42).

d. "Respect and reserve" toward "parents-in-law, especially of the opposite sex" (Slobodin 1962:42).

e. Menstrual seclusion in a hut away from camp. If a young woman during her first menstrual seclusion ventured out, she wore a conical head covering whose sides fell as far as her knees to prevent her from gazing at anything but the ground. She could not touch food, but ate with a pointed stick and drank water through a bird bone tube which hung around her neck, or which was attached to her mittens (McKennan 1965:58). A menstruating woman was not supposed to touch hunting or fishing gear or eat fresh meat (McKennan 1965:58). A menstruating woman should not gaze at men or have any contact with them (McKennan 1965:85). If boys and girls played too much together while growing up, boys would not become good hunters (McKennan 1965:85). Male puberty was not regarded as seriously as female, although some practices (a conical cap with fringe hanging over the eyes, a drinking tube, and mittens) paralleled practices for females (McKennan 1965:59). Boys at puberty were trained for several months in a group by respected men (McKennan 1965:52).

f. "Normally, an expectant father will go off to hunt during his wife's labor, but if necessary he will remain to assist" (Osgood 1936:146).

g. Arranged marriages (McKennan 1965:56).

Mountain (see also Slave, Hare)

a. Apparently bilateral (Gillespie 1981:334).

b. Bride service was expected until the birth of the first child (Gillespie 1981:336).

c. Reserve between siblings of the opposite sex (Gillespie 1981:336).

d. Insufficient evidence of mother-in-law avoidance.

e. Menstrual seclusion at puberty, involving a stricture that she must hide her face from view (Gillespie 1981 : 335). "Menstrual blood was always treated as dangerous to men's ability to kill animals" (Gillespie 1981 : 336). Menstruating women were restricted from contact with hunting weapons. There was no formal recognition of male puberty (Gillespie 1981 : 335).

f. "A woman gave birth away from camp or in a shelter with only women about her" (Gillespie 1981 : 335).

g. "Marriage contracts were often made between a man and a girl's parents when she was still a small child" (Gillespie 1981 : 336).

Sarsi

a. "Girls belonged to their mothers' bands, boys above the age of nine or ten to their fathers', though they still retained close contact with their mothers' kin; for since the bands were very small and freely intermarried there was no outward distinction between their members." "The bands, indeed, seem to have been very fluid" (Jenness n.d. : 10).

b. Matrilocal residence (Curtis 1964, XVIII, 102).

c. No evidence of cross-sex sibling avoidance.

d. Mother-in-law avoidance. "The taboo does not extend to father-in-law or daughter-in-law" (Curtis 1964, XVIII, 108).

e. No formal puberty rituals for either sex, but "menstruating females usually remained apart from the family tipi" (Curtis 1964, XVIII, 161).

f. Husbands could assist at childbirth (Curtis 1964, XVIII, 105–106). According to Jenness, however, "The first pangs of labour drove the mother into a separate tent, and brought to her aid three or four old women, one of them a medicine-woman. They warned away all men and unmarried girls" (Jenness n.d. : 26).

g. Marriages were arranged (Curtis 1964, XVIII, 107).

Sekani

a. Loose bilateral organization (Denniston 1981 : 433). At one time, the Sekani attempted to develop exogamous matrilineal phratries (Denniston 1981 : 438).

b. Matrilocal residence, with bride service until the birth of the first child (Denniston 1981 : 438).

c. No mention of cross-sex sibling avoidance.

d. No specific mention of mother-in-law avoidance, but "a newly married couple never lived under the same roof as their parents, for this would have been contrary to the dignity of both families" (Jenness 1937 : 54).

e. Menstrual seclusion at puberty with dietary restrictions on fresh meat and fish. Special cups were used by the young woman

(Denniston 1981:438). "Each night she camped apart for several days in a small brush hut, drinking from a special birchbark cup and supplied by her mother or female relatives with dried meat and dried fish. If she ate fresh meat or fish at this season, she would spoil the hunter's luck. Since even to look at a hunter would impair his success in the chase, she covered her eyes whenever she left her shelter. She might not walk in a hunter's trail, or touch his beaver net, though she could handle his knife, ax, or snowshoes" (Jenness 1937:56). If the group moved while she was in seclusion, she was compelled to walk through the brush behind rather than on the trail (Jenness 1937:524). Male puberty involved a vision quest. Restrictions were intended "to prevent any contact, physical or spiritual, between menstruating women and men or the animals they hunted: such contact would ruin the hunt" (Denniston 1981:438).

f. "A woman in labor camped away from her husband so that he would not have bad luck in hunting" (Denniston 1981:437).

g. Marriages were not arranged by parents (Denniston 1981:438).

Slave

a. Some suggestion of bifurcate merging and Iroquois kinship terms (Asch 1981:342, 344).

b. Matrilocal residence was most common; patrilocal residence was rare. Bride service was expected (Honigmann 1946:69, 71, 162).

c. "There was apparently little joking between brothers and sisters or between cousins," but no formal pattern of avoidance (Honigmann 1946:70).

d. "On the other hand respect was the keynote of the relationship between Ego and the mother-in-law. This respect did not extend to complete avoidance, the son-in-law and mother-in-law being permitted to eat together, for example" (Honigmann 1946:69).

e. Female puberty recognition involved seclusion for ten days. Males underwent a vision quest and a first game ceremony. For a woman in seclusion to look at a hunter would ruin his luck (Jenness 1937:56).

f. Childbirth was considered dangerous to men (Asch 1981:344; see also Honigmann 1946:83).

g. Marriage was often initiated by the groom, but it was subject to parental approval (Honigmann 1946:85).

Tanaina

a. Matrilineal clans organized in moieties, with bride service (Townsend 1981:632; see also Osgood 1937:137). Equal status for both sexes, with the belief that hunting "belongs" to men, while women are dominant in the home (Osgood 1937). There was a concept that "the home and the woman are fundamental whereas the man and the work he controls are contributory" (Osgood 1937:137).

b. Bride service expected to last for five years (Osgood 1937:162). "Ordinarily the suitor joins the girl's family for one to five years, exercising the privileges of a husband but at the same time giving his support to the aid of his wife's people. After that period he can move as he chooses" (Osgood 1937:164).

c. No mention of cross-sex sibling avoidance.

d. No mention of mother-in-law avoidance.

e. Female puberty observances involved seclusion for approximately one year in a small room attached to the dwelling, during which the young woman was not supposed to touch herself and wore a parka over her eyes (Townsend 1981). Seclusion lasted for one year (Townsend 1963:214). A young woman in seclusion was not allowed to prepare food or drink for herself, or to eat fresh meat or fish or bear meat in any form. She used a bone drinking tube and a special scratcher. It was forbidden for her to dress her own hair (Osgood 1937:160). She wore a hood of caribou skin to restrict her gaze, which could cause sickness (Osgood 1937:160). A young woman in seclusion who looked at a boy would cause him to be killed on a hunt (Townsend 1963:216).

f. Birth seclusion lasted five days (Osgood 1937:160).

g. Arranged marriages, with marriage to the father's sister's daughter preferred.

Tanana

a. Exogamous matrilineal descent groups organized in a tripartite system (McKennan 1981:571). The Kolchan had three exogamous matrilineal clans (Hosley 1981:620).

b. Bride service (McKennan 1981:571). Kolchan bride service was usually followed by continued matrilocal residence (Hosley 1981:620).

c. Insufficient evidence of cross-sex sibling avoidance.

d. Insufficient evidence of mother-in-law avoidance.

e. Regarding menstrual seclusion, "at this time she was compelled to live in a special menstrual hut, avoid gazing upon men or upon the sun, refrain from eating fresh meat, take her drinking water only through a bone tube, and observe other taboos of a similar nature" (Hosley 1981:572).

f. Insufficient evidence of birth practices.

g. In the Alaska Plateau region, "marriages were frequently arranged" (Hosley 1981:542).

Tutchone

a. Matrilineal descent, with exogamous moieties and Iroquois cousin terminology. The ideal marriage was to the father's sister's daughter (McClellan and Denniston 1981b:501).

b. Bride service (McClellan and Denniston 1981b:501).

c. "Strict cross-sex avoidance was enjoined between siblings who had reached puberty" (McClellan and Denniston 1981b:501).

d. "A man avoided his mother-in-law in looks and speech and behaved formally to his father-in-law" (McClellan and Denniston 1981b:501).

e. Menstrual seclusion at puberty involved the drinking tube and hood to restrict vision. "Her female physiology had now become a powerful force in relation to the pervasive spiritual aspects of the world about her. Her conduct would affect either favorably the state of the weather, mountains, rivers, and the animals and plants on which the welfare of the group depended" (McClellan and Denniston 1981b:500).

f. Insufficient evidence of birth practices.

g. Insufficient evidence of arranged marriage.

Pacific Coast Athapaskan

Hupa-Chilula-Whilkut

a. No principle of matrilineal descent. Inheritance was patrilineal (Goddard 1903–1904:58).

b. Although bride price was preferred, "half marriage," involving matrilocal residence, was allowed (Wallace 1978:172). Generally, residence was patrilocal.

c. Insufficient evidence of cross-sex sibling avoidance.

d. Insufficient evidence of mother-in-law avoidance.

e. The pubescent female was considered "unclean" and secluded for ten days, her head covered with a deerskin (Wallace 1978:172). During her seclusion she stayed in a special menstrual lodge (Goddard 1903–1904:17). The young woman's glance was considered to be contaminating. During the ten days of her seclusion, "she is not allowed to look up at the world about her nor is she allowed to look anyone in the face" (Goddard 1903–1904:53). During seclusion, the young woman was not allowed to drink cold water and had to use scratching sticks. "She is not allowed to drink water for the ten days." "She is careful not to touch her face or hair with her hands. A piece of bone or horn is worn suspended from her neck that it may be at hand for dressing her hair" (Goddard 1903–1904:53).

f. "Women gave birth alone or in the special menstrual lodge. Some woman made for her the required medicine" (Goddard 1903–1904:81). She lived in the lodge for thirty to sixty days (Goddard 1903–1904:18).

g. Insufficient evidence of arranged marriage.

Mattole

a. No evidence of matrilineal descent.

b. Patrilocal tendency, but "either in the beginning, or later, residence was matrilocal, patrilocal, or variable" (Elsasser 1978). If bride price was not paid, bride service with temporary matrilocal residence was expected (Nomland 1938:104).

c. Insufficient evidence of cross-sex sibling avoidance.

d. No evidence of mother-in-law avoidance.

e. Seclusion at first menstruation, with eyes covered, scratchers, and prohibitions on meat and cold water (Elsasser 1978). In the Bear River group, there was a token seclusion in a corner of the house. Scratching sticks were used to prevent sores. Deer meat was prohibited on the grounds that it would harm the girl (Nomland 1938:99). A young woman during this time had her hair pulled over her eyes and was not supposed to "look piercingly into the distance" or she might develop poor eyesight or go blind (Nomland 1938:99). She was not allowed to look at the sky for thirty days. Female puberty was given more complex ritual recognition than male.

f. Men were not allowed to be present at birth and were said to be "afraid" of newborn babies (Nomland 1938:102). Restrictions on eating meat and drinking cold water were associated with birth (Elsasser 1978:196).

g. Arranged marriages.

Tolowa

a. "Paternal kin, because they lived together," constituted the "basic social group" (Drucker 1937:248). No concept of "tribe," or any political unit larger than the village (Drucker 1937:222).

b. Patrilocal residence seen as the ideal, but matrilocal residence associated with "half-marriage" also possible (Gould 1978:132).

c. No mention of cross-sex sibling avoidance.

d. No mother-in-law avoidance (Drucker 1937:248).

e. Confinement for females at puberty; no initiation rituals for boys (Drucker 1937:254). Seclusion could be in the dwelling or in a separate hut. The young woman used head scratchers, since to touch herself would cause sores and skin disease. She was not allowed to drink cold water (Drucker 1937:254). A young woman in seclusion was not allowed to gaze at the sun, which would burn her eyes (Drucker 1937:254). A girl's puberty ceremony, held only for the daughters of rich men, involved token seclusion in the dance house, fasting, restriction on drinking cold water, a feather visor over the eyes, and a prohibition on "looking around" for ten days (Drucker 1937:263). Female puberty was observed among the Galice Creek group, but the drinking tube was not used. There was no puberty observance for males (Barnett 1937:194).

f. At a birth, both parents were prohibited from eating meat or drinking cold water. Birth took place in the dwelling, with both parents undergoing a subsequent "purification ceremony" (Drucker 1937:253).

g. "A marriage had to be arranged by a formal procedure of purchase" (Drucker 1937:250).

Wailaki-Nongatl-Lassik-Sinkyone-Kato

a. "Among the Kato, children were not regarded as belonging any more to the paternal than to the maternal side" (Curtis 1964, XIV, 11). Among the Sinkyone, "genealogies were recited to the great-great-grandfather in the male line" (Nomland 1935:159).

b. Bride price was preferred among the Sinkyone, and bride service for one year was a less desirable alternative (Nomland 1935:160).

c. Respect/avoidance relationships between siblings of the opposite sex were maintained among the Sinkyone (Nomland 1935).

d. Mother-in-law avoidance was practiced among the Sinkyone (Nomland 1935:159).

e. "At puberty a girl began to live for five months a very quiet and abstemious life, remaining always in or near the house, abstaining from meat, and drinking little water" (Curtis 1964, XIV, 11). Among the Wailaki, at puberty a young woman would sit in the middle of the dwelling with a deerskin draped over her head, taking little food or water. Older women would sit in a circle around her and sing. After a few days she was bathed in running water by her mother, with a general celebration (Curtis 1964, XIV, 29). A menstruating woman among the Wailaki did not cook for others but was not secluded (Curtis 1964, XIV, 29). Female puberty among the Sinkyone involved token seclusion in a corner of the dwelling. The young woman had to leave when deer meat was being cooked. She used a special head scratcher to avoid sores, a special drinking basket and tube, and fasted (Nomland 1935:162). During the period of puberty observance, a young Sinkyone woman had her hair pulled down over her face and was not supposed to look around or at the sun (Nomland 1935:162). Sinkyone women were not allowed to hunt. Violation of sexual abstinence before a hunt, during menstruation, or within five days after childbirth was thought to offend game (Nomland 1935:152).

f. Insufficient evidence of birth practices.

g. Marriages were arranged by the fathers (Curtis 1964, XIV, 29). Sinkyone marriage was negotiated "through a relative or friend acting as a go-between" (Nomland 1935:159).

Southern Athapaskan

General

a. Most Apachean groups emphasized descent bilaterally; but "in Apache kinship usages there was emphasis on the role of grandparents, particularly on the maternal side" (Opler 1983a:369).

b. All Apachean groups were matrilocal (cf. Opler 1983a:368, 369). "An Apache male was trained to feel that he should provide for his wife's parents and obey their instructions" (Opler 1983a:370).

c. Between siblings of the opposite sex in all Apachean groups, "great restraint in speech and behavior" was expected (Opler 1983a:369).

e. The use of the drinking tube in puberty rituals was ubiquitous among Apachean groups with the exception of the western Navajo, but otherwise rare in the Southwest and Basin. Fresh meat restrictions associated with female puberty were also "universal" (Driver 1941, Table 13).

g. Marriages were arranged, although individual preferences usually were taken into account (cf. Opler 1983a:370).

Chiricahua Apache

a. Bilateral kinship. "It is impossible to get any convincing assurance that one kind of relative is necessarily 'closer' than another" (Opler 1941a:54). However, "in normal circumstances the father's sisters and brothers will never be members of the same extended family as the child, though they may be living in the same local group or vicinity. Since their primary ties are with other family units, they have less contact with a child than the maternal relatives" (Opler 1941a:57). "The rule of matrilocal residence permits constant contact between the child and his mother's parents" (Opler 1941a:63). "The paternal grandparents usually cannot hope for a great deal of contact with their son's child" (Opler 1941a:64).

b. Matrilocal residence (see above), with bride service. "We speak of one who marries into our family as 'one who carries things in for me' in the sense of 'one who goes out and kills and carries in game for me.' The word means to me that in the old days a son-in-law would go out and kill game for his parents-in-law" (Opler 1941a:163). "A man lives near his in-laws and brings what he gets on the hunt back to them, all of it. His food is prepared at his mother-in-law's place anyway" (Opler 1941a:164).

c. "Siblings of the opposite sex, expecially after puberty, must show great respect and decorum when they are together" (Opler 1941a:57). "'If the mother and father aren't at home and your sister is alone, you must leave camp. You must stay somewhere else'" (Opler 1941a:60).

d. Mother-in-law avoidance (Opler 1941a:164–166). "'The camp of the young people is so arranged that the place of the parents-in-law cannot be seen; it might be behind some brush with the door facing the other way'" (Opler 1941a:164).

e. Symbolic seclusion for young women at puberty ceremony. Before the public ceremony, she stays in a hut for four days and is advised by an older woman. "'She tells her how to drink through the tube [of carrizo, suspended from the fringe of the dress on the right side], how to scratch herself with the stick [from a fruit or nut-bearing tree; the scratcher hangs on the left side of the dress]. She tells the girl that she must not scratch herself with her nails, because, if she does, it will leave scars, and she must not touch water with her lips but must use the tube for eight days or it will rain.'" "'She tells the girl not to eat too much, because she must stay in the tepee most of this time and she shouldn't go out in the brush much'" (Opler 1941a:90). During this time the young woman should go only where she is told and stay inside the dwelling most of the time for four days preceding and following the public ceremony. She should refrain from laughing and talk very little (Opler 1941a:90). A young woman during her puberty ceremony should not look at the sky, since it would cause rain clouds to gather (Opler 1941a:93). After the public ceremony, the young woman stayed at the grounds for four days with her family. "'During that time the girl can't wash and has to wear her costume. She must use the scratcher and reed for those four days too'" (Opler 1941a:133). Although there were no formal restrictions on women during menstruation, young women were "reminded of the effect of menstrual blood on men. They are told that it makes men paralyzed and deformed, unable to straighten their arms or legs" (Opler 1941a: 154).

f. Regarding childbirth, "When the time for delivery draws near, the husband leaves the home." "There is no definite rule which bars other men from being present . . ." but usually " 'men don't come to a birth because there are so many women around, and a man would feel funny.' Another factor which discourages their attendance is that discharges from the woman's body at childbirth are to some extent equated with menstrual blood, from which a man can contract painful swelling of the joints" (Opler 1941a: 7).

g. "Most marriages are arranged in terms of a conventional pattern in which the wishes of the families involved carry much weight" (Opler 1941a: 154). "Sometimes the parents of the boy and girl arrange the match and only tell the principals when all arrangements have been made" (Opler 1941a: 155).

Jicarilla Apache

a. It was believed possible for several men to contribute to the conception of a child (Opler 1936b). The Jicarilla recognized kin ties bilaterally, but had Iroquois cousin terminology (Opler 1936b: 216).

b. Matrilocal residence was the norm (Opler 1936b, 1936a: 620).

c. "Brothers and sisters are expected to act with great reserve in each other's presence" (Opler 1936b: 217).

d. Mother-in-law avoidance was expected (Opler 1936b: 220).

e. Puberty for females involved a four-day ceremony based on a pattern similar to that of other Apachean groups (Opler 1936b: 215). "The sight, smell or touch of menstrual blood is extremely dangerous to men" (Opler 1936b: 222).

f. Insufficient evidence regarding birth practices.

g. "A young man wishing to marry sends a near relation to procure the consent of the girl's parents, with whose decision the wishes of the daughter have little weight" (Curtis 1964, I, 55).

Kiowa Apache

a. Essentially bilateral, but matrilocal residence led to a close association of matrilineal kin (cf. McAllister 1955: 58).

b. "Also, residence seems to have been matrilocal more often than patrilocal" (McAllister 1955: 58).

c. Reserve/respect between siblings of the opposite sex (Opler 1936a).

d. "A man would never touch his mother-in-law, look at her, talk to her, call her name, or be alone with her in a tipi" (McAllister 1955: 130).

e. There was little formal recognition of the first menstruation. "For four days a girl was supposed to stay close to the tipi because she was 'ashamed'" (McAllister 1955:142).

f. Birth was attended by women. In the case of difficult labor, "a medicine man might be called in to perform a ceremony which would aid in delivery, but before the child was born he would rush from the tipi" (McAllister 1955:145).

g. Ideally, marriages were arranged (McAllister 1955:145).

Lipan Apache

a. The Lipan had bilateral organization, but practiced the levirate and sororate (Opler 1945:137).

b. The Lipan practiced matrilocal residence, with at least implicit bride service. "Relatives by marriage, particularly sons-in-law, are the mainstay of the family system of economy and protection" (Opler 1945:135).

c. Insufficient evidence for cross-sex sibling avoidance.

d. Insufficient evidence for mother-in-law avoidance, but see item d under "General" Apache features, above.

e. Insufficient evidence.

f. Insufficient evidence for birth practices.

g. "Marriage among the Lipan is an understanding between families rather than between individuals" (Opler 1945:135).

Mescalero Apache

a. "Women are the stable nucleus of the family group" (Opler 1969:39).

b. Matrilocal residence. "In spite of a theory of bilateral kinship, in practice there is a greater reliance on maternal relatives and more contact with them" (Opler 1969:39). Bride service (Opler 1969:147).

c. Avoidance between siblings of the opposite sex (Opler 1969:67).

d. Mother-in-law avoidance (Opler 1969:209).

e. The ceremonial structure for the girls' puberty ritual was located away from the dwellings (Opler 1969:98).

f. Insufficient evidence for birth practices.

g. Arranged marriages (Opler 1969:208).

Navajo

a. "The matrilineal clans of the Navajo are based on the mother-child bond." "The primary bond . . . in Navajo culture is found in the mother-child bond, which is the closest and strongest of all relationships in the Navajo social system" (Witherspoon 1983b:524, 525).

b. Although there is a range of option in residence choice, "there is a preference and an expectation that they will live at the wife's mother's unit" (Witherspoon 1983b: 526).

c. "Thus the relation between adult brother and sister, while one of deep affection, is marked by great reserve in physical contact and certain restrictions in speech" (Kluckhohn and Leighton 1947: 58).

d. Mother-in-law avoidance (Kluckhohn and Leighton 1947: 58).

e. Girls' puberty ceremony, incorporating Blessing Way chants (Kluckhohn and Leighton 1947: 149).

f. Birth usually took place in the dwelling, with the father present (Leighton and Kluckhohn 1947: 15–16).

g. Marriages were arranged (Kluckhohn and Leighton 1947: 58).

Western Apache

a. Matrilineal clans (Goodwin 1969). Women were considered more knowledgeable about kinship, "perhaps because of the descent traced through the mother and the functional dominance of kin on her side rather than the father's" (Goodwin 1969: 206). Women were seen as perpetuating relationships. "If you have only boys, the blood lineage dies out and you are left without relatives" (Goodwin 1969: 539). Kinship terms were extended to members of the same clan, but the strongest ties were with immediate kin; genealogies were not kept beyond the fourth generation. "After the fourth time the kinship is gone. It is no more, because no one can live longer than that" (Goodwin 1969: 205). Between the parents, the primary attachment was to the mother, and "the Apache feels closest to his maternal relatives" (Goodwin 1969: 208). The maternal grandmother is far more important than the other grandparents (Goodwin 1969: 218).

b. Matrilocal residence.

c. Respect/avoidance of opposite sex siblings (Goodwin 1969: 205, 255).

d. Mother-in-law avoidance (Goodwin 1969: 482).

e. There was no formal menstrual seclusion, but a puberty ceremony during which a drinking tube and scratching stick were hung around the young woman's neck (Goodwin 1969: 484). During the four days following her puberty ceremony, the young woman is not secluded, but must remain at the ceremonial grounds. "She may not wash herself, for it is thought that by doing so she would sacrifice her power. She may drink only through her drinking tube." She is required to touch herself only with a scratching stick (K. Basso 1966: 160). Avoidance of intercourse before hunting because "if you do that, the deer will smell the man and he will never kill any" (Goodwin 1969: 322). No comparable ceremony for male puberty, except for participation on first raid.

f. Insufficient evidence of traditional birth practices.

g. Arranged marriages.

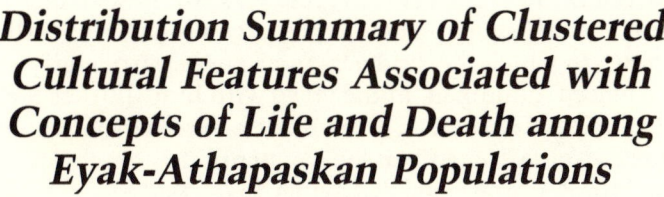

Distribution Summary of Clustered Cultural Features Associated with Concepts of Life and Death among Eyak-Athapaskan Populations

Aspects of the cluster:
a. A belief that "souls" have a dual aspect, with one especially threatening and associated wtih physical remains or places and the other transitory at death and associated with wind or air.
b. An emphatic physical and symbolic dissociation of the living from the dead, with quick removal of the corpse from the dwelling through a hole made in the wall, disposal of the remains at a distance away from human habitation, abandonment or purification of the dwelling to keep the ghost from returning, destruction or disposal of the property of the deceased at the gravesite, and a restriction on uttering the name of the deceased to avoid summoning the ghost.
c. An association of owls with the dead.
d. A concept of reincarnation.

Eyak
a. "The Eyak may have had a vague notion of two souls" (Birket-Smith and de Laguna 1938:231). One informant "supposed that it was the person's 'mind' which is reborn." "He does not know where the 'mind' stays when it is in the body, but supposes it is in the breath." "'The mind is just like the wind'" (Birket-Smith and de Laguna 1938:231, 232).
b. After death the body was kept in the house for four days, leaning in a sitting position against the wall of the sleeping room, dressed in his best clothes and completely covered with a blanket. "The eyes were closed, otherwise the deceased might look at his next of kin and make him die" (Birket-Smith and de Laguna 1938:163). "The Eyak do not like to touch a dead person, but it was the duty of the opposite moiety to dress the dead, since his own relatives dared (?) not touch him" (Birket-Smith and de Laguna 1938:163). "Boards were removed from the wall of the house so that the corpse could be carried out through a special opening. If it were

removed through the door, the relatives would soon die" (Birket-Smith and de Laguna 1938:165; de Laguna 1937:35). "All the belongings to which the dead person had been particularly attached were placed, unbroken, in the grave with him" (Birket-Smith and de Laguna 1938:165). "The name of a dead person who had not yet been reincarnated was never mentioned except at the potlatch" (Birket-Smith and de Laguna 1938:156).
c. Insufficient evidence regarding the possible association of owls with death.
d. Children were often given the same name as a sibling who had died. "The child was to them actual reincarnation of the namesake" (Birket-Smith and de Laguna 1938:153; see also above).
Athapaskan
Northern
Ahtna
a. Insufficient evidence regarding concepts of the soul.
b. The corpse was removed from the dwelling through a window or the smoke hole (de Laguna and McClellan 1981). It was forbidden to mention the name of the deceased. The house was "abandoned and burned with all its contents" (de Laguna and McClellan 1981:658). The ghost was believed to linger near the body for three days (de Laguna and McClellan 1981:658).
c. Unruly children were threatened by the owl (de Laguna and McClellan 1981:657).
d. It was believed that some individuals were reincarnated (de Laguna and McClellan 1981:659).
Bearlake
a. Insufficient evidence for belief in a dual soul, association with air.
b. The property of the deceased was destroyed or abandoned (Osgood 1932:81).
c. Insufficient evidence of association of owl with death.
d. Concept of reincarnation (Osgood 1932:75).
Beaver
a. Insufficient evidence regarding concepts of the soul.
b. Property of the deceased was destroyed at death (Goddard 1917:224).
c. Insufficient evidence regarding association of owls with death.
d. Insufficient evidence regarding belief in reincarnation.
Carrier

a. "The Carrier distinguished the soul, which occasionally left the body during dreams, from the ghost, which emerged only at death" (Tobey 1981:429). The being was considered to have three aspects: the warmth (*bizil*), which was an attribute of the living body that totally disappeared at death; the mind (*bini*); and shadow (*bitsen*) or shade (*bizul*) (Jenness 1937:535).

b. Cremation, box burial with potlatch, post with crest carving (Tobey 1981:429).

c. "The hooting of a small owl night after night near his camp fills him with dismay, for it is warning for him that a relative will soon die" (Jenness 1937:540–541).

d. Insufficient evidence for belief in reincarnation.

Chilcotin

a. "Every human being had a soul that could leave the body for short periods. Permanent soul loss caused death" (Lane 1981:409–410).

b. The house was abandoned after death (Lane 1981:409).

c. Owls were "taboo" (Lane 1981:405).

d. Insufficient evidence of a belief in reincarnation.

Chipewyan

a. Insufficient evidence regarding concepts of the soul.

b. After a death the camp was abandoned and the property of the deceased was destroyed (J. Smith 1981:279). "The name of a deceased person was not mentioned in the presence of relatives during a period of two or three years" (Curtis 1964, I, 44).

c. Owls were eaten (Hearne 1911:372).

d. It was believed that some people were reincarnated as wolves (J. Smith 1981:279).

Dogrib

a. Insufficient evidence regarding concepts of the soul.

b. An individual's property was destroyed after death (Helm 1981:301).

c. Insufficient evidence to associate owls with death.

d. Insufficient evidence of belief in reincarnation, although such a belief was shared by the linguistically close and geographically adjacent Bearlake and the nearby Hare (see appropriate listings).

Han

a. Insufficient evidence regarding concepts of the soul.

b. The clothing and property of the deceased were burned (Osgood 1971:52).

c. Insufficient evidence regarding association of owls with death.

d. Belief in reincarnation (Osgood 1971:47).

Hare (see also Slave, Mountain)

a. Insufficient evidence for dual concept of soul.

b. Ghosts were feared; the property of the deceased was destroyed (Savishinsky and Hara 1981:320).

c. Insufficient evidence for association of owls with death.

d. There was a belief in reincarnation; a child was often named after a recently deceased person (Savishinsky 1974:176).

Ingalik

a. In addition to the body, the individual was thought to consist of a "shadow (yeg)" and "speech" (Osgood 1937:106). Regarding the speech component, "the connection with the human voice is not altogether clear and perhaps it is the breath which is primarily involved" (Osgood 1959:107).

b. "At the death of a person, ideally, the house in which he lived and his cache are burned. Smaller and more personal things may be abandoned inside the coffin of the deceased. Frequently larger implements are tied up on a pole, at the head of the grave. Such things are reported by observers to be invariably broken" (Osgood 1959:73).

c. Owls were sometimes eaten (Osgood 1959:37).

d. It was believed that children could be reincarnated (Osgood 1959:107).

Kaska

a. The soul was thought to consist of two parts, one of which was associated with "wind" (Honigmann 1981b:448). Death involved the departure of both, but the shadow "did not leave the earth but remained around the scene of death or at a burial place. At night the shadow sometimes manifested itself as a ghost (tsune)" (Honigmann 1964:136).

b. Burial took place quickly (Honigmann 1981b:448). The corpse was removed through a back wall, and the dwelling was burned (Honigmann 1964:141). People returning from the grave circled the dwellings before entering to avoid the return of the ghost (Honigmann 1964:140). The personal property of the deceased was destroyed after death, but other items were distributed (Honigmann 1964:89). Among the Tahltan, however, feasts were given to honor the dead (MacLachlan 1981).

c. Owls were sometimes eaten (Honigmann 1964:146).

d. It was believed that the "wind" aspect of the soul could be reincarnated (Honigmann 1964:137).

Koyukon

a. The soul was believed to have dual aspects, one of which left only at death. One aspect, translated "it's out of you," was considered to be vulnerable and easily lost. The other, considered the primary aspect of the soul, could be dangerous, lingered near the body, and could be reborn (A. Clark 1970:81).

b. Elaborate ceremonialism associated with death, but ghosts were considered dangerous (A. Clark 1981:591). A dying person was taken to a small shelter away from the dwelling. People sat inside the dwelling with a fire burning to keep the dead from returning. The belongings of the deceased were left with the grave.

c. Insufficient evidence for association of owls with death.

d. Belief in reincarnation (see item a above).

Kutchin

a. Among the Crow River Kutchin, the shadow as a component of the soul "is said to have a spiritual existence of its own" (Osgood 1936:157).

b. After death the tent in which it occurred was torn down (McKennan 1965:59). The deceased's property was buried with the body (McKennan 1965:59). There was a general abandonment of the location in which a death had occurred (Osgood 1936:157).

c. Insufficient evidence for association of owls with death.

d. Beliefs in reincarnation among the Peel River and Crow River Kutchin (Osgood 1936:145).

Mountain (see also Slave, Hare)

a. Insufficient evidence.

b. Insufficient evidence.

c. Insufficient evidence.

d. Insufficient evidence.

Sekani

a. Insufficient evidence.

b. The place at which a death had occurred was abandoned (Denniston 1981:438; see also Jenness 1937:59). After death the property of the deceased was not destroyed but was divided among the relatives (Jenness 1937:59).

c. Insufficient evidence.

d. Insufficient evidence.

Slave

a. "Death was recognized as the loss of the individual's shadow" (Honigmann 1946:86).

b. The property of the deceased was left at the grave, burned, or discarded (Asch 1981:344). The dwellings in which death occurred usually were abandoned (Honigmann 1946:87).

c. Owls were eaten (Honigmann 1946:38).

d. Insufficient evidence for belief in reincarnation.

Sarsi

a. At death the spirit leaves the body and becomes the *tsunu.ga* ("bad spirit whistling") (Honigmann 1945:467). "Ghosts may appear as whirlwinds" (Honigmann 1945:468).

b. The relatives of the deceased abandoned the dwelling in which death had occurred (Honigmann 1945:469). The name of the deceased was avoided (Curtis 1964, XVIII, 110).

c. Insufficient evidence regarding association of owls with death.

d. Insufficient evidence regarding belief in reincarnation.

Tanaina

a. "The Tanaina believe that there are three component parts to an Indian's being, his body, his breath, and his shadow-spirit" (Osgood 1937:169). At death the "breath" left the body, while the shadow lingered nearby and was considered dangerous (Osgood 1933:715).

b. The possessions of the deceased were buried (Osgood 1937: 166). The name of the deceased was taboo (Osgood 1937: 166). The soul was believed to consist of "breath" and a "shadow-spirit," which was evil and lingered near the body for forty days (Osgood 1937:169).

c. Owls were believed to speak in human language and to warn of impending disasters and tragedies (Townsend 1963:217).

d. "The Tanaina believe in reincarnation" (Osgood 1937:160).

Tanana

a. Insufficient evidence.

b. Insufficient evidence.

c. Insufficient evidence.

d. Insufficient evidence.

Tutchone

a. Insufficient evidence for dual concept of soul.

b. Insufficient evidence for traditional practices.

c. Insufficient evidence for association of owls with death.

d. "Although the fleshly body died, the essential soul spirit of a person was reborn as a new individual" (McClellan and Denniston 1981b: 501).

Pacific Coast

Hupa-Chilula-Whilkut

a. Insufficient evidence of dual concept of soul.
b. The body was disposed of as quickly as possible, taken out through a hole in the house wall. The belongings of the deceased were left at the grave (Wallace 1978 : 193). The name of the deceased was taboo.
c. Insufficient evidence of association of owls with death.
d. Insufficient evidence of belief in reincarnation.

Mattole

a. Insufficient evidence for dual concept of soul.
b. The corpse was left in the house until buried; then disposed of some distance away from the dwelling (Elsasser 1978: 197). The personal property of the deceased was buried at the grave. The name of the deceased was taboo.
c. Insufficient evidence of association of owls with death.
d. Insufficient evidence of belief in reincarnation.

Tolowa

a. Whirlwinds associated with ghosts among the Tolowa, Chetco, Tutuni, and Sixes River groups (Barnett 1937 : 185). In the Galice Creek group, the soul was associated with "breath" (Barnett 1937 : 184). Soul loss could be caused by seeing a ghost, or the like, causing the victim to become "thin and weak" until the soul could be retrieved (Drucker 1937 : 275).
b. The body was taken from the house through the wall by removing a loose board (Gould 1978 : 134). The name of the deceased, as well as words and names that were thought to resemble the name of the deceased, were prohibited. If mentioned in the presence of relatives of the deceased, they could demand payment of damages (Drucker 1937 : 253). A child of five to ten years of age could be named after a deceased relative if the name were ritually purified (Drucker 1937 : 253). In the Chetco River group, soul loss could result from a sudden fright or from seeing a ghost (Drucker 1937 : 275).
c. Insufficient evidence of association of owls with death.
d. Insufficient evidence of belief in reincarnation.

Wailaki-Nongatl-Lassik-Sinkyone-Kato

a. Insufficient evidence of dual concept of soul.

b. Among the Sinkyone, the property of a deceased person was destroyed, and the dwelling was burned or abandoned (Nomland 1935 : 163). Utterance of the name of the deceased was prohibited for four to five years among the Sinkyone (Nomland 1935 : 163). The body was cremated immediately after death to prevent the return of the malevolent soul (Nomland 1935 : 163). The property of the deceased was given away before death or buried, since it could not be inherited (Nomland 1935 : 164). Among the Wailaki, at death the possessions of close relatives were thrown into the grave; the property of the deceased was given to guests (Curtis 1964, XIV, 30). Among the Kato the corpse was washed, dressed, wrapped in deerskins, and buried; sometimes, but not always, with belongings (Curtis 1964, XIV, 12). After a man's death, his dog was killed and thrown into the grave with him (Curtis 1964, XIV, 30).

c. Among the Sinkyone the dove and owl were seen as "transformed persons who mourned their dead relatives," and hence were not eaten (Nomland 1935 : 152).

d. Insufficient evidence of belief in reincarnation.

Apachean

Chiricahua

a. Insufficient evidence for dual concept of soul.

b. The body was buried as quickly as possible after death. The personal property of the deceased was destroyed (Opler 1941a : 472–475). The ghost was considered to linger near the grave or the place at which the death had occurred. Graves in general were avoided by most people, and the name of the deceased was not uttered (Opler 1941a : 235–236).

c. The owl was a form taken by ghosts and could cause sickness through fright (Opler 1941a : 229–232). "'If you hear an owl, you know a ghost is near by, for an owl is connected with the ghost. The ghost uses him, goes into his body. Owls talk the Chiricahua language'" (Opler 1941a : 230).

d. Insufficient evidence of belief in reincarnation.

Jicarilla

a. The soul was considered to have two components. "One is called 'breath,' and it is this which leaves the corpse via the sole of the foot in the form of a small whirlwind" (Opler 1936b : 222; see also Opler 1959 : 957). The malevolent ghost remained near the body. "This ghost is always thought of as malignant and vindictive, and the relatives of the dead, since it stays around the body for four days, and since they have to handle and bury the body, are in constant danger from it" (Opler 1936b:222).

b. The body was buried as quickly as possible. "The personal possessions of the dead are buried with him or burned and thrown away, for it is believed that otherwise the ghost will return to claim his belongings" (Opler 1936b:223). "The names of the dead are never mentioned by the Jicarilla" (Opler 1936b:220).

c. The owl had special powers for evil (Opler 1946:31).

d. Insufficient evidence of belief in reincarnation.

Kiowa Apache

a. The living being had multiple aspects, including a "vital force of animating spirit which continues as a neutral or harmless spirit after death; evil tendencies which develop during life and continue in association with the ghost in afterlife; and the ghost which comes into being at death and is a potential source of danger to the living thereafter" (Opler and Bittle 1961:388).

b. The body was disposed of quickly, removed through the side of the dwelling rather than through the doorway. The personal belongings of the deceased were buried with the body, and the grave site avoided (Opler and Bittle 1961:384). "Upon the return of the funeral party any remaining property of the deceased was destroyed." "If a family in which a death occurred had been camping with others, the entire group moved from the place where the person had died" (Opler and Bittle 1961:385–386). "His name could not be mentioned, particularly in the presence of his relatives, and words that were similar to or identical with his name could not be uttered" (Opler and Bittle 1961:386).

c. "If the ghost alters its appearance, it is as an owl that it is most likely to return." . . . "the hooting of an owl is interpreted as a threatening message" (Opler and Bittle 1961:390).

d. Insufficient evidence of belief in reincarnation.

Lipan

a. Both Lipan and Jicarilla Apache made a "distinction between the dreaded material remains of the dead and the more innocuous breath or spirit" (Opler 1975:185–186). "According to Lipan Apache doctrine, a small whirlwind enters the human body through the throat at birth and provides the vitalizing 'wind inside that keeps you alive.'" At death "'the wind comes out and you are gone'" (Opler 1945:123).

b. Burial took place as quickly as possible, often on the day of the death. The personal possessions of the deceased were buried in the grave or destroyed. People returning from the grave site took different paths (Opler 1945:124–125). The dwelling in which the death occurred was destroyed. "As soon as the burial is over, the immediate family moves camp, always in the opposite direction of the fresh grave." If this is not done, "the ghost of the dead or other ghosts will come back to bother them" (Opler 1945:126). The name of the deceased was avoided (Opler 1945:127).

c. "'When a mean person dies he goes to the afterworld like the others. Then his bad spirit comes back to earth and takes the form of an owl. Therefore we don't like to hear the owl hoot. They say it is just like a Lipan Indian's voice. People hear it say "I am your grandfather. I am your relative" (Opler 1945:134).

d. Insufficient evidence of belief in reincarnation.

Mescalero

a. Insufficient evidence of dual concept of soul.

b. The name of the deceased was not uttered (Opler 1969:229). The house in which death had occurred was abandoned (Opler 1969:232). The property of the deceased was destroyed (Opler 1969:253).

c. "The owl is associated with death and is believed to be the form assumed by dead witches. Consequently its hoot, which is often interpreted as a threatening message in the Mescalero Apache language, is feared and disliked" (Opler 1969:262).

d. Insufficient evidence of concept of reincarnation.

Navajo

a. "Death is described as the departing from the body of the breath (wind) of life" (Witherspoon 1983a:571). "The instanding wind soul is thought to be in total control of one's body, including one's thoughts and actions." "Like the inner forms of natural phenomena, these wind souls have an existence that is independent of the body that they occupy" (Witherspoon 1983a:573).

b. The corpse was removed from the dwelling through a hole in the wall (Opler 1983:378).

c. Ghosts appeared as owls (Kluckhohn and Leighton 1947: 127).

d. Although the name of the deceased was avoided, "the Navajo delight in talking about the life, good deeds, and accomplishements of the deceased. They are pleased when a child is said to resemble the recently dead or when an outsider reminds them of an event concerning him. Memory of the deceased could be seen as a form of spirit perpetuation" (Reichard 1950:45).

Western Apache

a. "Life and breath are one and the same." "The last breath of a dying person remains on earth in the form of a little wind. On the fourth day after death the life or breath and the shadow, conducted by ghost people, starts to the land of the dead somewhere to the north in an indefinite place" (Goodwin 1938:36).

b. After death the body was removed through a hole broken in the wall of the dwelling (Goodwin 1969:518). After death the dwelling was burned, with the property of the deceased, to prevent the ghost's return (Goodwin 1969:520). Participants in the burial spread ashes around the grave to keep the dead from leaving, and they returned from the grave by different paths to the site of the death, without looking back, before going to their homes. They bathed in smoke (Goodwin 1969:519). Uttering the name of the deceased was prohibited for at least fifteen years. Eventually a child might be named after a long-dead relative (Goodwin 1969:521, 528). Ghosts could cause sickness; fear resulting from an encounter with a ghost could cause fainting. Ghost sickness could be treated by inhaling smoke from pitchwood (Goodwin 1969:561).

c. Small children who misbehaved were sometimes threatened with Big Owl (Goodwin 1969:454, 457).

d. "On the other hand, the good luck, success, and prominence of a deceased person are reasons for naming a child after him, as it is thought these attributes may accompany the name" (Goodwin 1969:529).

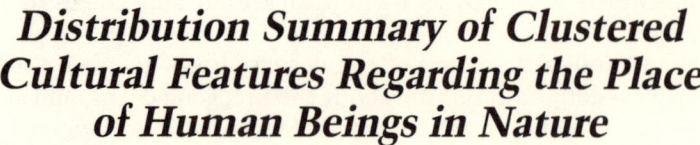

Distribution Summary of Clustered Cultural Features Regarding the Place of Human Beings in Nature

Aspects of the cluster:

a. A belief that all objects in nature are "alive" and sapient and that the universe is populated by capricious beings who are neither good nor evil, but potentially helpful or harmful and unpredictable.

b. A belief in personal power acquired through dreams that is variable and unstable within individuals, men in particular, and is associated with luck in gambling and the ability to influence game animals.

c. Ambivalence toward dogs and wolves.

Eyak

a. "Trees, rocks, plants, the sea, etc. have 'men or women' behind them. These souls are shaped like human beings, but he thought that animals' souls looked like the animals themselves" (Birket-Smith and de Laguna 1938:230).

b. Ambiguous evidence regarding the acquisition of power through dreams.

c. Dogs were viewed with ambivalence; they were not killed (de Laguna 1937:66).

Athapaskan

Northern

Ahtna

a. All creatures and objects were a potential source of power (de Laguna and McClellan 1981:661).

b. All shamanistic power was obtained by dreaming (de Laguna and McClellan 1981:661).

c. "To kill any dog or pup meant death to the slayer or his child" (de Laguna and McClellan 1981:648).

Bearlake

a. "The people are definitely animistic, living in a world of multitudinous spirits which influence or control their destinies" (Osgood 1932:81).

b. Communications with animal powers occurred through dreams (Osgood 1932:83).

c. "Of the animals, the most sacred position is taken by the wolf and dog, which are held to be sacred, and it is said that even in the worst straits of hunger, the people will not eat them" (Osgood 1932:83).

Beaver

a. Belief in capricious spirit helpers (Goddard 1917:226).

b. Plains type vision quest with medicine bundles (Ridington 1981:335–356).

c. Insufficient evidence regarding beliefs about dogs.

Carrier

a. "Belief centered on the concept of a world populated by a number of spirits, mostly animal" (Tobey 1981:428).

b. Communication with spirits took place during dreams (Tobey 1981:428).

c. Insufficient evidence of ambivalence toward dogs.

Chilcotin

a. Multiple spirits including "animals, birds, mythological figures, ghosts, and natural phenomena such as thunder, lightning, rainbows, or winds" (Lane 1981:405).

b. "Boys and girls might acquire spirit power" during puberty training (Land 1981:405). "Anyone could seek a guardian spirit although not everyone did and not all those who sought were successful" (Lane 1981:409).

c. The wolf was a "special animal feared by most people." Contact with this animal could cause "serious illness and, ultimately, death" (Lane 1981:409).

Chipewyan

a. There were beliefs in several kinds of spiritual beings "called by them Nant-e-na, whom they frequently say they see, and who are supposed by them to inhabit the different elements of earth, sea, and air, according to their several qualities." To these "they usually attribute any change in their circumstances for the better or worse" (Hearne 1911: 327).

b. "Traditional magico-religious beliefs were based on the concept of . . . power given in dreams by spirit-animal beings" (J. Smith 1981:279).

c. It was customary to avoid killing wolves (Hearne 1911: 325).

Dogrib
a. Insufficient evidence.
b. "Power was given to men or women by animal-spiritual beings, who directed them in curing, divination, or controlling
game and weather" (Helm 1981:302).
c. Insufficient evidence of ambivalence toward dogs.

Han
a. Insufficient evidence (cf. Osgood 1971:39).
b. "Power was derived from a variety of sources, though commonly it was from an animal being seen in a dream" (Crow
and Obley 1981:509).
c. "The Indians never ate wolf or dog meat; they would rather
starve" (Schmitter 1910:7, quoted in Osgood 1932:111).

Hare
a. "'The medicine men knew about animals, ground, trees,
anything on the earth. Anything that is on the earth could
sing to the medicine man and then he would have it for his
helper'" (Savishinsky 1974:63).
b. "The Hare continue to place a strong emphasis on the pre-
dictive efficacy of dreams, and they stress this as an important source of the old medicine men's power" (Savishinsky
1974:63).
c. Wolves, wolverines, and dogs were prohibited as food, based
on "the belief that dogs were 'dirty' animals and that wolves
and wolverines ate them" (Savishinsky and Hara 1981:320).

Ingalik
a. "For the Ingalik, the universe is a continuum in which all
determinate things are possessed of a spirit or soul known as
a yeg. Not only has each man and animal a yeg, but even
each tree and rock has one also" (Osgood 1959:102). "Everything in the universe is alive and rocks are no exception"
(Osgood 1959:50). "The Ingalik universe is distinguished by
its animation and the modesty with which the Indians regard man's place in the natural order" (Osgood 1959:167).
b. Incantations and "songs" were used to "exert the necessary
influence for support when it is needed" (Osgood 1959:167).
c. There were no particular taboos regarding dogs, but they
were not considered edible (Osgood 1959:26).

Kaska
a. There was a concept of "certain normally unseen and un-
sensed entities, including counterparts or souls of the empirically sensed animals. Other sensed events, like stones or
clouds, also possessed a transcendental character such as

they perhaps warrant designation of Kaska thinking as animatistic" (Honigmann 1981b: 101). There were numerous spiritual beings who could be either harmful or helpful to humans (Honigmann 1964: 101).

b. Power was acquired through animal "sponsors" and was variable among individuals (Honigmann 1964: 107).

c. The wolf was given special respect (Honigmann 1964: 108, 148).

Koyukon

a. There was "a belief that all humans and animals as well as many inanimate objects also had spirits, which could be turned to good or evil practice at the whim of their owners" (A. Clark 1981: 593). All objects were believed to have spirits with a whimsical or unpredictable nature (A. Clark 1970: 80). "Natural entities are endowed with spirits and with spiritually based power" (Nelson 1983: 228).

b. "Each person is thought to have some supernatural ability," but shamans had especially strong power (A. Clark 1981: 593–595).

c. Insufficient evidence of ambivalence toward dogs.

Kutchin

a. "The Kutchin were encompassed by myriad supernatural beings, friendly, hostile, and unpredictable" (Slobodin 1981: 527). "The Peel River Kutchin appear to be definitely animatistic." "This 'liveliness' of the surroundings demands a respectful attitude but is not always fearful" (Osgood 1936: 154).

b. Relationships with animal spirits were developed through dreaming (Slobodin 1981: 527). "Power is acquired through animal association" (Osgood 1936: 158).

c. Dogs, foxes, wolves, wolverines, ravens, and eagles were never eaten (McKennan 1965: 84).

Mountain (see also Slave, Hare)

a. Insufficient evidence.

b. Insufficient evidence.

c. Insufficient evidence.

Sarsi

a. Insufficient evidence.

b. Personal power was obtained either through a Plains-type vision quest or through dreams (Brant 1953: 202; see also Curtis 1964, XVIII, 112).

c. Insufficient evidence.

Sekani

a. "There was a pervasive belief among the Sekani that man and the animal world were linked by a mystic bond, and that animals possessed special powers that they could grant a seeker" (Denniston 1981:439). Both animate and inanimate objects could be sources of power for the individual (Jenness 1937:72).

b. Powers were transmitted through dreams (Denniston 1981: 439; Jenness 1937:72).

c. Insufficient evidence.

Slave

a. "There was a belief in multiple spirits that could disperse power to or create danger for mortals" (Asch 1981:344).

b. "Dreams could also be the source of power and dared never be revealed" (Honigmann 1946:77).

c. "The prevailing attitude toward the wolf and otter was one of fear" (Honigmann 1946:76).

Tanaina

a. "The Tanaina believe that all natural objects are animatistic and have a power relatively greater than that of human beings" (Osgood 1937:169).

b. Insufficient evidence.

c. Insufficient evidence.

Tanana

a. Insufficient evidence.

b. Insufficient evidence.

c. There was a special reverence for the dog (McKennan 1981:439).

Tutchone

a. "Each Tutchone had somehow to relate to a world full of superhuman power made manifest in spiritualized aspects of mountains, rivers, plants and—most particularly—of animals and certain other nonhuman beings. It was a world marked too by fluidity of the forms and functions of spirits and of uncertainty as to the consequences of human behavior" (McClellan and Denniston 1981b:502).

b. Young men "tried to strengthen their personal powers both through vigorous physical exercise and by acquiring spirit helpers" (McClellan and Denniston 1981b:500).

c. "Dogs were categorized separately from other animals and after Christian teaching was introduced in the second half of the nineteenth century, they were usually linked with the devil" (McClellan and Denniston 1981b:502).

Pacific Coast

Hupa

a. Insufficient evidence.
b. Insufficient evidence.
c. "They think it hazardous to talk much to dogs for fear they might reply. This would cause the death of those who hear. Pains are taken to keep dogs from the vicinity of a dance or religious feast" (Goddard 1903–1904:6–7).

Mattole

a. Insufficient evidence.
b. Insufficient evidence.
c. Canids were not killed or eaten (Nomland 1938:111).

Tolowa

a. "One receives the impression that every outcrop of rock, every trickle of water, every little clearing in the brush had power for good or evil, or figured in some event in mythological times" (Drucker 1937:228).
b. Insufficient evidence.
c. Food prohibitions included dogs, coyotes, wildcats, grizzly and black bears, snakes, frogs, all birds of prey and carrion, seagulls, and doves (Drucker 1937:232). Ambivalence toward dogs, which were valued but considered magically potent for evil (Drucker 1937:240).

Wailaki-Nongatl-Lassik-Sinkyone-Kato

a. In Sinkyone belief, "All things animate and inanimate had souls" (Nomland 1935:169).
b. Insufficient evidence.
c. Dogs were seen by the Sinkyone as transformed human beings (Nomland 1935:152). Birds of prey, grizzly bears, coyotes, wolves, weasels, minks, and otters were not eaten by the Kato (Curtis 1964, XIV, 6).

Apachean

General

a. "Underlying all ceremonies, whether shamanistic or priestly, was the conception of supernatural power that pervaded the universe and could be utilized for human purposes by ritual procedures known to priests or learned in personal revelation by shamans" (Opler 1983a:373).

Chiricahua

a. "Any object or force of the external world is potentially animate for the candidate for supernatural power" (Opler 1941a:206). "'The old people tell stories that show that all things have life—trees, rocks, the wind, mountains'" (Opler 1941a:206).

b. Dreams could be a source of power (Opler 1941a:192).

c. Ambivalence about dogs. "'The dog was classed with the coyote, wolf, and fox. We felt that all of them could cause you trouble'" (Opler 1941a:226). "'If you have a little child crawling around and suddenly a dog barks at it, they say that the fright will go inside that child and make its heart sick. So they don't like dogs around much. If you have one, some man might come along and say "Why do you have that dog around? It might scare your children and make them sick"'" (Opler 1941a:14).

Jicarilla

a. "Animal life is part of the personified universe whose efforts were primarily concerned with the well-being and happiness of the Jicarilla tribe" (Opler 1936b:208).

b. Insufficient evidence.

c. Insufficient evidence.

Kiowa Apache

a. Insufficient evidence.

b. Power was obtained through a Plains-style vision quest or through dreams. "Among the Kiowa Apache, the latter mode seems to have been much more frequent and important" (Brant 1953:199).

c. "It is said that the coyote howls before a death occurs and that the howling of a dog or wolf is also a warning of death or bad luck. For this reason howling dogs are often driven from camp" (Opler and Bittle 1961:390).

Lipan

a. Insufficient evidence.

b. Insufficient evidence.

c. The Lipan refused to eat dog meat (Opler 1975:189).

Mescalero

a. "Both Chiricahua and Mescalero Apache conceive of the universe being suffused with supernatural power, potentially useful to man for curing illness, confounding the enemy, finding lost objects, and so on" (Opler 1969:42). "Everything in the Mescalero universe is thought of as potentially animate and a possible source of supernatural power" (Opler 1969:61).

b. Dreams were an important source of power (Opler 1969:96).

c. The coyote was viewed with ambivalence as potentially

dangerous in a supernatural sense (Opler 1969:78). Dogs were viewed with suspicion, and "most people are afraid to touch a wolf" (Opler 1969:154).

Navajo

a. "There are numerous things or powers in the universe that are indifferent or good when under control and in harmony with man but that may be potentially evil when uncontrolled" (Wyman 1983:536). "Natural phenomena such as earth and sky, sun and moon, rain and water, lightning and thunder, have inner forms. They are referred to as . . . that (animate being) which lies within it" (Witherspoon 1983:573).

b. "Most dreams are thought to have prognostic value" (Kluckhohn and Leighton 1947:142).

c. Insufficient evidence.

Western Apache

a. "Sources of power are numerous, and include all parts and phenomena of the universe already discussed, as well as many objects such as stones, shells, plants, and animals" (Goodwin 1938:28). If a child were to unknowingly touch "a ceremonial article charged with power or something else which could cause sickness, the result may be dangerous, for the power or sickness does not discriminate between children and adults" (Goodwin 1969:466).

b. Although ceremonies were handed down through tradition, a person might "have direct contact with the source of power, either by dreams or more direct experience, whereby additional power and songs are acquired" (Goodwin 1938:28).

c. Dogs were not highly valued (Goodwin 1969:554, 555). Snake sickness can result from contact with a discarded snake skin (Goodwin 1969:467).

Notes

Preface

1. For a discussion of this theoretical issue, see M. E. Smith (1982: 127–142).

2. Ellis (1974, I, 124, editor's pagination), in her study of Navajo culture history, notes that "none of the Southwestern Indians have been 'time minded' and that keeping exact count of years passed even since relatively recent events has not been their forte."

3. Schroeder (1974, IV, 482) argues that clans were introduced to the Western Apache by the Navajo some time after 1863. It is most likely that, even though matrilineal descent groups are an ancient Apache characteristic, most of the specific named clans of the Western Apache have more recent origins.

4. See Lee's (1950) classic discussion, as well as Whorf (1941).

5. Grenville Goodwin still was remembered with affection and high regard by some older people in San Carlos in 1963. See also Opler's (1973) *Grenville Goodwin among the Western Apache* for more insights into Goodwin's work.

1. From the Present into the Past

1. The early separation of Kiowa Apache has been disputed by Brant (1949, 1953), but a number of others, including Mooney (1898), have supported such a postulate. This seems greatly strengthened by the linguistic evidence that Hoijer (1971) discusses. See also Young (1983) for a summary of the present evidence, which further substantiates an early split, and Gunnerson and Gunnerson (1971) for a fuller discussion of the Plains Apache issue.

2. See Forbes (1959) for a discussion of this issue, and Schroeder (1974, I) for a painstaking analysis of the archival evidence for the identification of early Apachean groups.

3. These differences, discussed by Goodwin (1969: 7, 8), are dealt with in detail by Durbin (1964) on the basis of field work carried out several decades later in 1963.

4. Recent archaeological work in northwestern New Mexico, however,

has revealed likely Navajo sites that appear to date as early as the late fourteenth century (Hogan 1989).

5. Young (1983) presents a summary of recent evidence to substantiate the divergence of Kiowa Apache from the other Apachean dialects.

6. The centrality of their position with regard to the other Apache groups is suggested not only by the geographic location of the Chiricahua and Mescalero in the nineteenth century but also by their intermediate position with regard to linguistic innovations shared with the other Apachean divisions. It should be noted, however, that during the early reservation period the Chiricahua, in particular, incorporated other Apachean groups who were known variously as Mogollon, Mimbres, Warm Springs, and Coppermine Apache, and more generally as Gila Apache and who were not apparently closely related to them before that time (see Schroeder 1974, I, 263).

7. Schroeder (1974, I, 229; IV, 512–513) argues that the Apachean expansion into Arizona was from the east and perhaps even from the southeast. This issue will be discussed more fully in chapter 7.

8. Schroeder argues that Goodwin's San Carlos and other groupings are products of the reservation period.

9. Goodwin (1969:61) refers to the San Carlos Reservation as a "Western Apache melting-pot," but he suggests that as of the 1930s the people of San Carlos were still quite aware of their band affiliations.

10. The term *genetic* in this context, of course, is a metaphor to suggest that these languages share a common origin in a single parent language. It does not preclude later mutual influences among these languages, which undoubtedly have been significant.

11. Greenfeld observes that, even after centuries of contact, there appear to be few loan words from Pueblo languages in Western Apache, and the number of borrowed Spanish words is suprisingly small (personal communication; see also Greenfeld 1973).

12. Jorgensen (1980:61), in his analysis of comparative data on native groups of western North America, notes the tendency for migrating groups to seek environments similar to those they had left, necessitating minimal adjustments in their survival strategies.

2. The Athapaskan-speaking Peoples

1. This statement is based predominantly on lexicostatistical data (see Dyen and Aberle 1974:10–14) but tends to be compatible with observations regarding mutual intelligibility. Krauss and Golla (1981:72) point out that Tanaina is mutually unintelligible with regard to all of its neighbors. In the same volume, Townsend (1981:621) states further that Tanaina is one of the "most internally diverse Alaska Athapaskan languages" as well, which suggests a long occupancy in that region.

2. This perception of degrees of divergence is based to some extent on percentages of shared cognates as seen in Hoijer's tables presented in Dyen

and Aberle (1974:12). The sources do not agree on the number of Athapaskan languages or where the linguistic boundaries should be drawn.

3. See also Krech (1980) for a general discussion of recent research on early Athapaskan social organization.

4. See Goldman (1941) for a discussion of the Carrier case and Honigmann (1964:85 n. 13) for comments regarding the origins of Kaska moieties. References to earlier Carrier social organization are from Kobrinsky (1977).

5. Bishop (1987) also argues that the aboriginal Carrier egalitarian matrilineal organization altered as a result of the influx of European goods and intensified trade with coastal groups. Rubel and Rosman (1983) posit the development of the elaborate Northwest Coast social organizations from a simpler Athapaskan-type organization, stimulated by the greater resources of the Pacific Coast.

6. There has been a great deal of controversy over the antiquity of bilateral organization among the eastern Athapaskan groups (e.g., Krech 1980). On the basis of ethnohistorical evidence, Yerbury (1986:163) argues that "the genesis of an overall bilateral organization lay in the kind of life determined by Euro-Canadian exploitation and trade."

7. Among the many sources that attest to this, data from the unpublished field notes of Catherine McClellan (1966) on the seasonal food quest of the Southern Tutchone, discussed by Workman (1978:84–89), present a detailed picture of the subsistence base in the southwestern Yukon Territory. See also McClellan (1964:9).

8. See, for example, Honigmann's (1946:61, 62) comments on the value of individualism among the Fort Nelson Slave and Slobodin's (1969) observations on Kutchin participation in a trapping party. VanStone (1988:68) comments that individualism was a predominant characteristic of northern Athapaskan belief systems.

9. Osgood (1937:169) equates this with Marett's classic concept of animatism. See also Osgood (1936:154, 157).

10. See E. Basso (1978) for a detailed discussion of the *nakani* belief in the western Subarctic.

11. McDonnell (1984:44) also notes a belief among the Kaska that women drain or draw off the "power" of men.

12. See, for example, Osgood (1937:162). Among the Ahtna such restrictions surrounding the first menstruation lasted a year (de Laguna and McClellan 1981:657).

13. Osgood (1937:162) writes of the Tanaina that "of a series of taboos probably the most important is that forbidding the girl to look at anyone." He adds that it was believed that "the eyes of a menstruating woman cause sickness." McClellan and Denniston (1981a:385) attribute this pattern to the Cordilleran Athapaskan groups in general.

14. Cruikshank (1975:6) quotes a central Yukon informant, who states, "When the girl gets better they make party for her. Everybody eat and dance because she is finished with her training. It's not like a potlatch—more like a party."

15. This, of course, is an interpretation based on the insights of Bronislaw Malinowski, as expressed in his classic work *Magic, Science, and Religion*. See McDonnell (1984) for an analysis of Kaska thought in this vein.

16. This clearly seems to be the case among some of the Tanaina subgroups (see Osgood 1937:162, 163). See also de Laguna and McClellan (1981: 657) for an Ahtna example, and Townsend (1981:633) for additional discussion of the Tanaina case.

17. There are exceptions to this. Among the Ingalik it was the "breath" component of the soul that was a source of danger, indicating some "free play" within a more stable, general cognitive framework (see Osgood 1959:107).

18. This appears to be yet another symbolic dissociation of the realms of life and death (see VanStone 1974:84).

19. See Workman (1978:82) for a discussion of the variety of methods practiced in one small area of the western Subarctic, including simple burial, burial with a grave house erected over the site, cremation, log caches, and disposal of the bones in bark baskets hung in trees.

20. See Osgood's (1937:162) statement that, in Tanaina belief, "the eyes of a menstruating woman can cause sickness."

21. See, however, Janes (1973), Townsend (1979), and Smith and Burch (1979) for fuller discussions of the complexities of these relationships.

22. F. G. Cooch (personal communication). Kunz (1977) also notes incidents of recent conflict between Nunamiut Inuit and Kutchin.

23. Simeone (1982:16–18) notes that Ingalik and Koyukon Athapaskans were involved in a Russian-sponsored trade network based on the Kolyma River in Siberia near the beginning of the nineteenth century.

24. See also A. Clark (1977) for discussion of this trade. The Tanaina may have been the earliest Athapaskans to have had contact with Russians (Simeone 1982:39).

25. Yerbury (1986:10–11, 49–50) notes that the Chipewyan were at least indirectly involved in the fur trade by 1680. He also suggests the importance of firearms with their advantage over bows and arrows, which might have contributed to intergroup competition.

26. VanStone (1988:68) notes of Alaskan Athapaskans that "aboriginal subsistence activities did not involve extensive trapping, and most of the fur-bearing animals were not suitable for food."

27. This is based on rather informal, though perhaps accurate, assessments by observers of the region. It seems unlikely, however, that trapping will disappear as a supplementary source of subsistence in the region in the foreseeable future.

28. Asch (1984:17) points out that contemporary Athapaskans in the Great Slave Lake area "were able to sustain their meat needs at a level equal to that of the average Canadian without making one purchase from the store." The Berger Report, publishing the findings of a commission headed by Chief Justice Berger (1977) of the British Columbia Supreme Court, which was set up to assess the social and environmental impact of a proposed pipeline through the Mackenzie River Valley, is useful evidence with

regard to the continued importance of trapping in the region. See also Van-Stone (1976) and Krech (1976, 1978) for analyses of the effects of the trade in the western Subarctic.

29. Jorgensen (1980) suggests that dialects spoken in regions where resources are dense and compartmentalized may tend to differentiate at a more rapid rate than those in areas where more mobility brings population segments into frequent contact. This clearly suggests that the degree of similarity among dialects may be an extremely unreliable gauge of the time depth of their divergence.

30. This may have been the case with the Hupa.

31. Barnett (1937:159) perceives far greater influence from California groups among the Pacific Coast Athapaskans than from the northern coastal region. See also Elsasser (1978:193).

32. These distances are based on Hoijer's cognate tables presented by Dyen and Aberle (1974:12–13).

33. See, for example, Gunnerson (1969). Schroeder (1974, I) notes the frequent mention of farm plots among most of these groups and also mentions these plots in a brief summary of the Apache pattern.

34. Schroeder (1974, I, 437) disputes the assertion of significant Pueblo influence on the Jicarilla. This is a bit puzzling, since he presents a good deal of data to show a long period of contact between the two populations.

35. See Goodwin (1945) for a discussion of Navajo and Western Apache ceremonials. Reichard (1945) presents an additional discussion of Navajo ritual. Ellis (1974:106) gives a detailed account of the evidence for Navajo and Pueblo interactions and population mergers.

36. See, for example, Sanday (1973). More recently Schlegel and Barry (1986) have substantiated this rough correlation between women's contributions to subsistence and their social status.

3. Subarctic Beginnings

1. See, for example, Laughlin and Wolf (1979:5). Szathmary (1979a:203) also states that "successive waves of migration" seem most likely. Based on a comparison of linguistic, dental, and genetic data, Greenberg, Turner, and Zegura (1986) posit at least three waves of migration involving Eskimo/Aleut, greater Northwest Coast including Na-Dene, and the rest of the native American population.

2. The appearance of Asian pottery techniques in Alaska during the Choris stage of the Norton Tradition is a clear example of intercontinental contact long after the close of the Pleistocene (see Dumond 1977:63). See also Powers (1973). With regard to prehistoric developments in this part of North America, Powers states that "all main elements of early North Pacific assemblages have parallels in the Diuktai Culture of northeastern Asia."

3. Swadesh (1959) has suggested that, although most native American languages may share remote ties with Indo-European, Athapaskan and Eskimo-Aleutian could not be included in this grouping. In any case, a rela-

tively shallow differentiation among Athapaskan languages compared with other major language families in North America suggests that a shorter period of time has been involved.

4. According to the language boundaries set by Dyen and Aberle (1974), four of the eight existing Athapaskan languages are spoken in Alaska.

5. Fowler (1977:103) notes that "the linguistic data are inherently consistent and offer valuable clues to Athapaskan prehistory."

6. Levine (1971) challenges the basis for including Haida, and Greenberg (1987) takes issue with Levine's method and conclusions.

7. According to Spuhler (1979:154–155), probabilities of a genetic relationship for Haida and Tlingit populations with Athapaskan speakers are .666 and .749, respectively. This is far higher than the probability of their linkage with any other populations. Comparable figures for the probability of Na-Dene and Eskimo relationships are from 0.00 to .039. Szathmary (1977: 118) also concludes that, based on gene frequencies for twenty-four blood-group genes, Athapaskan, Haida, and Tlingit speakers form a distinct cluster within a broader North American sample. See also Szathmary (1979:41).

8. The Hypsithermal in this area is thought to have begun after 4000 B.C., or roughly six thousand years ago. With regard to the earlier period at the close of the Pleistocene, Hopkins (1979:35) notes, "The drastic changes in vegetation and in the ungulate population during the interval 14,000 to 10,000 years ago must have placed great stress upon nomadic hunting populations. This seems to be the interval during which major ethnic or demographic changes would be most likely to occur."

9. Driver (1966:141) states that "only with control of genetic language classification is it possible to distinguish heritage from subsequent diffusion of cultural phenomena."

10. De Laguna (1975:133) notes correspondences in social structure between Athapaskans and Samoyeds.

11. Workman (1977a:37) also notes apparent ties to the coast in the Ahtna region from the second millennium A.D.

12. Wilmeth (1977:101) suggests that the White River Ash Fall may have been a factor in the southward migrations of Athapaskan peoples.

13. Bacon (1977:9), however, suggests that the Itkillik "may represent the final Denali tradition."

14. Taylor and Meighan (1978:44) also point out a significant break in cultural continuity before 1200 B.P. and consider that the validity of an Athapaskan Tradition is "yet to be proven." See Dumond (1979) for another interpretation. D. Clark (1981:113) refers to an "Athapaskan Tradition" consisting of Tuktu and Denali.

15. Fowler (1977:104) argues on the basis of linguistic evidence that "Tanaina is probably located where Proto-Athapaskans began to diverge."

4. Proto-Athapaskan Culture

1. See, for example, the Onion Portage site in northern Alaska (Anderson 1968).

2. Krech (1980) presents a synthesis of published research on early Athapaskan social organization. See Perry (1989) for a more detailed argument pertaining to the Athapaskan case.

3. See Dyen and Aberle (1974) for a discussion of the diffusion of matrilineality, and Service (1972) for another influential perspective on social organization in hunting societies. Regarding matrilocal residence, on the basis of extensive North American comparative data, Jorgensen (1980: 153) notes a "tendency toward composing hunting groups primarily of affines among the people most dependent on large game of all types (large herd and small herd animals)." See also Hosley (1980: 14–15). A subsequent paper by Aberle (1974) makes a strong case for matrilineal organization among other early North American hunting and gathering groups as well.

4. Driver (1966: 145) substantiates the association of mother-in-law avoidance with unilineal descent but argues that it is derived from contact with other peoples, largely because he accepts a bilateral reconstruction of Proto-Athapaskan social organization. Since mother-in-law avoidance occurs in all three areas and clearly is compatible with matrilocal residence, it is presented here as a Proto-Athapaskan feature.

5. Based on Hoijer's figures presented in Dyen and Aberle (1974: 12, Table 2.1). This is based partly on the assumption that the percentage of shared cognates is inversely related to the length of time that speakers of these languages have been separated. In any case, the extreme differences between Tanaina and Apachean within Athapaskan do not appear to be in any doubt.

6. Philip Greenfeld notes that Apache women maintain a downward gaze in a variety of contexts (personal communication).

7. Greenfeld (1973) notes that owl beliefs might have led to differing rates of phonological change in Apache.

8. Savishinsky (1974) discusses in some detail the Hare attitudes toward dogs. Sherwood (1958: 51) states that dogs were few among Northern Athapaskan groups in the early days of contact and that their more recent increase put a strain on the carrying capacity of the land.

9. See also Greenfeld (1973) for discussion of the linguistic treatment of wolves, coyotes, and foxes in Western Apache. Greenfeld (personal communication) notes, however, that dogs are not included in this category but are linked with horses.

10. See Douglas (1969) for a discussion of the significance of anomalies in symbolic classification.

5. The Early Divergences

1. The language classifications used here are those presented in Dyen and Aberle (1974). Krauss (1979) divides Northern Athapaskan into more separate languages; see also Krauss and Golla (1981).

2. See Jorgensen (1980: 74). Donohue (1975: 55) sees a "Plateau pattern" in the archaeological record of central British Columbia established at least four thousand years ago.

3. Relationships, again, are based on lexicostatistical data. See Derry (1975).

4. Dyen and Aberle (1974:14) consider this to be a relatively unified subgrouping of Canadian Athapaskan. It should be pointed out, however, that Krauss (1979:107–108) has raised serious objection to the "branching" or "genetic" model suggested in much of the use of lexicostatistics and has asserted that in the Athapaskan case, particularly, an "isogloss" model is more appropriate. Such a model takes into account the spread of innovations within a dialect group. According to Krauss (1973b:919), "Athapaskan must be viewed as a dialect complex with many convergence ('wave') as well as divergence (Stammbaum) relationships." He considers the Pacific Coast Athapaskan languages and Apachean to be "themselves dialect complexes which are in turn parts of the greater Athapaskan dialect complex."

5. Kutchin and Hare share cognates at 74 percent and are probably not mutually intelligible. Kutchin and Nabesna, however, share cognates at the level of 82 percent (Dyen and Aberle 1974:12).

6. Hare shares cognates with Chipewyan at 83 percent, with Slave at 85 percent, and with Dogrib at 86 percent (Dyen and Aberle 1974:12).

7. This appears very clearly in Dumond's (1969:859) map of the distribution of languages that constituted the formerly recognized Na-Dene phylum in Alaska and northwestern Canada.

8. Specifically, the Punuk and Birnirk.

6. In the Mountain Corridor

1. This complex was named by Wettlaufer (1955) for a site in Saskatchewan.

2. It could be pointed out that, while caribou are fairly easy to kill and not particularly dangerous (see Burch 1972), buffalo are not only larger but also more formidable in many ways. Hence, a hunting technique that incapacitated the animals or killed them outright would have become more important in a buffalo-hunting context.

3. Frison (1988:155) states that "Avonlea is the first formalized manifestation of a cultural group presumed to have been involved with the first appearance of the bow and arrow on the Northern Plains."

4. Smith (1987) shows that Cree inhabited lands as far west as the Pace River during the early historic period.

5. Opler (1975:184) takes issue rather strongly with Mooney's version of the Kiowa Apache–Kiowa alliance.

6. Wilcox (1981:223) offers his Black Hills hypothesis as a model to explain a purported High Plains migration of Apache into the Southwest, seeing the Black Hills as a jumping-off point to the south. As Brugge (1981:283) points out in the same volume, however, the evidence for an Athapaskan Black Hills presence centers only on the Kiowa Apache, and the model may only account for the movements of that particular sector of the population. The position taken in this book, of course, is that just such a division be-

tween the Kiowa Apache and the rest took place in that area, but that the general Proto-Apachean population remained associated with the mountains.

7. See, for example, Bolton (1916:183) and Hammond and Rey (1953: 484, 814). The Benavides statement is quoted in Young (1983:394). Brugge (1981) suggests that Dobyns' (1966) principles for estimating population size indicate a very large Athapaskan population before diseases introduced through European contact took their toll.

7. On the Fringes of the Southwest

1. Jorgensen (1980:151), incidentally, asserts that the use of tanned hide clothing was exclusively an Apache trait in the Southwest.

2. Various observers (e.g., Sherwood 1958 and Hardisty 1867) assert that dogs were rare among Northern Athapaskan groups during early contact times.

3. The Gunnersons (Gunnerson and Gunnerson 1971; J. Gunnerson 1968) argue strongly for an Apachean association with the Dismal River sites, although Opler (1971) has taken issue with this interpretation.

4. See, for example, Hester (1962); see Wilcox (1981) for a very complete summary of this debate.

5. There are Spanish references to probable Apache in the Plains bordering the Southwest by the 1600s.

6. It is generally accepted that Apaches were in the Southwest at least by the late 1500s.

7. See Schroeder (1974, I, 436) for a dissenting view.

8. Hickerson (1988) identifies one group who have sometimes been suggested as Apaches, the Jumano, as Tiwa speakers whose language was closely related to the people of Piro Pueblo.

9. Sylvester Mowry in an 1858 report to the commissioner of Indian Affairs (quoted in Schroeder 1974, IV, 182).

10. Ellis (1974:106, 114, 119) sees clans as a late addition to Navajo social organization and notes that many of them result from the amalgamation of various Pueblo groups into the Navajo population. On the other hand, she notes that, even after those clans with apparent Pueblo origins are discounted, forty-nine remain that appear to be purely Navajo.

11. Greenfeld agrees with the *katcina* influence on the historic form of the *gaan* but suggests that they also represent a more general sense of "power" with origins in the North (personal communication). See also Boyer (1979:87–91) for an analysis of the *gaan* myth from a psychological perspective.

8. The Western Apache

1. The distinctive eight-sided and older forked-stick hogans are quite different from the Apache dome-shaped dwellings.

2. Workman (1977b:24) states that fish were not particularly well liked

by the Tutchone, and Jenness (1972:379) notes that the Sekani viewed "fisheaters" with disdain.

3. Both whitetail and mule deer abound in Western Apache territory.

4. From a letter by Goodwin to Morris E. Opler dated January 1934 (quoted in Opler 1972:1137).

5. Evidence of Puebloan influences on Navajo culture is, of course, far greater. Not only did the Navajo experience long and, at times, intensive contact with Puebloan peoples, but also, as Goodwin points out, even their territory shows much greater similarity to Pueblo territory; hence, they coped with many of the same ecological problems (Opler 1972:1137).

6. See Goodwin (1969:97–122 and appendixes) and Kaut (1956, 1957, 1974) for detailed analyses of the clan system.

7. Some writers have suggested Caddoan or Yuman affinities for Jocome, and Naylor (1981), on the basis of an analysis of the names of Suma rebels executed in 1685, suggests that they were Uto-Aztecan speakers.

8. See Goodwin and Basso (1971) for nineteenth-century accounts of this pattern.

9. Hall (1989:219) points out that Congress did not outlaw Navajo slavery in New Mexico until 1867, several years after the Emancipation Proclamation.

10. Hall (1989:159) notes that the opening of the Santa Fe Trail had the effect of incorporating the Southwest into the world economy, which had profound repercussions for the Apache.

11. In 1850 Kit Carson and General Philip Kearny traveled through Arizona and visited some of the Western Apache bands.

12. One of the more astonishing blots on the history of early relations was the beating of the respected Apache leader Mangas Coloradas by prospectors. Colyer's (1971) report of 1872 for President Grant's Peace Commission argues strongly that the Apache were inclined to seek peaceful relationships throughout this period. There is considerable support for this in Griffen (1988), Cole (1988), and Cortés (1988).

13. See Spicer (1962:249–250) for a fuller account of this attack.

9. The Reservation Years

1. See Thrapp (1968) for a more detailed account of these episodes.

2. Much of the succeeding discussion of the contemporary situation is based on the author's field research.

3. See the Meriam Report (Institute for Government Research 1928:682) for a discussion of these settlements.

4. Letter, Congressman Morris K. Udall to Wayne N. Aspinall, Chairman, Interior and Insular Affairs Committee, House of Representatives, March 6, 1967 (Carl Hayden Papers, Arizona State University, Tempe, Box 331, folder 19).

Bibliography

Aberle, David F.
    1963   "Some Sources of Flexibility in Navajo Social Organization." *Southwestern Journal of Anthropology* 19:1–8.
    1974   "Historical Reconstruction and Its Explanatory Role in Comparative Ethnology: A Study in Method." In *Comparative Studies by Harold E. Driver and Essays in His Honor*, ed. J. G. Jorgensen, 63–79. New York: HRAF Press.
    1980   "Navajo Exogamic Rules and Preferred Marriages." In *The Versatility of Kinship*, ed. Linda Cordell and Stephen Beckerman, 105–143. New York: Academic Press.

Ackerman, Robert E., and Lillian A. Ackerman
    1973   "Ethnoarchaeological Interpretation of Territoriality and Land Use in Southwestern Alaska." *Ethnohistory* 20:315–334.

Adair, John, and Evon Z. Vogt
    1949   "Navaho and Zuni Veterans: A Study of Contrasting Modes of Culture Change." *American Anthropologist* 51:547–561.

Adams, William Y.
    1971   "The Development of San Carlos Apache Wage Labor to 1954." In *Apachean Culture History and Ethnology*, ed. Keith H. Basso and Morris E. Opler, 116–128. Tucson: University of Arizona Press.

Adams, William Y., Dennis O. Van Gerven, and Richard S. Levy
    1978   "The Retreat from Migrationism." In *Annual Review of Anthropology*, ed. Bernard J. Siegel, A. R. Beals, and S. A. Tyler, 483–532. Palo Alto: Annual Reviews.

Anderson, Douglas D.
    1968   "A Stone Age Campsite at the Gateway to America." *Scientific American* 218 (June) 24–33.
    1970   "Athapaskans in the Kobuk Arctic Woodlands, Alaska?" *Canadian Archaeological Association Bulletin* 2:3–12.

Antevs, Ernst
    1955   "Geologic Climatic Dating in the West." *American Antiquity* 20:317–335.

Asch, Michael

    1981   "Slavey." In *Handbook of North American Indians.* Vol. VI, *Sub-arctic,* ed. June Helm, 338–349. Washington, D.C.: Smithsonian Institution.

    1984   *Home and Native Land: Aboriginal Rights and the Canadian Constitution.* Toronto: Methuen.

Bacon, Glen H.

    1977   "The Prehistory of Alaska: A Speculative Alternative." In *Problems in the Prehistory of the North American Subarctic: The Athapaskan Question,* ed. James W. Helmer, S. Van Dyke, and Francois J. Kense, 1–10. Calgary: University of Calgary.

Barnett, H. G.

    1937   "Culture Element Distribution: VII Oregon Coast." *University of California Anthropological Records* 1:155–204.

Basso, Ellen

    1978   "The Enemy of Every Tribe: 'Bushman' Images in Northern Athapaskan Narratives." *American Ethnologist* 5:690–709.

Basso, Keith H.

    1966   *The Gift of Changing Woman.* Bureau of American Ethnology Bulletin 196. Washington, D.C.: Smithsonian Institution.

    1970   *The Cibecue Apache.* New York: Holt, Rinehart and Winston.

    1971   Introduction. In *Western Apache Raiding and Warfare.* Grenville Goodwin and Keith H. Basso. Tucson: University of Arizona Press.

    1973   "A Western Apache Writing System: The Symbols of Silas John." *Science* 180(4090):1013–1022.

    1983   "Western Apache." In *Handbook of North American Indians.* Vol. X, *Southwest,* ed. Alfonso Ortiz, 462–488. Washington, D.C.: Smithsonian Institution.

Benavides, Alonso de

    1965   *The Memorial of Fray Alonso de Benavides, 1630,* trans. E. E. Ayer. Albuquerque: Horn and Wallace.

Benedict, James E.

    1975a   "The Murray Site: A Late Prehistoric Game Drive System in the Colorado Rocky Mountains." *Plains Anthropologist* 20:161–174.

    1975b   "Scratching Deer: A Late Prehistoric Campsite in the Green Lakes Valley, Colorado." *Plains Anthropologist* 20:267–278.

Berger, Thomas R.

    1977   *Northern Frontier, Northern Homeland: The Report of the Mackenzie Valley Pipeline Inquiry.* Ottawa: Minister of Supply and Services Canada.

Birket-Smith, Kai, and Frederica de Laguna

    1938   *The Eyak Indians of the Copper River Delta.* Copenhagen: Levin and Munksgaard.

Bishop, Charles A.

    1987   "Coast-Interior Exchange: The Origins of Stratification in Northwestern North America." *Arctic Anthropology* 24(1):72–83.

Bishop, Charles A., and Shepard Krech III
  1980   "Matri-Organization: The Basis of Aboriginal Sub-Arctic Social
            Organization." *Arctic Anthropology* 17(2):34–45.
Boas, Franz
  1910   "Ethnological Problems of Canada." *Journal of the Royal Anthro-
            pological Institute* 40:529–539.
  1940   *Race, Language, and Culture.* New York: Macmillan.
Bogoras, Waldimar
  1902   "The Folk-Lore of North Eastern Asia as Compared with That of
            North Western America." *American Anthropologist* 4:577–683.
Bolton, Herbert E.
  1916   *Spanish Explorations in the Southwest, 1542–1706.* New York:
            Charles Scribner's Sons.
Boyer, L. Bryce
  1979   *Childhood and Folklore: A Psychoanalytic Study of Apache Per-
            sonality.* New York: Library of Psychological Anthropology.
Brant, Charles S.
  1949   "The Cultural Position of the Kiowa Apache." *Southwestern
            Journal of Anthropology* 5:56–61.
  1953   "Kiowa Apache Culture History." *Southwestern Journal of An-
            thropology* 9:195–202.
Brugge, David M.
  1981   "Comments on Athabaskans and Sumas." In *The Protohistoric
            Period in the North American Southwest, A.D. 1450–1700,* ed.
            David R. Wilcox and W. Bruce Masse, 282–290. Anthropological
            Research Papers no. 24. Tempe: Arizona State University.
  1983   "Navajo Prehistory and History to 1850." In *Handbook of North
            American Indians.* Vol. X, *Southwest,* ed. Alfonso Ortiz, 489–
            501. Washington, D.C.: Smithsonian Institution.
Bryson, Reid A., and Wayne M. Wendland
  1967   "Tentative Climatic Episodes in Central North America." In *Life,
            Land, and Water,* ed. William Mayer-Oakes, 271–298. Winnipeg:
            University of Manitoba Press.
Burch, Ernest S., Jr.
  1972   "The Caribou/Wild Reindeer as a Human Resource." *American
            Antiquity* 37:339–368.
Castetter, Edward F., and Morris E. Opler
  1936   *The Ethnobotany of the Chiricahua and Mescalero Apache.* Eth-
            nobiological Studies in the American Southwest no. 111. Biologi-
            cal Series IV, 5. Albuquerque: University of New Mexico Press.
Clark, Annette McFadyen
  1970   "Koyukon Athabascan Ceremonialism." *Western Canadian Jour-
            nal of Anthropology* 2(1):80–88.
  1977   "Trade at the Cross Roads." In *Problems in the Prehistory of the
            North American Subarctic: The Athapaskan Question,* ed. James
            W. Helmer, S. Van Dyke, and Francois J. Kense, 130–134. Calgary:
            University of Calgary.

1981   "Koyukon." In *Handbook of North American Indians*. Vol. VI, *Subarctic*, ed. June Helm, 582–601. Washington, D.C.: Smithsonian Institution.

Clark, Donald W.
1981   "Prehistory of the Western Subarctic." In *Handbook of North American Indians*. Vol. VI, *Subarctic*, ed. June Helm, 107–129. Washington, D.C.: Smithsonian Institution.

Clum, Woodworth
1936   *Apache Agent*. Boston: Houghton Mifflin.

Cole, D. C.
1988   *The Chiricahua Apache, 1846–1876: From War to Reservation*. Albuquerque: University of New Mexico Press.

Colyer, Vincent
1971   *Peace with the Apaches of New Mexico and Arizona*. Freeport, N.Y.: Books for Libraries Press (orig. 1872).

Cook, John P.
1969   "The Early Prehistory of Healy Lake, Alaska." Ph.D. diss., University of Wisconsin.
1975   "The Archaeology of Interior Alaska." *Western Canadian Journal of Anthropology* 5(3–4): 125–133.

Cortés, José
1988   *Views from the Apache Frontier: Report on the Northern Provinces of New Spain*. Norman: University of Oklahoma Press.

Crow, John R., and Philip R. Obley
1981   "Han." In *Handbook of North American Indians*. Vol. VI, *Subarctic*, ed. June Helm, 506–513. Washington, D.C.: Smithsonian Institution.

Cruikshank, Julie
1975   "Becoming a Woman in Athapaskan Society: Changing Traditions on the Upper Yukon River." *Western Canadian Journal of Anthropology* 5(2): 1–14.

Curtis, E. S.
1964   *The North American Indian*. New York: Johnson Reprint.

Czaplicka, M. A.
1914   *Aboriginal Siberia: A Study in Social Anthropology*. Oxford: Clarendon Press.
1934   "Samoyed." In *Encyclopedia of Religion and Ethics*, ed. James Hastings, XI, 172–177. New York: Charles Scribner's Sons.

Davidson, D. S.
1937   "Snowshoes." *Memoir of the American Philosophical Society* 6: 1–207.

Davis, Leslie B.
1988   "Avonlea Three Decades Later: An Introduction." In *Avonlea Yesterday and Today: Archaeology and Prehistory*, ed. Leslie B. Davis, 5. Saskatoon: Saskatchewan Archaeological Society.

de Laguna, Frederica
1937   *A Preliminary Sketch of the Eyak Indians of the Copper River*

Delta, Alaska. Philadelphia: Philadelphia Anthropological Society.

1975 "Matrilineal Kin Groups in Northwestern North America." In *Proceedings: Northern Athapaskan Conference, 1971,* ed. Annette McFadyen Clark, 120–190. Mercury Series Paper no. 27. Ottawa: National Museum of Man.

de Laguna, Frederica, and Catherine McClellan

1981 "Ahtna." In *Handbook of North American Indians.* Vol. VI, *Subarctic,* ed. June Helm, 641–663. Washington, D.C.: Smithsonian Institution.

Denniston, Glenda

1981 "Sekani." In *Handbook of North American Indians.* Vol. VI, *Subarctic,* ed. June Helm, 433–441. Washington, D.C.: Smithsonian Institution.

Derry, David E.

1975 "Later Athapaskan Prehistory: A Migration Hypothesis." *Western Canadian Journal of Anthropology* 5(3–4):134–147.

Dixon, E. James

1985 "Cultural Chronology of Central Interior Alaska." *Arctic Anthropology* 22:47–66.

Dobyns, Henry F.

1966 "Estimating Aboriginal American Populations: An Appraisal of Techniques with a New Hemispheric Estimate." *Current Anthropology* 7(4):346–365.

Donohue, Paul F.

1975 "Concerning Athapaskan Prehistory in British Columbia." *Western Canadian Journal of Anthropology* 5(3–4):21–63.

1977 "Prehistoric Relationships between the Plains, Boreal Forest, and Cordilleran Regions." In *Problems in the Prehistory of the North American Subarctic: Athapaskan Question,* ed. James W. Helmer, S. Van Dyke, and Francois J. Kense, 84–89. Calgary: University of Calgary.

Douglas, Mary

1969 *Purity and Danger: An Analysis of Concepts of Pollution and Taboo.* London: Routledge and Kegan Paul.

Driver, Harold E.

1939 "Culture Element Distribution: X Northwest California." *University of California Anthropological Records* 1:297–433.

1941 "Girls' Puberty Rites in Western North America: Culture Element Distribution: XVI." *University of California Anthropological Records* 6(2):21–90.

1961 *Indians of North America.* Chicago: University of Chicago Press.

1966 "Geographical-Historical versus Psycho-Functional Explanations of Kin Avoidance." *Current Anthropology* 7:131–182.

Drucker, Philip

1937 "The Tolowa and Their Southwest Oregon Kin." *University of*

California Publications in American Archaeology and Ethnology 36:221–300.

DuBois, Cora
  1932 "Tolowa Notes." *American Anthropologist* 34:248–262.

Dumond, Don E.
  1969 "Toward a Prehistory of the Na-Dene with a General Comment on Population Movements among Nomadic Hunters." *American Anthropologist* 71:857–863.
  1977 *The Eskimos and Aleuts.* London: Thames and Hudson.
  1979 "Eskimo-Indian Relationships: A View from Prehistory." *Arctic Anthropology* 16(2):3–22.

Dupre, Wilhelm
  1974 *Religion in Primitive Cultures: A Study in Ethnophilosophy.* The Hague: Mouton.

Durbin, Marshall E.
  1964 "A Componential Analysis of the San Carlos Dialect of Western Apache." Ph.D. diss., State University of New York at Buffalo.

Dyen, Isidore, and David F. Aberle
  1974 *Lexical Reconstruction: The Case of the Proto-Athapaskan Kinship System.* Cambridge: Cambridge University Press.

Dyk, Walter
  1966 *Son of Old Man Hat: A Navajo Autobiography.* Lincoln: University of Nebraska Press.

Eggan, Fred
  1954 "Social Anthropology and the Method of Controlled Comparison." *American Anthropologist* 56:743–763.

Ellis, Florence
  1974 *American Indian Ethnohistory.* Vol. I, *Navajo Indians,* ed. David Agee Horr. New York: Garland.

Elsasser, Albert B.
  1978 "Mattole, Nongatle, Sinkyone, Lassik, and Wailaki." In *Handbook of North American Indians.* Vol. VIII, *California,* ed. Robert F. Heizer, 190–204. Washington, D.C.: Smithsonian Institution.

Farmer, Malcolm F.
  1940 "Navaho Archaeology of the Upper Blanco and Largo Canyons, Northern New Mexico." *American Antiquity* 8:65–79.

Fitzhugh, William W., and Aron Crowell, eds.
  1988 *Crossroads of Continents: Cultures of Siberia and Alaska.* Washington, D.C.: Smithsonian Institution.

Fladmark, K. R.
  1979 "Routes: Alternative Migration Corridors for Early Man in North America." *American Antiquity* 44:55–67.

Foor, Thomas A.
  1988 "Avonlea Systematics and Culture History." In *Avonlea Yesterday and Today: Archaeology and Prehistory,* ed. Leslie B. Davis, 257–263. Saskatoon: Saskatchewan Archaeological Society.

Forbes, Jack D.
1959   "Unknown Athapaskans: The Identification of the Jano, Jocome, Jumano, Manso, Suma, and Other Indian Tribes of the Southwest." *Ethnohistory* 6:97–158.
Fowler, William R., Jr.
1977   "Linguistic Evidence for Athapaskan Prehistory." In *Problems in the Prehistory of the North American Subarctic: The Athapaskan Question,* ed. James W. Helmer, S. Van Dyke, and Francois J. Kense, 102–105. Calgary: University of Calgary.
Fredlund, Lynn B.
1988   "Distribution and Characteristics of Avonlea South of the Yellowstone River in Montana." In *Avonlea Yesterday and Today: Archaeology and Prehistory,* ed. Leslie B. Davis, 171–182. Saskatoon: Saskatchewan Archaeological Society.
Frison, George C.
1962   "Wedding of the Waters Cave: A Stratified Site in the Bighorn Basin of Northern Wyoming." *Plains Anthropologist* 7:246–265.
1971   "The Buffalo Pound in Northwestern Plains Prehistory, Site 48CA302, Wyoming." *American Antiquity* 36:77–91.
1978   *Prehistoric Hunters of the High Plains.* New York: Academic Press.
1988   "Avonlea and Contemporaries in Wyoming." In *Avonlea Yesterday and Today: Archaeology and Prehistory,* ed. Leslie B. Davis, 155–170. Saskatoon: Saskatchewan Archaeological Society.
Gillespie, Beryl C.
1975   "Territorial Expansion of the Chipewyan in the Eighteenth Century." In *Proceedings: Northern Athapaskan Conference, 1971,* ed. Annette McFadyen Clark. Mercury Series Paper no. 27. Ottawa: National Museum of Man.
1981   "Territorial Groups before 1821: Athapaskans of the Shield and the Mackenzie Drainage." In *Handbook of North American Indians.* Vol. VI, *Subarctic,* ed. June Helm, 161–168. Washington, D.C.: Smithsonian Institution.
Gluckman, Max
1968   "The Utility of the Equilibrium Model in the Study of Social Change." *American Anthropologist* 70:219–237.
Goddard, Pliny Earle
1903–   "The Life and Culture of the Hupa." *University of California Pub-*
1904   *lications in American Archaeology and Ethnography* 1:1–95.
1917   "The Beaver Indians." *Anthropological Papers of the American Museum of Natural History* 10(4):201–293.
Goldenweiser, Alexander
1910   "Totemism, an Analytical Study." *Journal of American Folklore* 23:179–293.
Goldman, Irving
1941   "The Alkatcho Carrier: Historical Background of Crest Prerogatives." *American Anthropologist* 43:396–408.

Goodwin, Grenville G.
1938   "White Mountain Apache Religion." *American Anthropologist* 40:24–37.
1945   "A Comparison of Navajo and White Mountain Apache Ceremonial Forms and Categories." *Southwestern Journal of Anthropology* 1:498–506.
1969   *The Social Organization of the Western Apache.* Tucson: University of Arizona Press.
Goodwin, Grenville G., and Keith H. Basso
1971   *Western Apache Raiding and Warfare.* Tucson: University of Arizona Press.
Goodwin, Grenville G., and Charles R. Kaut
1954   "A Native Religious Movement among the White Mountain and Cibecue Apache." *Southwestern Journal of Anthropology* 10:385–404.
Gordon, Bryan H. C.
1975   *Of Men and Animals in Barrenland Prehistory.* Mercury Series Paper no. 28. Ottawa: National Museum of Man.
1977   "Chipewyan Prehistory." In *Problems in the Prehistory of the North American Subarctic: The Athapaskan Question,* ed. James W. Helmer, S. Van Dyke, and Francois J. Kense, 72–76. Calgary: University of Calgary.
Gould, Richard A.
1978   "Tolowa." In *Handbook of North American Indians.* Vol. 8, *California,* ed. Robert F. Heizer, 128–136. Washington, D.C.: Smithsonian Institution.
Greenberg, Joseph H.
1987   *Language in the Americas.* Stanford: Stanford University Press.
Greenberg, Joseph H., Christy G. Turner, and Stephen L. Zegura
1986   "The Settlement of the Americas: A Comparison of the Linguistic, Dental, and Genetic Evidence." *Current Anthropology* 27(5):477–497.
Greenfeld, Philip J.
1973   "Cultural Conservatism as an Inhibitor of Linguistic Change: A Possible Apache Case." *International Journal of American Linguistics* 39(2):98–104.
Gregory, David A.
1981   "Western Apache Archaeology: Problems and Approaches." In *The Protohistoric Period in the North American Southwest, A.D. 1450–1700,* ed. David R. Wilcox and W. Bruce Masse. Anthropological Research Papers no. 24. 257–274. Tempe: Arizona State University.
Griffen, William B.
1988   *Utmost Good Faith: Patterns of Apache-Mexican Hostilities in Northern Chihuahua Border Warfare, 1821–1848.* Albuquerque: University of New Mexico Press.

Gunnerson, Dolores A.
1974   *The Jicarilla Apaches: A Study in Survival.* DeKalb: Northern Illinois University Press.

Gunnerson, James H.
1968   "Plains Apache Archaeology: A Review." *Plains Anthropologist* 13:167–189.
1969   "Apache Archaeology in Northeastern New Mexico." *American Antiquity* 34:23–39.

Gunnerson, James H., and Dolores A. Gunnerson
1971   "Apachean Culture: A Study in Unity and Diversity." In *Apachean Culture History and Ethnology*, ed. Keith H. Basso and Morris E. Opler, 7–33. Tucson: University of Arizona Press.

Gurvich, I. S.
1979   "An Ethnographic Study of Cultural Parallels among the Aboriginal Populations of Northern Asia and Northern North America." *Arctic Anthropology* 16(1):32–38.
1988   "Ethnic Connections across Bering Strait." In *Crossroads of Continents: Cultures of Siberia and Alaska*, ed. William W. Fitzhugh and Aron Crowell, 17–21. Washington, D.C.: Smithsonian Institution.

Haas, Mary R.
1968   "Notes on a Chipewyan Dialect." *International Journal of American Linguistics* 34:165–175.

Hajdu, Peter
1963   *The Samoyed Peoples and Languages.* Indiana University Publications: Uralic and Altaic Series 14. Bloomington: Indiana University Press.

Hall, Edward T.
1944   "Recent Clues to Athabascan Prehistory in the Southwest." *American Anthropologist* 46:98–105.

Hall, E. Raymond, and Keith R. Kelson
1958   *Mammals of North America.* New York: Ronald Press.

Hall, Thomas D.
1989   *Social Change in the Southwest, 1350–1880.* Abilene: University of Kansas Press.

Hallowell, A. Irving
1926   "Bear Ceremonialism in the Northern Hemisphere." *American Anthropologist* 28:1–175.

Hammerich, Louis L.
1960   "Some Linguistic Problems of the Arctic." *Acta Arctica* 12:83–91.

Hammond, George, and Agapito Rey
1953   *Don Juan de Oñate, Colonizer of New Mexico, 1595–1628.* Albuquerque: University of New Mexico Press.

Hardisty, William L.
1867   "The Loucheux Indians." *Annual Report of the Smithsonian*

Institution, 1866, 311–320. Washington, D.C.: Smithsonian Institution.

Harp, Elmer, Jr.

1978   "Pioneer Cultures of the Sub-Arctic and the Arctic." In *Ancient Native Americans*, ed. Jesse D. Jennings, 95–129. San Francisco: Freeman.

Haskell, J. Loring

1987   *Southern Athapaskan Migration, A.D. 200–1750*. Tsaile, Ariz.: Navajo Community College Press.

Hatt, Gudmund

1916   "Moccasins and Their Relationships to Asiatic Footwear." *Memoirs of the American Anthropological Association* 3:149–250.

Hearne, Samuel

1911   *A Journey from Prince of Wales's Fort in Hudson's Bay to the Northern Ocean in the Years 1769, 1770, 1771, and 1772*. Toronto: Champlain Society.

Helm, June

1965   "Bilaterality in the Socio-Territorial Organization of the Arctic Drainage Dene." *Ethnology* 4:361–385.

1981   "Dogrib." In *Handbook of North American Indians*. Vol. VI, *Subarctic*, ed. June Helm, 291–309. Washington, D.C.: Smithsonian Institution.

Helmer, James W.

1977   "Points, People, and Prehistory: A Preliminary Synthesis of Culture History in North Central British Columbia." In *Problems in the Prehistory of the North American Subarctic: The Athapaskan Question*, ed. James W. Helmer, S. Van Dyke, and Francois J. Kense, 90–96. Calgary: University of Calgary.

Hester, James J.

1962   *Early Navajo Migrations and Acculturation in the Southwest*. Museum of New Mexico Papers in Anthropology. Santa Fe: Museum of New Mexico.

1971   "Navajo Culture Change, 1550 to 1960 and Beyond." In *Apachean Culture History and Ethnology*, ed. Keith H. Basso and Morris E. Opler, 51–68. Tucson: University of Arizona Press.

Hickerson, Nancy

1988   "The Linguistic Position of Jumano." *Journal of Anthropological Research* 44(3):311–326.

Hockett, Charles F.

1977   "Review of *Lexical Reconstruction* by Dyen and Aberle." *Current Anthropology* 18:84–91.

Hogan, Patrick

1989   "Dinetah: A Reevaluation of Pre-Revolt Navajo Occupation in Northwest New Mexico." *Journal of Anthropological Research* 45(1):51–67.

Hoijer, Harry

1938 "The Southern Athapaskan Languages." *American Anthropologist* 40:75–87.

1956 "The Chronology of the Athapaskan Languages." *International Journal of American Linguistics* 22:219–232.

1971 "The Position of the Apachean Languages in the Athapaskan Stock." In *Apachean Culture History and Ethnology*, ed. Keith H. Basso and Morris E. Opler, 3–6. Tucson: University of Arizona Press.

Holmes, Charles E.

1971 "A Northern Athapaskan Environmental System in Diachronic Perspective." *Western Canadian Journal of Anthropology* 5(3–4): 92–124.

1977 "Three Thousand Years of Prehistory of Minchumina: The Question of Cultural Boundaries." In *Problems in the Prehistory of the North American Subarctic: The Athapaskan Question*, ed. James W. Helmer, S. Van Dyke, and Francois J. Kense, 11–15. Calgary: University of Calgary.

Honigmann, John J.

1945 "Northern and Southern Athapaskan Eschatology." *American Anthropologist* 47:467–469.

1946 *Ethnography and Acculturation of the Fort Nelson Slave.* Anthropology Publication no. 33. New Haven: Yale University Press.

1964 *The Kaska Indians: An Ethnographic Reconstruction.* Anthropology Publication no. 51. New Haven: Human Relations Area Files Press, Yale University.

1981a "Expressive Aspects of Subarctic Indian Culture." In *Handbook of North American Indians*. Vol. VI, *Subarctic*, ed. June Helm, 718–738. Washington, D.C.: Smithsonian Institution.

1981b "Kaska." In *Handbook of North American Indians*. Vol. VI, *Subarctic*, ed. June Helm, 442–450. Washington, D.C.: Smithsonian Institution.

Hopkins, David M.

1979 "Landscape and Climate of Beringia during Late Pleistocene and Holocene Times." In *The First Americans: Origins, Affinities, and Adaptations*, ed. William S. Laughlin and Albert B. Harper, 15–41. New York: Gustav Fischer.

Hosley, E. H.

1977 "A Reexamination of the Salmon Dependence of the Pacific Drainage Culture Athapaskans." In *Problems in the Prehistory of the North American Subarctic: The Athapaskan Question*, ed. James W. Helmer, S. Van Dyke, Francois J. Kense, 124–129. Calgary: University of Calgary.

1980 "The Aboriginal Social Organization of the Pacific Drainage Dene: The Matrilineal Basis." *Arctic Anthropology* 17:12–16.

1981 "Environment and Culture in the Alaska Plateau." In *Handbook of North American Indians.* Vol. VI, *Subarctic,* ed. June Helm, 533–555. Washington, D.C.: Smithsonian Institution.

Huscher, Betty H., and Harold A. Huscher
1942   "Athapaskan Migration via the Intermontane Region." *American Antiquity* 8:80–88.

Institute for Government Research
1928   *The Problem of Indian Administration.* Baltimore: Johns Hopkins University Press.

Janes, Robert R.
1973   "Indian and Eskimo Contact in the Southern Keewatin: An Ethnohistorical Approach." *Ethnohistory* 20:39–54.

Jenness, Diamond
n.d.   *The Sarcee of Alberta.* National Museums of Canada Bulletin no. 90. Ottawa: Canada Department of Mines.
1937   *The Sekani Indians of British Columbia.* National Museums of Canada Bulletin no 84. Ottawa: Canada Department of Mines and Resources.
1943   "The Carrier Indians of the Bulkley River: Their Social and Religious Life," *Bureau of American Ethnology Bulletin* 133: 469–586.
1956   "The Chipewyan Indians: An Account by an Early Explorer." *Anthropologica* 3:15–33.
1972   *The Indians of Canada.* National Museums of Canada Bulletin no. 65. Ottawa: National Museum of Man.

Jochelson, Waldemar
1928   *Peoples of Asiatic Russia.* New York: American Museum of Natural History.

Johnson, Ann M.
1988   "Parallel Ground Ceramics: An Addition to Avonlea Material Culture." In *Avonlea Yesterday and Today: Archaeology and Prehistory,* ed. Leslie B. Davis, 137–143. Saskatoon: Saskatchewan Archaeological Society.

Jones, Strachan
1867   "The Kutchin Tribes." *Annual Report of the Smithsonian Institution, 1866,* 320–327. Washington, D.C.: Smithsonian Institution.

Jorgensen, Joseph G.
1980   *Western Indians: Comparative Environments, Languages, and Cultures of 172 Western American Indian Tribes.* San Francisco: Freeman.
1983   "Comparative Traditional Economics and Ecological Adaptations." In *Handbook of North American Indians.* Vol. X, *Southwest,* ed. Alfonso Ortiz, 684–710. Washington, D.C.: Smithsonian Institution.

Kaut, Charles R.
1956   "Western Apache Clan and Phratry Organization." *American Anthropologist* 58:140–161.

1957   *The Western Apache Clan System: Its Origins and Develop-
        ment.* Publications in Anthropology no. 9. Albuquerque: Univer-
        sity of New Mexico Press.
1974   "The Clan System as an Epiphenomenal Element of Western
        Apache Social Organization." *Ethnology* 13:45–70.
Kehoe, Thomas F., and Alice B. Kehoe
1968   "Saskatchewan." In *The Northwestern Plains: A Symposium.*
        Occasional Papers no. 1, 21–35. Billings, Mont.: Center for In-
        dian Studies, Rocky Mountain College.
Kehoe, Thomas F., and Bruce A. McCorquodale
1961   "The Avonlea Point: Horizon Marker for the Northwestern
        Plains." *Plains Anthropologist* 6:179–188.
Keim, de Benneville Randolph
1887   *Sheridan's Troopers on the Border: A Winter Campaign on the
        Plains.* Philadelphia: D. McKay.
Kelley, Clara B.
1980   "Navajo Political Economy before Fort Sumner." In *The Versatil-
        ity of Kinship,* ed. Linda Cordell and Stephen Beckerman, 307–
        332. New York: Academic Press.
Kluckhohn, Clyde C., and Dorothea Leighton
1947   *The Navajo.* Cambridge: Harvard University Press.
Kobrinsky, Vernon H.
1977   "The Tsimshianization of the Carrier Indians." In *Problems in
        the Prehistory of the North American Subarctic: The Athapas-
        kan Question,* ed. James W. Helmer, S. Van Dyke, Francois J.
        Kense, 201–210. Calgary: University of Calgary.
Krauss, Michael E.
1973a   "Eskimo-Aleut." In *Current Trends in Linguistics.* Vol. X, *Lin-
        guistics in North America,* ed. Thomas A. Sebeok, 796–902. New
        York: Humanities Press.
1973b   "Na-Dene." In *Current Trends in Linguistics.* Vol X, *Linguistics
        in North America,* ed. Thomas A. Sebeok, 903–978. New York:
        Humanities Press.
1979   "Na-Dene and Eskimo-Aleut." In *The Languages of Native North
        America: Historical and Comparative Assessment,* ed. Lyle
        Campbell and Marianne Mithun, 803–901. Austin: University of
        Texas Press.
Krauss, Michael E., and Victor K. Golla
1981   "Northern Athapaskan Languages." In *Handbook of North Amer-
        ican Indians.* Vol. VI, *Subarctic,* ed. June Helm, 67–85. Washing-
        ton, D.C.: Smithsonian Institution.
Krech, Shepard, III
1976   "The Eastern Kutchin and the Fur Trade, 1800–1860." *Ethno-
        history* 23:213–235.
1978   "Disease, Starvation, and Northern Athapaskan Social Organiza-
        tion." *American Ethnologist* 5:710–732.

1980   "Northern Athapaskan Ethnology in the 1970's." In *Annual Review of Anthropology*, ed. Bernard J. Siegel, A. R. Beals, S. A. Tylor, XI, 83–100. Palo Alto: Annual Reviews.

Kroeber, A. L., ed.

1925   *Handbook of the Indians of California*. Bureau of American Ethnology Bulletin no. 78. Washington, D.C.: Smithsonian Institution.

Krutz, Gordon V.

1971   "San Carlos Apache Wage Labor in 1970." In *Apachean Culture History and Ethnology*, ed. Keith H. Basso and Morris E. Opler, 129–133. Tucson: University of Arizona Press.

Kunz, Michael

1977   "Athapaskan/Eskimo Interfaces in the Central Brooks Range." In *Problems in the Prehistory of the North American Subarctic: The Athapaskan Question*, ed. James W. Helmer, S. Van Dyke, Francois J. Kense, 135–144. Calgary: University of Calgary.

Lamphere, Louise

1977   *To Run After Them: The Social Bases of Cooperation in a Navajo Community*. Tucson: University of Arizona Press.

Lampl, Michelle, and Baruch S. Blumberg

1979   "Blood Polymorphisms and the Origins of New World Populations." In *The First Americans: Origins, Affinities, and Adaptations*, ed. William S. Laughlin and Albert B. Harper, 107–123. New York: Gustav Fischer.

Lane, Robert B.

1981   "Chilcotin." In *Handbook of North American Indians*. Vol. VI, *Subarctic*, ed. June Helm, 402–412. Washington, D.C.: Smithsonian Institution.

Laughlin, William S.

1979   "Problems in the Physical Anthropology of North American Indians, Eskimos, and Aleuts." *Arctic Anthropology* 16(1): 165–178.

1980   *Aleuts: Survivors of the Bering Land Bridge*. New York: Holt, Rinehart and Winston.

Laughlin, William S., and Susan J. Wolf

1979   "Introduction. The First Americans: Origins, Affinities, and Adaptations." In *The First Americans: Origins, Affinities, and Adaptations*, ed. William S. Laughlin and Albert B. Harper, 1–11. New York: Gustav Fischer.

Lee, Dorothy

1950   "Lineal and Nonlineal Codification of Reality." *Psychosomatic Medicine* 12:89–97.

Leighton, Dorothea, and Clyde C. Kluckhohn

1947   *Children of the People*. Cambridge: Harvard University Press.

Levin, Maksim G., and Leonid P. Potapov, eds.

1964   *The Peoples of Siberia*. Chicago: University of Chicago Press.

Levine, Robert D.

1979   "Haida and Na-Dene: A New Look at the Evidence." *International Journal of American Linguistics* 45 : 157–170.

Lowie, Robert H.
1923   "The Buffalo Drive and Old World Hunting Practice." *Natural History* 23 : 280–282.
1970   *Primitive Society.* New York: Liveright.

McAllister, J. Gilbert
1955   "Kiowa-Apache Social Organization." In *Social Anthropology of North American Tribes,* ed. Fred Eggan, 99–169. Chicago: University of Chicago Press.

McClellan, Catherine
1964   "Culture Contacts in the Early Historic Period in Northwestern North America." *Arctic Anthropology* 2(2) : 3–15.
1981   "Environment and Culture in the Cordillera." In *Handbook of North American Indians.* Vol. VI, *Subarctic,* ed. June Helm, 372–386. Washington, D.C.: Smithsonian Institution.

McClellan, Catherine, and Glenda Denniston
1981a   "Tagish." In *Handbook of North American Indians.* Vol. VI, *Subarctic,* ed. June Helm, 481–492. Washington, D.C.: Smithsonian Institution.
1981b   "Tutchone." In *Handbook of North American Indians.* Vol. VI, *Subarctic,* ed. June Helm, 493–506. Washington, D.C.: Smithsonian Institution.

McDonnell, Roger F.
1984   "Symbolic Orientations and Systematic Turmoil: Centering on the Kaska Symbol of Dene." *Canadian Journal of Anthropology* 4(1) : 39–56.

McKennan, Robert
1935   "Anent the Kutchin Tribes." *American Anthropologist* 37 : 369.
1959   *The Upper Tanana Indians.* Anthropology Publication no. 55. New Haven: Yale University Press.
1965   *The Chandalar Kutchin.* Technical Paper no. 17. Washington, D.C.: Arctic Institute of America.
1969   "Athapaskan Groupings and Social Organization in Central Alaska." In *Contributions to Anthropology: Band Societies,* ed. David Damas. National Museums of Canada Bulletin no. 223, Anthropological Series no. 84, 93–115. Ottawa: National Museums of Canada.
1981   "Tanana." In *Handbook of North American Indians.* Vol. VI, *Subarctic,* ed. June Helm, 562–576. Washington, D.C.: Smithsonian Institution.

MacLachlan, Bruce B.
1981   "Tahltan." In *Handbook of North American Indians,* Vol. VI, *Subarctic,* ed. June Helm, 458–468. Washington, D.C.: Smithsonian Institution.

McNeley, James E.
1981   *Holy Wind in Navajo Philosophy*. Tucson: University of Arizona Press.

Madsen, David B.
1975   "Dating Paiute-Shoshoni Expansion in the Great Basin." *American Antiquity* 40:82–86.

Malinowski, Bronislaw
1948   *Magic, Science, and Religion and Other Essays*. Glencoe, Ill.: Free Press.

Marett, Robert R.
1912   *Anthropology*. New York: Holt, Rinehart.

Meiklejohn, Christopher
1977   "Genetic Differentiation and Deme Structure: Considerations for an Understanding of the Athapaskan/Algonkian Continuum." In *Problems in the Prehistory of the North American Subarctic: The Athapaskan Question*, ed. James W. Helmer, S. Van Dyke, Francois J. Kense, 106–110. Calgary: University of Calgary.

Meyer, David, Olga Klinko, and James Finnigan
1988   "Northernmost Avonlea in Saskatchewan." In *Avonlea Yesterday and Today: Archaeology and Prehistory*, ed. Leslie B. Davis, 33–42. Saskatoon: Saskatchewan Archaeological Society.

Milne, Laurie Ann
1988   "The Larson Site (DiOn-3) and the Avonlea Phase in Southeastern Alberta." In *Avonlea Yesterday and Today: Archaeology and Prehistory*, ed. Leslie B. Davis, 137–143. Saskatoon: Saskatchewan Archaeological Society.

Montefiore, A.
1895   "Notes on the Samoyads of the Great Tundra, Collected from the Journals of F. G. Jackson, F.R.G.S." *Journal of the Royal Anthropological Institute* 24:388–410.

Mooney, James
1898   "Calendar History of the Kiowa Indians." *Bureau of American Ethnology Annual Report* 17:141–445. Washington, D.C.: Smithsonian Institution.

Morice, A. G.
1914   "Northwestern Denes and Northeastern Asiatics: A Study of the Origins of the Former." *Transactions of the Royal Canadian Institute* 10:131–193.

Morlan, Richard E.
1972   *The Later Prehistory of the Middle Porcupine Drainage, Northern Yukon Territories*. Mercury Series Paper no. 11. Ottawa: National Museum of Man.

Naylor, Thomas N.
1981   "Athapaskans They Weren't: The Suma Rebels Executed at Casas Grandes in 1685." In *The Protohistoric Period in the North American Southwest, A.D. 1450–1700*, ed. David R. Wilcox and

W. Bruce Masse, Anthropological Research Papers no. 24, 275 –
281. Tempe: Arizona State University.

Nelson, Richard K.
1983   *Make Prayers to the Raven: A Koyukon View of the Northern
Forest.* Chicago: Univeristy of Chicago Press.

Noble, William C.
1977   "The Taltheilei Shale Tradition: An Update." In *Problems in the
Prehistory of the North American Subarctic: The Athapaskan
Question,* ed. James W. Helmer, S. Van Dyke, Francois J. Kense,
65–71. Calgary: University of Calgary.
1981   "Prehistory of the Great Slave Lake and Great Bear Lake Region."
In *Handbook of North American Indians.* Vol. VI, *Subarctic,* ed.
June Helm, 97–106. Washington, D.C.: Smithsonian Institution.

Nomland, Gladys A.
1935   "Sinkyone Notes." *University of California Publications in
American Archaeology and Ethnology* 36:149–178.
1938   "Bear Lake Ethnography." *University of California Anthropological Records* 2(2):91–126.

Ogle, R. F.
1970   *Federal Control of the Western Apache, 1848–1886.* Albuquerque: University of New Mexico Press.

Opler, Morris E.
1936a   "The Kinship Systems of the Southern Athabaskan-Speaking
Tribes." *American Anthropologist* 38:620–633.
1936b   "A Summary of Jicarilla Apache Culture." *American Anthropologist* 38:202–223.
1937   "Apache Data concerning the Relation of Kinship Terminologies
to Social Classification." *American Anthropologist* 39:201–212.
1938   *Dirty Boy: A Jicarilla Tale of Raid and War.* Memoirs of the
American Anthropological Association no. 52. Menasha, Wis.:
American Anthropological Association.
1941a   *An Apache Life-Way: The Economic, Social, and Religious Institutions of the Chiricahua Indians.* Chicago: University of Chicago Press.
1941b   "A Jicarilla Apache Expedition and Scalp Dance." *Journal of
American Folklore* 54:10–23.
1944   "The Jicarilla Apache Ceremonial Relay Race." *American Anthropologist* 46:75.
1945   "The Lipan Apache Death Complex and Its Extensions." *Southwestern Journal of Anthropology* 1:122–141.
1946   *Childhood and Youth in Jicarilla Apache Society.* F. W. Hodge
Anniversary Publishing Fund, no. 5. Los Angeles: Southwest
Museum.
1959   "Component, Assemblage, and Theme in Cultural Integration
and Differentiation." *American Anthropologist* 61:955–964.
1965   "An Interpretation of Ambivalence in Two American Indian

Tribes." In *A Reader in Comparative Religion*, ed. William A. Lessa and Evon Z. Vogt, 421–432. New York: Harper and Row.

1969 *Apache Odyssey: A Journey between Two Worlds.* New York: Holt, Rinehart and Winston.

1971 "Pots, Apache, and the Dismal River Complex." In *Apachean Culture History and Ethnology*, ed. Keith H. Basso and Morris E. Opler, 29–33. Tucson: University of Arizona Press.

1972 "Cause and Effect in Apachean Agriculture, Division of Labor, Residence Patterns, and Girls' Puberty Rites." *American Anthropologist* 74:1133–1146.

1973 *Grenville Goodwin among the Western Apache: Letters from the Field.* Tucson: University of Arizona Press.

1975 "Problems in Apachean Culture History, with Special Reference to the Lipan Apache." *Anthropological Quarterly* 48:182–192.

1983a "The Apachean Culture Pattern and Its Origins." In *Handbook of North American Indians*. Vol. X, *Southwest*, ed. Alfonso Ortiz, 368–392. Washington, D.C.: Smithsonian Institution.

1983b "Mescalero Apache." In *Handbook of North American Indians*. Vol. X, *Southwest*, ed. Alfonso Ortiz, 419–439. Washington, D.C.: Smithsonian Institution.

Opler, Morris E., and William E. Bittle

1961 "The Death Practices and Eschatology of the Kiowa Apache." *Southwestern Journal of Anthropology* 17:383–394.

Osgood, Cornelius

1932 *The Ethnography of the Great Bear Lake Indians.* Canada Department of Mines Bulletin no. 70. Ottawa: National Museum of Man.

1933 "Tanaina Culture." *American Anthropologist* 35:695–717.

1936a *Contributions to the Ethnography of the Kutchin.* Anthropology Publication no. 14. New Haven: Yale University Press.

1936b "The Distribution of the Northern Athapaskan Indians." *Yale University Publications in Anthropology* 7:3–23.

1937 *The Ethnography of the Tanaina.* Anthropology Publication no. 16. New Haven: Yale University Press.

1959 *Ingalik Mental Culture.* Anthropology Publication no. 56. New Haven: Yale University Press.

1971 *The Han Indians: A Compilation of Ethnographic and Historical Data on the Alaska-Yukon Boundary Area.* Anthropology Publication no. 74. New Haven: Yale University Press.

Perry, Richard J.

1972 "Structural Resiliency and the Danger of the Dead: The Western Apache." *Ethnology* 11:380–385.

1977 "Variations on the Female Referent in Athapaskan Cultures." *Journal of Anthropological Research* 33:99–118.

1979 "The Fur Trade and the Status of Women in the Western Subarctic." *Ethnohistory* 26:363–375.

1980 "The Apachean Transition from the Subarctic to the Southwest." *Plains Anthropologist* 25:279–296.

1989   "Matrilineal Descent in a Hunting Context: The Athapaskan
        Case." *Ethnology* 28(1):33–51.
Powers, William R.
1973   "Paleolithic Man in Northeast Asia." *Arctic Anthropology* 10:
        1–106.
Price, John A.
1978   *Native Studies: American and Canadian Indians.* Toronto:
        McGraw-Hill Ryerson.
Prokof'yeva, E. D.
1964   "The Nentsy." In *The Peoples of Siberia*, ed. Maksim G. Levin and
        Leonid P. Potapov, 547–570. Chicago: University of Chicago
        Press.
Ray, Arthur J.
1974   *Indians in the Fur Trade: Their Role as Trappers, Hunters, and
        Middlemen in the Lands Southwest of Hudson Bay, 1660–1870.*
        Toronto: University of Toronto Press.
Ray, Verne F.
1939   *Cultural Relations in the Plateau of Northwestern North Amer-
        ica.* F. W. Hodge Anniversary Publishing Fund, no. 3. Los Angeles:
        Southwest Museum.
Reeves, Brian O. K.
n.d.   *Culture Change in the Northern Plains, 1000 B.C.–A.D. 1000.*
        Archaeological Survey of Alberta Occasional Paper no. 20. Cal-
        gary: Alberta Culture Historical Resources Division.
1983   *Culture Change in the Northern Plains, 1000 B.C.–A.D. 1000.*
        Occasional Paper no. 20. Edmonton: Archaeological Survey of
        Alberta.
Reger, Douglas
1977   "Prehistory in the Upper Cook Inlet, Alaska." In *Problems in the
        Prehistory of the North American Subarctic: The Athapaskan
        Question*, ed. James W. Helmer, S. Van Dyke, Francois J. Kense,
        16–21. Calgary: University of Calgary.
Reichard, Gladys
1945   "Distinctive Features of Navajo Religion." *Southwestern Journal
        of Anthropology* 1:199–220.
1950   *Navaho Religion: A Study of Symbolism.* Chicago: University of
        Chicago Press.
Ridington, Robin
1969   "Kin Categories vs. Kin Groups: A Two-Section System without
        Sections." *Ethnology* 8:460–467.
1981   "Beaver." In *Handbook of North American Indians*. Vol. VI, *Sub-
        arctic*, ed. June Helm, 350–360. Washington, D.C.: Smithsonian
        Institution.
Rogers, Edward S., and James G. E. Smith
1981   "Environment and Culture in the Shield and Mackenzie Border-
        lands." In *Handbook of North American Indians*. Vol. VI, *Sub-*

arctic, ed. June Helm, 130–145. Washington, D.C.: Smithsonian Institution.

Rubel, Paula G., and Abraham Rosman
1983   "The Evolution of Exchange Structures and Ranking: Some Northwest Coast Examples." *Journal of Anthropological Research* 39(1):1–25.

Ruebelmann, George N.
1988   "The Henry Smith Site: An Avonlea Bison Procurement and Ceremonial Complex in Northern Montana." In *Avonlea Yesterday and Today: Archaeology and Prehistory*, ed. Leslie B. Davis, 191–202. Saskatoon: Saskatchewan Archaeological Society.

Sanday, Peggy
1973   "Toward a Theory of the Status of Women." *American Anthropologist* 75:1682–1700.

Sapir, E.
1936   "Internal Linguistic Evolution Suggestive of the Northern Origins of the Navajo." *American Anthropologist* 38:224–235.

Savishinsky, Joel S.
1974   *The Trail of the Hare*. New York: Gordon and Breach.

Savishinsky, Joel S., and Hiroko Sue Hara
1981   "Hare." In *Handbook of Native American Indians*. Vol. VI, *Subarctic*, ed. June Helm, 458–468. Washington, D.C.: Smithsonian Institution.

Schaafsma, Curtis F.
1981   "Early Apacheans in the Southwest: A Review." In *The Protohistoric Period in the North American Southwest, A.D. 1450–1700*, ed. David R. Wilcox and W. Bruce Masse, 291–320. Anthropological Research Papers no. 24. Tempe: Arizona State University.

Schlegel, Alice, and Herbert Barry III
1986   "The Cultural Consequences of Female Contribution to Subsistence." *American Anthropologist* 88:142–150.

Schlesier, Karl H.
1972   "Rethinking the Dismal River Aspect and the Plains Athapaskans, A.D. 1692–1768." *Plains Anthropologist* 17:101–133.

Schmitter, Ferdinand
1910   "Upper Yukon Native Customs and Folk-Lore." *Smithsonian Miscellaneous Collections* 56(4):1–30.

Schroeder, Albert H.
1974   *A Study of the Apache Indians*. Vols. I, IV. New York: Garland Publishing.

Secoy, Frank
1953   *Changing Military Patterns on the Great Plains*. American Ethnological Society Monograph no. 21. Seattle: University of Washington Press.

Service, Elman R.
1962   *Primitive Social Organization*. New York: Random House.

Sherwood, Angus
  1958   "Some Remarks about the Athabascan Indians." *Anthropologica*
         6:51–56.
Sherzer, Joel
  1973   "Areal Linguistics in North America." In *Current Trends in Lin-
         guistics*. Vol. X, *Linguistics in North America*, ed. Thomas A.
         Sebeok, 749–795. New York: Humanities Press.
Shinkwin, Anne D.
  1977   "The 'Archaeological Visibility' of Northern Athapaskans in the
         Tanana River Area, Central Alaska." In *Problems in the Pre-
         history of the North American Subarctic: The Athapaskan Ques-
         tion*, ed. James W. Helmer, S. Van Dyke, and Francois J. Kense,
         40–45. Calgary: University of Calgary.
  1979   *Dakah de'nin's Village and the Dixthada Site: A Contribution to
         Northern Athapaskan Prehistory*. Mercury Series Paper no. 91.
         Ottawa: National Museum of Man.
Shipley, William F.
  1978   "Native Languages of California." In *Handbook of North Ameri-
         can Indians*. Vol. VIII, *California*, ed. Robert F. Heizer, 80–90.
         Washington, D.C.: Smithsonian Institution.
Simeone, William E.
  1982   *A History of Alaskan Athapaskans: A History of Alaskan Atha-
         paskans Including a Description of Athapaskans and a Histori-
         cal Narrative, 1785–1971*. N.p.: Alaska Historical Commission.
Sjoberg, Andree F.
  1953   "Lipan Apache Culture in Historical Perspective." *Southwestern
         Journal of Anthropology* 9:76–98.
Slobodin, Richard
  1962   *Band Organization of the Peel River Kutchin*. National Mu-
         seums of Canada Bulletin 179, Anthropological Series no. 55. Ot-
         tawa: National Museums of Canada.
  1969   "Leadership and Participation in a Kutchin Trapping Party."
         In *Contributions to Anthropology: Band Societies*, ed. David
         Damas, 56–92. National Museums of Canada Bulletin no. 228,
         Anthropological Series no. 84. Ottawa: National Museums of
         Canada.
  1981   "Kutchin." In *Handbook of North American Indians*. Vol. VI,
         Subarctic, ed. June Helm, 514–532. Washington, D.C.: Smithso-
         nian Institution.
Smith, James G. E.
  1973   "The Chipewyan Hunting Group in a Village Context." In *Cul-
         tural Ecology*, ed. Bruce Cox, 315–322. Toronto: McClelland and
         Stewart.
  1981   "Chipewyan." In *Handbook of North American Indians*. Vol. VI,
         Subarctic, ed. June Helm, 271–284. Washington, D.C.: Smithso-
         nian Institution.

1987   "The Western Woods Cree: Anthropological Myth and Historical Reality." *American Ethnologist* 14(3):434–448.

Smith, James G. E., and Ernest S. Burch, Jr.
1979   "Chipewyan and Inuit in the Canadian Subarctic, 1613–1977." *Arctic Anthropology* 16(2):76–101.

Smith, M. Estellie
1982   "The Process of Sociocultural Continuity." *Current Anthropology* 23(2):127–142.

Snow, Jeanne H.
1981   "Ingalik." In *Handbook of North American Indians*. Vol. VI, *Subarctic*, ed. June Helm, 602–617. Washington, D.C.: Smithsonian Institution.

Spicer, Edward H.
1962   *Cycles of Conquest*. Tucson: University of Arizona Press.

Spuhler, James N.
1979   "Genetic Distances, Trees, and Maps of North American Indians." In *The First Americans: Origins, Affinities, and Adaptations*, ed. William S. Laughlin and Albert B. Harper, 135–183. New York: Gustav Fischer.

Swadesh, Morris
1959   "Principle in Comparative Linguistics." *Anthropological Linguistics* 1:7–14.

Szathmary, Emoke J. E.
1977   "Genetic Characteristics of Athapaskan-Speakers: The Problem of Genetic Relationships." In *Problems in the Prehistory of the North American Subarctic: The Athapaskan Question*, ed. James W. Helmer, S. Van Dyke, Francois J. Kense, 111–119. Calgary: University of Calgary.

1979a   "Blood Groups of Siberians, Eskimos, Subarctic, and Northwest Coast Indians: The Problem of Origins and Genetic Relationships." In *The First Americans: Origins, Affinities, and Adaptations*, ed. William S. Laughlin and Albert B. Harper, 185–209. New York: Gustav Fischer.

1979b   "Eskimo and Indian Contact: Examination of Craniometric, Anthropometric and Genetic Evidence." *Arctic Anthropology* 16(2): 23–48.

Szathmary, Emoke J. E., and Nancy Ossenberg
1978   "Are the Biological Differences between North American Indians and Eskimos Truly Profound?" *Current Anthropology* 19: 673–701.

Taylor, R. E., and Clement W. Meighan
1978   *Chronologies in New World Archaeology*. New York: Academic Press.

Thrapp, Dan
1968   *The Conquest of Apacheria*. Norman: University of Oklahoma Press.

Tiller, Veronica
   1983   *The Jicarilla Apache Tribe.* Lincoln: University of Nebraska Press.
Tobey, Margaret J.
   1981   "Carrier." In *Handbook of North American Indians.* Vol. VI,
            Subarctic, ed. June Helm, 413–432. Washington, D.C.: Smithso-
            nian Institution.
Townsend, Joan B.
   1963   "Ethnographic Notes on the Pedro Bay Tanaina." *Anthropologica*
            5:209–223.
   1970   "The Tanaina of Southwestern Alaska: An Historical Synopsis."
            Western Canadian Journal of Anthropology 1:2–16.
   1973   "Ethnoarchaeology in Nineteenth-Century Southern and West-
            ern Alaska: An Interpretive Model." *Ethnohistory* 20:393–412.
   1979   "Indian or Eskimo? Interaction and Identity in Southern Alaska."
            Arctic Anthropology 16(2):160–182.
   1981   "Tanaina." In *Handbook of North American Indians.* Vol. VI, *Sub-
            arctic,* ed. June Helm, 621–640. Washington, D.C.: Smithsonian
            Institution.
Turner, William W.
   1852   "The Apaches." *Literary World* 10(272):281–282.
Tweedie, M. Jean
   1968   "Notes on the History and Adaptations of the Apache Tribes."
            American Anthropologist 70:1132–1142.
Underhill, Ruth
   1953   *Red Man's America: A History of Indians in the United States.*
            Chicago: University of Chicago Press.
Vansina, Jan
   1973   "Cultures through Time." In *A Handbook of Method in Cultural
            Anthropology,* ed. Raoul Naroll and Ronald Cohen, 165–179.
            New York: Columbia University Press.
VanStone, James W.
   1974   *Athapaskan Adaptations.* Chicago: Aldine.
   1976   "The Yukon River Ingalik: Subsistence, the Fur Trade, and a
            Changing Resource Base." *Ethnohistory* 23:199–212.
   1988   "Northern Athapaskans: People of the Deer." In *Crossroads of
            Continents: Cultures of Siberia and Alaska,* ed. William W. Fitz-
            hugh and Aron Crowell, 64–68. Washington, D.C.: Smithsonian
            Institution.
Vogt, Evon Z.
   1961   "Navaho." In *Perspectives in American Indian Culture Change,*
            ed. Edward H. Spicer, 278–336. Chicago: University of Chicago
            Press.
Wallace, William J.
   1978   "Hupa, Chilula, and Whilkut." In *Handbook of North American
            Indians.* Vol. VIII, *California,* ed. Robert F. Heizer, 164–179.
            Washington, D.C.: Smithsonian Institution.

Wedel, Waldo R.
  1978   "The Prehistoric Plains." In *Ancient Native Americans,* ed. Jesse D. Jennings, 183–219. San Francisco: Freeman.
Wedel, Waldo R., Wilfred M. Husted, and John H. Moss
  1968   "Mummy Cave: Prehistoric Record from Rocky Mountains." *Science* 160:184–196.
Wettlaufer, Boyd
  1955   *The Mortlach Site in the Besant Valley of Central Saskatchewan.* Saskatchewan Department of Natural Resources, Anthropological Series 1. Regina: Saskatchewan Museum of Natural History.
Whorf, Benjamin Lee
  1941   "The Relation of Habitual Thought and Behavior to Language." In *Language, Culture, and Personality: Essays in Honor of Edward Sapir,* ed. Leslie Spier, A. I. Hallowell, and Stanley S. Newman, 75–93. Menasha, Wis.: Sapir Memorial Publications Fund.
Wilcox, David R.
  1981   "The Entry of Athapaskans into the American Southwest: The Problem Today." In *The Protohistoric Period in the North American Southwest, A.D. 1450–1700,* ed. David R. Wilcox and W. Bruce Masse. Anthropological Research Paper no. 24, 213–256. Tempe: Arizona State University.
  1988   "Avonlea and Southern Athapaskan Migrations." In *Avonlea Yesterday and Today: Archaeology and Prehistory,* ed. Leslie B. Davis, 273–280. Saskatoon: Saskatchewan Archaeological Society.
Wilmeth, Roscoe
  1975   "The Proto-Historic and Historic Athapaskan Occupation of British Columbia: The Archaeological Evidence." *Western Canadian Journal of Anthropology* 5(3–4):4–20.
  1977   "Chilcotin Archaeology: The Direct Historic Approach." In *Problems in the Prehistory of the North American Subarctic: The Athapaskan Question,* ed. James W. Helmer, S. Van Dyke, and Francois J. Kense, 97–101. Calgary: University of Calgary.
  1978   *Anaheim Lake Archaeology and the Early Chilcotin Indians.* Mercury Series Paper no. 83. Ottawa: National Museum of Man.
Witherspoon, Gary
  1977   *Language and Art in the Navajo Universe.* Ann Arbor: University of Michigan Press.
  1983a   "Language and Reality in Navajo World View." In *Handbook of North American Indians.* Vol. X, *Southwest,* ed. Alfonso Ortiz, 570–578. Washington, D.C.: Smithsonian Institution.
  1983b   "Navajo Social Organization." In *Handbook of North American Indians.* Vol. X, *Southwest,* ed. Alfonso Ortiz, 524–535. Washington, D.C.: Smithsonian Institution.
Worcester, Donald
  1979   *The Apaches: Eagles of the Southwest.* Norman: University of Oklahoma Press.

Workman, William B.
1977a "Ahtna Archaeology: A Preliminary Report." In *Problems in the Prehistory of the North American Subarctic: The Athapaskan Question*, ed. James W. Helmer, S. Van Dyke, and Francois J. Kense, 22–45. Calgary: University of Calgary.

1977b "The Prehistory of the Southern Tutchone Area." In *Problems in the Prehistory of the North American Subarctic: The Athapaskan Question*, ed. James W. Helmer, S. Van Dyke, and Francois J. Kense, 46–54. Calgary: University of Calgary.

1978 *Prehistory of the Aishihik-Kluane Area, Southwest Yukon Territory*. Mercury Series Paper no. 74. Ottawa: National Museum of Man.

Wormington, H. M., and Richard G. Forbis
1965 *An Introduction to the Archaeology of Alberta, Canada*. Proceedings no. 11. Denver: Denver Museum of Natural History.

Wright, Gary A.
1978 "The Shoshonean Migration Problem." *Plains Anthropologist* 23:113–137.

1984 *People of the High Country: Jackson Hole before the Settlers*. New York: Peter Lang.

Wright, James V.
1976 *Six Chapters in Canada's Prehistory*. Toronto: Van Nostrand.

Wyman, Leland C.
1983 "Navajo Ceremonial System." In *Handbook of North American Indians*. Vol. X, *Southwest*, ed. Alfonso Ortiz, 536–557. Washington, D.C.: Smithsonian Institution.

Yerbury, J. C.
1976 "The Post-Contact Chipewyan: Trade Rivalries and Changing Political Boundaries." *Ethnohistory* 23:237–263.

1980 "Protohistoric Canadian Athapaskan Populations: An Ethnohistorical Reconstruction." *Arctic Anthropology* 17(2):17–33.

1986 *The Subarctic Indians and the Fur Trade, 1680–1860*. Vancouver: University of British Columbia Press.

Young, Robert W.
1983 "Apachean Languages." In *Handbook of North American Indians*. Vol. X, *Southwest*, ed. Alfonso Ortiz, 393–400. Washington, D.C.: Smithsonian Institution.

Index